Replicating the Past

Replicating the Past

The Art and Science of the Archaeological Experiment

Stephen C. Saraydar

State University of New York College, Oswego

WAVELAND
PRESS, INC.
Long Grove, Illinois

For information about this book, contact:
Waveland Press, Inc.
4180 IL Route 83, Suite 101
Long Grove, IL 60047-9580
(847) 634-0081
info@waveland.com
www.waveland.com

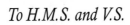

To H.M.S. and V.S.

CONTENTS

PREFACE

My interest in experimental archaeology goes back to my undergraduate days at Cornell University in the late 1960s when Professor Robert Ascher introduced me to an especially intriguing approach to reconstructing the past. Learning how ancient people might have done things, such as make and use stone tools, transport heavy objects, and construct dwellings, by imitating their actions had instant appeal, which led me to perform a number of experiments of my own (with varying degrees of success) and eventually devote my doctoral dissertation to the subject.

At the time that I began my studies, information about the many experiments carried out by amateur and professional archaeologists over a span of time exceeding 100 years was hard to come by as there was no comprehensive overview of the field and reports often appeared in obscure journals. This changed in 1973 with the publication of an extensive bibliography compiled by Thomas Hester and Robert Heizer. In that same year, John Coles published a book that surveyed the subject matter and results of a large number of experiments, which he organized according to the type of ancient technology replicated. In 1979 Coles produced an updated and expanded version of his book that, though now long out of print, stands as the most recent comprehensive treatment of the subject. Today, in some respects, the circumstances facing those seeking an in-depth introduction to experimental archaeology parallel those I experienced as a student. I wrote this book in an attempt to remedy that situation.

Most students today get their first exposure to experiments in introductory archaeology courses. That exposure is typically quite limited, with experimental archeology appearing in the context of discussions on the use of analogy in the interpretation of the archaeological record. This book is designed to supplement comprehensive textbooks and also serve as a stand-alone text for a course on experimental archaeology. It differs significantly from Coles' treatments in that, rather than presenting an encyclopedic account, it is highly selective, with an emphasis on contemporary archaeological theory, the scientific method, and how to distinguish between a better and a worse experiment and argument. It is structured around "Case Studies" in which investigations that provide particularly good insight into the nature of archaeological experimentation are examined in detail and critiqued. My goal has been to provide a clear sense of the range of subject matter covered by archaeological experiments and to show how they are used to achieve some of the diverse goals of modern archaeology.

ACKNOWLEDGMENTS

I thank Robert Ascher for his friendship and the inspiration he has always provided. I am grateful for the time and effort he generously devoted to helping me improve the first draft of my manuscript. I also thank John Whittaker for his thorough review of my work and his many valuable comments and suggestions. Roger Hedge provided generous and much needed assistance with my research on the Butser Ancient Farm and early metallurgy, for which I am most grateful. I also thank Fergus Milton for sharing his knowledge on the smelting of ores. I am especially grateful to my wife, Mary Rolland, for her contributions to the artwork, her careful proofreading, and most of all for her encouragement and support throughout this project.

CHAPTER 1

APPROACHES TO THE PAST

No belief can be established with finality and no knowledge is based upon knowing all the facts. Neither analogy, the imitative experiment, or any other tool which the archaeologist now has at his disposal, can be used conclusively to establish a belief about the past. The archaeologist must work with what Pareto (1935:319) has called "facts in scant numbers." The challenge of archaeology is in transforming hypotheses based upon scant data into legitimate inferences. It is hoped that the results of this study will encourage archaeologists to use one of the few mechanisms which can secure such transformations with confidence and clarity. (Ascher 1961:812)

INTRODUCTION

Popular images of archaeologists and the work they perform are shaped in important ways by films, television programs, and a variety of publications produced by people who generally lack archeological training.[1] While some of those images are entirely fanciful, others contain kernels of truth. Much the same can, of course, be said about popular views of other academic disciplines and their practitioners. In the case of archaeology, think about the picture that might emerge if we were to solicit and obtain descriptions of archaeologists on the job from an assortment of people strolling through a mall or emerging from a movie theater on a weekend afternoon. I feel confident that many of the responses would feature adventurous men and women attired in khaki or denim and wearing pith helmets or Indiana Jones–style fedoras. Most of those imaginary archaeologists would undoubtedly be situated in exotic and possibly dangerous locales—deserts and tropical forests are good bets—and they would be engaged in tedious efforts to unearth and recover valuable relicts of the past buried long ago. Despite a tendency to overromanticize the field and underestimate the amount of work archaeologists perform within the tamer confines of the academy, I believe that most of the responses would at least contain the essentially correct idea that archaeologists, by one means or another, "dig up" the past.

Let's compare these hypothetical results with the ones we might receive if our question concerned chemists rather than archaeologists. The chemists described to us would most likely be dressed in white lab coats and situated in laboratories filled with exotic instruments and glassware. They would probably be hard at work mixing chemicals or preparing solutions and heating them over Bunsen burners to discover what sort of reaction might occur. In the popular imagination, danger for the chemist would surely present itself in the ever-present possibility of poisonous fumes and explosions, in contrast to the rattlesnakes, booby-traps, unfriendly natives, and ruthless competitors thought to plague the archaeologist.

If we push this exercise one step further, we can see an apparent difference in the ways that knowledge is acquired in each of these disciplines: despite their exertions and adventures in the field, archaeologists "receive" their primary data through an essentially passive enterprise (the archaeological record contains what it contains—"facts in scant numbers"—and archaeologists merely recover them), while chemists actively "create" theirs. In other words, chemistry is an experimental science and archaeology is not. This is a fair enough assessment of most archaeology and some forms of chemistry at least, but there *are* archaeologists who regularly perform experiments, and those experiments provide valuable insights on the past that are unobtainable by other methods.

While it isn't surprising that the experimental side of archaeology fails to make an appearance in popular images, its low profile in many archaeology texts and frequent absence altogether in anthologies containing exemplars of theory and research (see, for example, Heizer 1959; Leone 1972; Peregrine, Ember, and Ember 2002; Preucel and Hodder 1996) are less easy to justify.[2] Although experiments are not the primary means of advancing our knowledge of the past, many have been performed over the last 120 or so years, and they have provided and continue to provide a very useful and unique means of supplementing knowledge obtained through survey and excavation. On this basis alone, they are worthy of greater prominence in the professional literature than they have been granted to date.

Before I proceed to make my case for increased recognition of experimental archaeology, I need to specify what is and is not covered by that term. It could quite reasonably include an experiment that compares two methods of excavation to determine if one allows for more effective data recovery than the other. Or, it might be applied to the work of lab-coated archaeologists when they test various types of chemical treatments of artifacts and ecofacts in attempts to extract as much information as possible from the evidence brought to light by their excavations. But neither of those investigations would fit normal usage. Experimental archaeology instead refers to a distinct category of experiment known as *imitative* (Ascher 1961) or *replicative*. This type of experiment is one in which the archaeologist attempts to re-create some aspect of the past in order to understand it better. Such an experiment might, for instance, involve replicating a particular type of stone tool to determine how it might have been made and/or used.

In contemporary archaeology, this kind of experimentation falls within a category of method that has come to be known as *actualistic studies*. Actualistic studies are ones in which the relationships between behavior and potentially observable material traces of that behavior are carefully examined. This "connective tissue" linking past and present is the primary subject matter of explorations carried out under the banners of ethnoarchaeology and experimental archaeology. Ethnoarchaeology is simply ethnography performed by an archaeologist for the purpose of interpreting the archaeology record. Although ethnographic accounts produced by cultural anthropologists are often of considerable value to archaeologists, they generally lack the detailed information relating to material culture that an archaeologist would most like to have. This isn't surprising, because the focus of such studies is normally on the nonmaterial aspects of human behavior: religious beliefs, kinship, marriage, and so on. Detailed accounts of tool manufacture, use, and discard, for instance, are not the stuff of which most ethnographies are made. To gather information of direct relevance to interpretation of the archaeological record, archaeologists sometimes carry out fieldwork involving observation of living populations to learn about how they do such things as make, use, and discard stone tools; butcher animals and dispose of the remains; use symbols to mark important social boundaries; and so on (see Binford 1978, 2002; Gould 1978, 1980; Hodder 1982; Kramer 1979; Longacre and Skibo 1994; Rathje 1974; and Stout 2002, for examples). In the case of experimental archaeology, the archaeologist moves from the role of essentially passive observer, to actor—taking matters, quite literally, into his or her own hands.

The classic definition of the archaeological experiment has been provided by Robert Ascher. He describes it as a category of experiment that

> entails operations in which matter is shaped, or matter is shaped and used, in a manner simulative of the past. . . . The aim of imitative experiments is testing beliefs about past cultural behavior. (1961:793)

My definition is slightly broader. I include experiments that are designed to replicate non-cultural processes relevant to the formation and content of the archaeological record (e.g., the burial of a set of organic and inorganic materials to investigate how they change in form, composition, and location over time).[3]

As the case studies in this book will show, when carrying out experiments that replicate past behaviors and processes, the activities of archaeologists may align more closely with popular images of scientists, although in most cases the experimental trials take place in the great outdoors and white lab coats only occasionally make an appearance. It was, in fact, this unique combination of traditional experimental methods ("lab science") and reenactments of interesting aspects of ancient life that led me to make archaeology the focus of my undergraduate major in anthropology. A pivotal experience was designing and performing an experiment in which a fellow student and I compared the performance of a stone and a steel axe (described in detail in chapter 4). Prior to this, my knowledge of stone tools had been largely abstract. I had learned about the methods ancient people used to manufacture them and modern archaeologists used to classify them. I had seen stone tools of various kinds (including axes) in photographs and gained greater appreciation for and understanding of them by examining actual specimens. As important as all this was to my archaeological education, it could not compare to the experience of actually making a haft (handle) for a stone axe head, fitting the two together and then setting off for the woods to use this implement to cut down several small trees. Through this experience, my muscles and my brain learned things about stone axes that could never be forgotten and no written or visual source could ever adequately convey. Attributes used to describe these tools such as blade length, edge angle, grooved/ungrooved, chipped/ground stone, and so on became significant in ways they had not been when they were merely terms that appeared in books and articles. And the people who made and used these tools no longer seemed quite so remote in time and space. I was hooked on archaeology!

In retrospect, I consider it fortunate that I performed my first experiments before I participated in my first dig. My experiences working with axes and other tools gave me an appreciation I would not otherwise have had for the human significance of the artifacts and features I encountered when I participated in the excavation of an 800-year-old pueblo in Arizona a short time later.

ARCHAEOLOGY IN THE TWENTIETH AND TWENTY-FIRST CENTURIES

Before we delve into the design of archaeological experiments, a short (and selective) history lesson is in order as is an examination of the logic that underlies contemporary archaeological inquiry and interpretation. This will help to clarify the role of experimental archaeology within the discipline and suggest how it might be used in the future. To gain a thorough understanding of how archaeology developed and why it's done the way it is today, I heartily recommend *The Idea of Prehistory* by Glyn Daniel (1964), *A History of Archaeological Thought* by Bruce Trigger (1989), and *A History of American Archaeology* by Gordon Willey and Jeremy Sabloff (1993). For briefer, but up-to-date overviews, I suggest *Archaeology: Discovering Our Past* by Robert Sharer and Wendy Ashmore (2003:42–118) and *Archaeology: Theories, Methods, and Practice* by Colin Renfrew and Paul Bahn (2004:21–52). Here I discuss a few key issues and developments as they relate to the guiding models (paradigms) that define the problems to be investigated and the approaches to be taken to solve them.

CULTURAL HISTORICAL ARCHAEOLOGY

Through much of the first half of the twentieth century the primary goal of most archaeological studies was to establish chronologies.[4] Accordingly, the questions archaeologists sought to answer typically concerned the what, when, and where of the past. This required precise excavation methods that paid close attention to stratification (the layering of deposits that, when undisturbed, presents a temporal sequence with the oldest layer or stratum underneath the next oldest and so on), followed by classification of artifacts and features into types that reflected changes through time and revealed regional differences. The results of these efforts at establishing what is known as *cultural history* were readily summarized in charts or grids in which the vertical axis represented time and the horizontal axis represented location. The resulting time-space was divided up into archaeological cultures and traditions delimited according to the similarities and differences in the artifacts and features they contained (Figure 1-1).

Although filling out time-space grids with increasing precision was a preoccupation of many archaeologists during this period, explanation—which required tackling questions concerning the "how" and "why" of the past—was also attempted, albeit on a limited scale. Imitative experiments, while never a mainstream approach, proved useful in such efforts, as they provided a means of moving from straightforward description and classification of artifacts and features on the basis of age, style, form, and the materials from which they were made, to testing ideas about how they might have been produced, their possible functions, and their modes of operation. In combination with judiciously selected analogies from the ethnographic literature and excavation methods and interpretation that paid greater attention to the context of finds, the results of experiments improved understanding of how technology functioned in the daily lives of ancient people and reflected their adaptation to the environment.

Another approach that likewise focused on context and function involved the study of ancient settlement patterns. A pioneering effort to understand the logic behind the location of settlements of various types on a landscape was made by Gordon Willey in a study of the Virú Valley of Peru. The basis of Willey's approach lay in his recognition that

> settlements reflect the natural environment, the level of technology on which the builders operated, and various institutions of social interaction and control which the culture maintained. Because settlement patterns are, to a large extent, directly shaped by widely held cultural needs, they offer a strategic starting point for the functional interpretation of archaeological cultures. (Willey 1953:1)

Not surprisingly, the interest in regional patterns of site distribution that Willey's study helped spark led in turn to greater emphasis on the reconstruction of ancient environments, because understanding the functional significance of a settlement pattern required that the individual sites each be placed in the context of their physical, biological, and cultural settings (see discussion in Willey and Sabloff 1993:176–182).

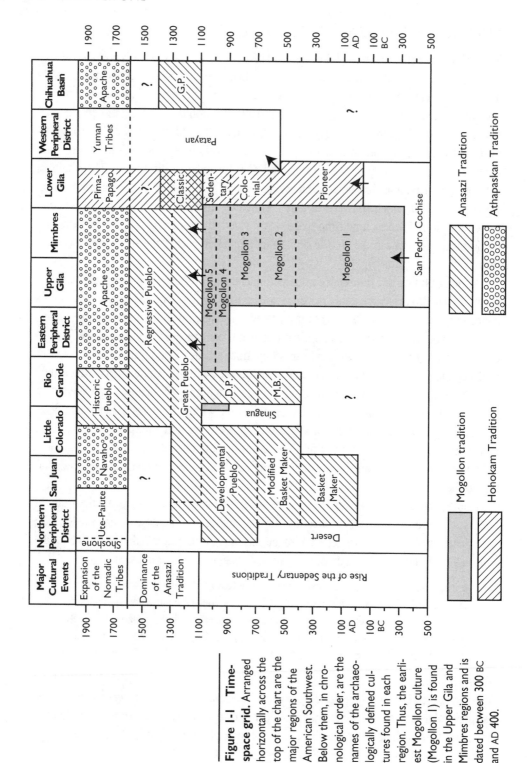

Figure 1-1 Time-space grid. Arranged horizontally across the top of the chart are the major regions of the American Southwest. Below them, in chronological order, are the names of the archaeologically defined cultures found in each region. Thus, the earliest Mogollon culture (Mogollon 1) is found in the Upper Gila and Mimbres regions and is dated between 300 BC and AD 400.

Over the course of the era in which the cultural historical approach held sway, archaeologists succeeded in learning a great deal about the adaptations of ancient societies and their interactions with one another. But progress on the particularly difficult problem of *why* changes had occurred in the social, ideological, technological, and economic systems of past cultures was less impressive, and it was only near the end of this period that the tentative explanations that were put forward began to be based less on speculation and more on directly relevant data (see Martin 1974 for a first person account; see also Willey and Sabloff 1993:204–220). Those explanations typically focused on the source(s) of change, which were classified as either internal or external. Internal sources relied on mechanisms such as invention, drift (random loss of cultural traits over time), and revival (the reintroduction of traits from an earlier time), while external sources drew on ones such as diffusion (the spread of ideas from one culture to another), trade, migration of human populations, invasion, conquest, and variations in climate (see Sharer and Ashmore 2003:557–568). More sophisticated and multidimensional investigations of how, why, and under what circumstances processes such as these might operate and also interact with one another to produce change would come later, with the emergence of processual archaeology.

PROCESSUAL ARCHAEOLOGY

By the mid-1960s the explanation of cultural change became a major focus of what was later to be called the *new archaeology*. This development was in large part an outgrowth of the dissatisfaction felt by a number of younger archaeologists with what they saw as the sterility of cultural-historical archaeology (with its strong emphasis on fact gathering for the purposes of describing, classifying, and arranging in sequences) and the lack of a properly scientific approach to research design and interpretation.[5] Their stated goal was to increase archaeology's relevance to anthropology as a whole by developing sufficiently rigorous theory and methods to permit full exploitation of the archaeological record's potential to provide answers to questions about human behavior and cultural evolution (see Binford and Binford 1968). It was time, they argued, to seek an anthropologically informed understanding of the internal dynamics of ancient cultures and work toward explanation of the *process* of change in ancient societies (hence the term "processual archaeology" that is now applied to this approach). In their quest to understand change over both the short and the long term, these archaeologists frequently relied on cultural-ecological models, which entailed close attention to the ways that ancient societies had interacted with and adapted to the many interrelated aspects of their environments.

Along with the resulting shift in emphasis from description and chronological ordering to explanation came a series of efforts aimed at making the discipline more *explicitly* scientific in its methods.[6] A key demand of the new archaeologists was for methods of inquiry and modes of presentation of results that closely modeled those of the natural sciences. Of particular significance was their strong support for a positivist approach to research based on the use of hypothesis testing (the hypothetico-deductive method), with the ultimate goal of establishing general ("covering") laws of human behavior (see Binford 1968; Spaulding 1968; Watson, LeBlanc, and Redman 1971). The search for such laws soon proved unproductive, but an approach based on formulation and testing of hypotheses has remained central to research carried out under this paradigm.

Simply put, a hypothesis is a possible explanation for a given phenomenon. It is a proposition that requires careful investigation, specifically, the gathering of evidence that can be applied to evaluate a particular situation. Imagine, for example, that we offer the hypothesis that climate change was largely responsible for the abandonment of a particular region by the farmers who had long inhabited it. That statement can't be evaluated directly. To investigate this possibility with archaeological data, we need to start with some serious thinking (always a good idea). Before any shovels or trowels hit the ground, we need to figure out what relevant evidence we should be able to extract from the archaeological record that would either support or refute our hypothesis. To use the proper terminology, we need to develop test implications. Test implications specify the type of evidence we need to collect in order to evaluate the hypothesis; they typically specify what should be found in the archaeological record if the hypothesis is valid. In the case of our present hypothesis, we would need test implications that point to evidence of a deteriorating climate, such as changes in the type of pollen found in the sites and in the width of tree rings in wood samples from fireplaces and structural timbers in houses. If our hypothesis specified an extended drought period as a factor in the abandonment, we would expect to find a change in pollen that reflected a shift to more drought-resistant plants and a pattern of increasingly narrow tree rings (we wouldn't stop with just two test implications, of course, and we'd also want to propose some alternative hypotheses and evaluate them as well). If our test implications are all supported by the evidence, our hypothesis is also supported. If, however, the evidence points strongly to no change in climate, we would consider our hypothesis refuted. This example points to the special place occupied by falsification in the work of the scientist. A hypothesis can clearly be disproved (disqualified), but no amount of confirmatory evidence can prove it to be true.[7]

When this approach is followed and then well documented in the report of the investigations, evaluation by other archaeologists of what was done and how the stated conclusions were reached is facilitated. If the set of test implications was logically flawed or simply insufficient, improvements can be suggested. Alternative conclusions based on the evidence collected might also be made. For many archaeological problems, this approach to investigation works quite well. Its essence lies in a problem having first been clearly defined, the evidence believed to be suitable for investigating it specified and, ultimately, produced for scrutiny by others (this is known as *public verifiability*). As much of the process as possible is out in the open and available for evaluation. Assuming that we've done a good job of selecting our test implications and obtaining reliable data, we might be able to offer a highly persuasive argument in favor of a climate change playing a significant role in the abandonment of the region in question. This would lead, ideally, to further investigations of the timing, scope, and nature of the environmental changes, the strategies the people developed to cope with them, and so on. A research design based on the formulation of hypotheses that are then carefully evaluated on the basis of data relevant to an assessment of their tenability helps us to understand the past in ways that the annotated chronologies and untested speculations typical of the strict cultural history approach do not.

This emphasis on the investigation of process through the testing of hypotheses led to some increased interest in imitative experiments. This can probably be attributed in part to the fact that the experimental method itself was seen as a hallmark of the kind of science processual archaeologists were striving to emulate. While many of the experiments performed since the mid-1960s have continued to focus in familiar ways on artifact manufacture and use, others have been specifically designed to produce quantitative data relating to the cultural and noncultural processes associated with life in the past as well as site formation and transformation (e.g., the relative efficiencies of stone and metal axes, the productivity of ancient agricultural systems, and the movement and modification of artifacts in sites caused by human and nonhuman agents).

POSTPROCESSUAL ARCHAEOLOGY

Much as the cultural history approach was found to be wanting in the mid-1960s, the processual archaeology that became increasingly the norm by the end of that decade came under fire in the early 1980s. The reasons are many, varied, and complex, so I must limit myself to a brief examination of the most salient aspects of the critique that led to what has come to be known as *postprocessual archaeology* (see Hodder 1991 and Johnson 1999 for clear introductions to postprocessualism; see also Hodder 1986, and Shanks and Tilley 1987). One of the key criticisms leveled at the processual approach centered on its preference for explaining the past in materialist terms rather than seeking an understanding of its meaning, that is, the significance of archaeological materials to the people who created the evidence archaeologists study. A related criticism concerned the invisibility of the individual person in processual studies, whose focus is typically on long-term changes in cultural systems; in contrast, postprocessualists have argued that understanding ancient societies requires that individuals be seen as active agents of stability and change, rather than as passive figures who merely conformed to behavioral norms and adapted en masse to changing circumstances. In addition, the notion of science as a privileged means of knowing was challenged, positivist science was rejected, and the efficacy of hypothesis testing was called into question. What has emerged from this critique of processualism is a more humanistically oriented archaeology, with an emphasis on flexibility in approach and openness to interpretations based on multiple points of view. Although the term *postprocessual archaeology* has been widely adopted to refer to the nonprocessual studies that have appeared with increasing frequency in the last 25 years, postprocessual archaeologies would be more accurate in view of their considerable diversity in subject matter, theoretical orientation, and methodology (see Preucel and Hodder 1996 for a well-chosen set of examples that reflects this diversity).[8]

I return to some of the issues associated with the processual/postprocessual debate (which continues to this day) in chapter 6, but one requires examination here because it is particularly relevant to experimental archaeology: is the method of hypothesis testing appropriate for archaeology? Although taken for granted by many archaeologists, Hodder and other postprocessualists would avoid research designs in which hypotheses are evaluated by means of test implications. One reason given is:

> During excavation, unexpected lines of enquiry are opened up and any rigid adherence to the testing of initial hypotheses . . . would involve ignoring evidence that may be relevant to the question in hand or that might be of interest to other archaeologists. In fieldwork, the questions are always changing and new lines of argument become available. (Hodder 1999:21)

Another concerns artificiality and a certain rigidity:

> There is supposed to be a controlled and linear process from hypothesis to conclusion. Data are supposed to confront theory in a direct and verifiable manner. There is little room here for the description of subjective thought processes, hunches and mistakes—the serendipitous processes of the practice of archaeology. Most reports of excavations have been "cleaned-up"—the debates and intuitions condemned to the margins, present if at all in acknowledgements, asides, or in diaries lost in archives.
>
> This inability to see "what really went on" in [the doing of archaeology] . . . is one of the most important critiques of the legacy of processual . . . archaeology. (Hodder 1999:30–31)

These objections clearly span several levels of archaeological enterprise. Easiest to address is Hodder's concern that an archaeologist might commit the error of slavishly limiting her or his data collection to whatever was specified in the initial test implications. No archaeologist, indeed no scientist, humanist, or investigator of any kind should ever do that. It should be obvious as well that this would be especially poor practice in a field in which the source of evidence is routinely destroyed by the process of acquiring the data! The fact that there are specific questions that the excavator is particularly interested in investigating should not compete with the need to learn as much as possible about the past. The best scientists are open to whatever may present itself to them in their investigations—serendipitous discoveries may ultimately prove more significant than anything specified in the original research design.

The second concern seems easily addressable as well. Hodder is certainly correct about the reality of doing fieldwork (or laboratory research in chemistry for that matter): the process is far less "clean" and linear than typical research reports would indicate.[9] Sometimes the "thick and rich" version will be of no relevance to the scientific community at large—just so many inconsequential, uninteresting details of the experience—and other times it will add measurably to an understanding of the results and provide food for thought that may lead to alternative interpretations and perhaps even to new avenues of inquiry. There is no reason why what anthropologists (after Clifford Geertz) call "thick description" should be seen as incompatible with a research design that centers on the investigation of specific hypotheses. In the case of typical imitative experiments, conveying the results adequately may actually demand a detailed account of the experience in which "objective" and "subjective" descriptions are skillfully integrated.

Perhaps the most serious charge leveled at processual methodology by Hodder and other postprocessualists is that "the idea of 'testing' is inappropriate in archaeology because the data are partly constructed within theory and most archaeology is not an experimental discipline" (Hodder 1999:59–60). The second part of this assertion clearly does not apply to experimental archaeology, which Hodder acknowledges follows an "experimental procedure" (1999:28). As to the tie between data and theory, Hodder is certainly correct: there is no such thing as a value-free fact. Data are never completely objective no matter how unbiased, straightforward and obvious they may appear to us—they exist because of theory and therefore cannot (in archaeology, chemistry, or any other discipline) be totally independent of theory. This does raise the issue of circular reasoning if one contends, for instance, that theories are tested against (independent) data:

> Theories in general . . . are confirmed by appeal to observations, and observations in general are understood and verified with the support of theories. Observations are theoretically influenced claims about specific situations. Theories are claims which go beyond particular perceptions of observations. Individual observations are interpreted by appeal to theories which are themselves put together and supported by observations. (Hodder 1999:28)

It is important to recognize that this relationship between theory and observation holds in all fields. In archaeology, the degree to which the absence of complete independence is felt to compromise an approach based on hypothesis testing appears to depend, in part, on where one stands with respect to the processual–postprocessual divide.

Nonetheless, there are clear and significant differences in testing hypotheses in fields that concern themselves with natural phenomena (which occur or can be made to occur repeatedly) and those that deal with the infinitely more complex and unique past behavior of human beings. Since archaeologists most often cannot, in the strictest sense, "test" a hypothesis about something they can never directly observe (past human behavior), should they abandon the hypothesis testing format for all but experimental archaeology (and perhaps ethnoarchaeology)? In a word, no. Used intelligently, that is, with its limitations clearly in mind, it is a highly useful tool for structuring research—experimental or otherwise—for reasons made clear in chapter 2.

COMMON GROUND?

Debates in archaeology can be interesting, infuriating, and enlightening. The current ones lead to at least one noncontroversial conclusion: regardless of theoretical orientation, all archaeologists strive to craft well-supported arguments that present their best thinking on the problems they have investigated. What the postprocessualists typically offer as an alternative to an approach in which archaeologists test hypotheses against objective data, is an interpretive process known as *hermeneutic "fitting"* in which "the data are always both subjective and objective" (Hodder 1999:64; see also Shanks and Tilley 1987:103–115).

Hermeneutics is in a broad sense a philosophy or body of theory concerned with the interpretation of meaning in things and events to which we do not have direct access, because of distance in time, space, or culture. It embodies a recognition that purely objective interpretations are impossible, thereby forcing serious consideration of the culture content the observer brings to the problem. Philosophical hermeneutics tells us that the process of understanding involves a circular or spiral-like movement rather than a unilinear progression toward some ultimate truth. Moving around the "hermeneutic circle" involves alternating back and forth between the general and the particular, from recapitulation to reassessment, with no interpretation necessarily final and all interpretation historically and culturally situated (Bauman 1978:17, 42–47).[10] According to Richard Rorty:

> We will never be able to avoid the "hermeneutic circle"—the fact that we cannot understand the parts of a strange culture, practice, theory, language, or whatever, unless we know something about how the whole thing works, whereas we cannot get a grasp on how the whole works until we have some understanding of the parts. This notion of interpretation suggests that coming to understand is more like getting acquainted with a person than following a demonstration. In both cases we play back and forth between guesses about how to characterize particular statements or other events, and guesses about the point of the whole situation, until gradually we feel at ease with what was hitherto strange. The notion of a culture as a conversation rather than as a structure erected upon foundations fits well with this hermeneutical notion of knowledge. (1979:319)

None of this means that there are no standards for judging the validity of an interpretation or that interpretive social science plunges us into "irrationality and subjectivism," as Jennings (1983:19) argues in a related context. It only means that progress in the enlargement of scientific and intellectual discourse through interpretation is problematic in ways that are neither recognized nor reconciled by conventional science and its arch-positivist practitioners. Postprocessual archaeology has served to emphasize that interpretive social science is "largely a rhetorical or persuasive medium," in which "literary, figurative, and stylistic considerations play a much more important role . . . than in positivist social analysis" (Jennings 1983:16).

A hermeneutic model in which archaeologists repeatedly move back and forth between theory and data as they struggle to interpret what they discover more realistically portrays the actual process of investigation than the cleaned-up, linear versions of the reasoning process that make their way into the conclusions section of the typical site report. But it must be understood that while postprocessualists may have introduced hermeneutics as a formal concept to archaeology, they did not initiate its use in the discipline—the interpretive process has always, of necessity, been hermeneutical. The method of hermeneutic fitting is not unique to any particular approach to archaeology; furthermore, it is equally a facet of the interpretive process in history, sociology, and the natural sciences.[11]

Similarities between the processual and postprocessual approaches are also to be found in other aspects of methodology. For instance, Kosso (1991) has asserted that the method of justification and the standard of objectivity are shared. In particular, he makes the important point that both rely on "a requirement of consistency and coherence" as well as "a constraint of independence in the accounting for evidential claims" (1991:626). The latter requirement means that although all evidence (facts) are tied to some theory, avoiding complete circularity entails seeking support for those claims outside the theories for which they provide supporting evidence. Nonetheless, even if common ground is to be found here, important differences between processual and postprocessual archaeology most certainly remain with respect to choice of subject matter and mode of presentation, as even a casual perusal of a representative sample of their products will easily demonstrate.

Experiments are "neutral" in this debate—they may serve either a processual or a postprocessual master. The reasons are simple. They have always been used by archaeologists seeking to move beyond description to understanding. Furthermore, the kinds of problems to which they have typically been applied have a significance that transcends theoretical orientation. For instance, it seems a fair assumption that knowing how an artifact may have been made and used is worthwhile to anyone seriously interested in the past. And of course, as the discussion above has shown, the use of hypothesis testing in experimental archaeology is far less controversial than it is in more typical investigations. While the content of imitative experiments performed after the emergence of postprocessual perspectives does not appear to have undergone a shift in content and application of even the limited magnitude that followed the rise of processual archaeology, imitative experiments have "postprocessual potential" that remains largely untapped—a subject to which we will return in chapter 6.

A LOOK AHEAD

The next chapter provides additional context for the use of experiments in archaeology by first examining their role in the sciences and then exploring the logic of archaeological interpretation. Next, the criteria for the design, execution, and evaluation of archaeological experiments are laid out. In the chapters that follow, I have organized experiments largely (but somewhat loosely) by the scale of the enterprise.[12] I have not attempted to present an encyclopedic account of the many experiments that have been performed in each category (for that I recommend Coles 1979, supplemented by Renfrew and Bahn 2004) but instead have chosen to focus on the problem to be solved (the hypothesis to be tested, the process to be observed, etc.) and the research design and its implementation. My primary goal is to provide a sense of the range of archaeological experiments, the logic that determines their design and execution, and the ways in which they serve the diverse goals of modern archaeology. I have also chosen to begin, for the most part, with experiments that are simpler, in the sense that they contain fewer distinct imitative steps, and progress to ones that have more and, in some cases, actually combine several discrete experiments to replicate complex, multicomponent behaviors. Chapter 3 focuses on examples that provide especially clear illustrations of how experiments are used to test what had previously been mere conjectures about the operation of ancient tools, the functions of features, and the methods used by ancient people to do such things as smelt copper and extract brains from corpses prior to mummification. The experiments in chapter 4 focus on activities that are generally composed of a greater number of operations (e.g., casting copper bells and moving and erecting megaliths). Chapter 5 is devoted to experiments that explore the construction of large architectural features and re-create ancient agricultural systems. Chapter 6 examines the scientific and humanistic aspects of experiments in light of the concerns of processual and postprocessual approaches to archaeology and also explores the role experiments may play in education (the development of critical-thinking skills, in particular) and in making archaeology more accessible to the general public.

NOTES

[1] Images of archaeologists tend to vary in the general public's eye from the swashbuckler to the absentminded professor. The best known fictional archaeologist is, of course, Indiana Jones. Jones presents a mix of these two types: he's primarily an adventurer, out to find valuable artifacts, but he's also a professor who does such mundane things as teach in a university setting. When we compare contemporary images with those identified by A. V. Kidder in the late 1940s, it becomes clear that little has changed since then (see Ascher 1960).

[2] Renfrew and Bahn (2004) provide significantly greater coverage of experiments than is to be found in other introductory texts. Awareness of the experimental side of archaeology by the general public has undoubtedly increased to some degree as a result of documentaries such as Discovery Channel's "Children of the Moai," NOVA's "This Old Pyramid" and its series *Secrets of Lost Empires.*

[3] Broader still, and certainly defensible, is the definition of Ingersoll, Yellen, and MacDonald, which includes "not only [1] replicative studies . . . but also [2] tests of method and theoretical principles relating to them" as well as "[3] studies of the processes of site formation and deterioration and [4] studies of the relationships between material and nonmaterial culture in societies functioning at present" (1977:xii; numbers added). I have chosen to exclude the second and fourth types of study and combine the third with the first. All can quite reasonably be labeled "experimental" but only the first and third normally feature imitative experiments. Experimental approaches to the investigation of site formation and the ways in which sites change over time typically make use of simulated sites and some include reconstructions of ancient structures, such as the example Ingersoll, Yellen, and MacDonald include of an experimental earthwork. The purpose of this experiment was to measure precisely the deterioration of the full-scale model to gain insight into the processes that transformed ancient earthworks in Britain (see discussion in chapter 4). Another example from this category, one that did not replicate a structure but nonetheless attempted to re-create past conditions, is a simulation

analysis of the effect of temperature on protein decay in bone. I see no reason not to place both of these experiments and others like them in the imitative/replicative group. The second category identified by Ingersoll, Yellen, and MacDonald is clearly distinct. Two examples from their collection include a test of methods used by archaeologists to estimate human population on the basis of meat consumption at an eighteenth century fort and an examination of possible distortions that may compromise seriations based on changes in the popularity of stylistic attributes over time, in which eighteenth and early nineteenth century gravestones in New England served as dated controls. The fourth category is simply ethnoarchaeology.

4 Willey and Sabloff (1993) refer to this as the Classificatory-Historical Period and divide it into two parts, each receiving a full chapter in their book: "The Concern with Chronology (1914–1940)" and "The Concern with Context and Function (1940–1960)."

5 Dissatisfaction with the cultural history approach predates the 1960s. For example, in 1948 Walter Taylor published *A Study of Archaeology* in which he criticized his profession for not moving beyond time-space systematics. The goal of his "conjunctive" approach was the reconstruction of the dynamics of ancient life. He was interested in discovering what the patterning found in archaeological remains could tell us about how ancient societies functioned. In other words, he wanted to pursue the "how" and "why" of the past in addition to the "what," "when," and "where."

6 In fairness to many earlier archaeologists and to a number of those at the time who rejected the new archaeology, it must be acknowledged that logical problem solving had always been a part of serious archaeological inquiry (even a casual reading of the selections in *The Archaeologist at Work* [Heizer 1959] will make this point clearly). But the processes that led from data to higher-level inferences were normally hidden from easy view; that is, they were not often made explicit. In addition, as Martin (1971, 1974) has argued, explanation, when it was attempted, generally appeared as an afterthought or by-product of the investigation.

7 Although philosophers of science such as Karl Popper have made a strong argument for the primacy of falsification in scientific research, many scientists exhibit a clear bias in favor of the pursuit of confirmation (see discussion in Tweney, Doherty, and Mynatt 1981:115–128).

8 For an excellent, comprehensive overview of the various theoretical orientations to be found in contemporary North American archeology see Hegmon 2003.

9 Peter Medawar, a biologist and Nobel Laureate went so far as to claim that the scientific paper is a "fraud because it misrepresents the processes of thought that accompanied or gave rise to the work that is represented in the paper. . . . The scientific paper in its orthodox form does embody a totally mistaken conception, even a travesty, of the nature of scientific thought" (1963:377).

10 Bauman (1978:42) includes two pertinent statements by historians Benedetto Croce and R. G. Collingwood in his discussion:

[Croce:]
The past fact does not answer to a past interest, but to a present interest, in so far as it is unified with an interest of the present life.
[Collingwood:]
The peculiarity which makes [an object] historical is not the fact of its happening in time, but the fact of its becoming known to us by our rethinking the same thought which created the situation we are investigating, and thus coming to understand that situation.

11 I find it interesting that this back and forth process bears some resemblance to what apparently happens at a deeper level as our brains manipulate prototypes and perceptions in a process of "match-mismatch" as we attempt to classify the objects we encounter in daily life (Rosch 1977). A process of fitting that involves alternation between two poles of some kind would appear to be universal to the way humans make sense of the world.

12 The experiments that have been performed in the service of archaeology are quite varied in subject matter, goals, and degree of complexity. As with a classification of artifacts, we may lump many together into just a

few basic categories or split them into many quite specific groups according to our purposes. Coles' *Archaeology by Experiment* (1973), features just three primary categories: Food Production, Heavy Industry, and Light Industry. In the chapter on Food Production we find experiments on "forest clearance and crops," "ploughing," "harvesting," "storage of food," and "preparation and consumption of food." Heavy Industry summarizes experiments on "house-building and destruction," "earthworks and erosion," "transport and erection of stones," and "boats and voyages," while Light Industry covers "stone-working," "wood-working and weapons," "working in bone, antler and shell," "working with metals," "hides, leathers and textiles," "pottery manufacture," "painting and paper," and "musical instruments." In Coles' updated and expanded volume (1979), the subcategories were deleted in favor of a revised set of primary categories: Discovery and Exploration, Subsistence, Settlement, Arts and Crafts, and Life and Death. By comparison, Hester and Heizer in their extensive bibliography (1973), divide imitative experiments into 18 categories that roughly parallel the 17 subheadings in Coles' earlier book.

CHAPTER 2

THE EXPERIMENT IN THE SCIENCES AND ARCHAEOLOGY

INVESTIGATION BY EXPERIMENT

Experiments have long played a crucial role in scientific investigation. They appeared in essentially modern form in the work of pioneering scientist Francis Bacon in the early seventeenth century. It is significant that in an evaluation of Bacon's work dating to 1830, F. W. Herschel recognized the "utility of experiment as distinguished from mere passive observation" for testing hypotheses and, ultimately, falsifying all but one (1830:144). These observations anticipated the later development by Chamberlin of a method entailing the deliberate creation of "multiple working hypotheses" for the purpose of bringing "into distinct view every rational explanation of the phenomenon in hand and to develop into working form every tenable hypothesis of its nature, cause or origin, and to give each of these a due place in the inquiry" (1904:69–70). Chamberlin's approach, in turn, provided the basis for the "strong inference" that Platt (1964) associated with rapid advances in knowledge in fields such as molecular biology and high-energy physics. Strong inference is based on the creative use of experiments to eliminate one or more competing hypotheses and consists of the following steps: devising alternative hypotheses, devising an experiment (or experiments) that will falsify one or more of the hypotheses, carrying out the experiment, and then recycling this procedure to further investigate whatever possibilities remain (1964:347).

Experiments also have other important functions in science. In a wide-ranging examination of the use of "experiments and observations" in the "fact-gathering" aspect of normal scientific investigation, Kuhn (1970:25–29) identified three primary areas of application: determining with greater precision facts that a particular paradigm has identified as being particularly important; determining facts used in comparisons with predictions from the paradigm theory; and, most important of all in his view, "articulating the paradigm theory, resolving some of its residual ambiguities and permitting the solution of problems to which it had previously only drawn attention." In the latter case, he pointed to experiments in the "more mathematical sciences" that are directed toward determination of physical constants and quantitative laws. But he also noted that experiments may serve to produce qualitative information when scientists pursue the matter of how a paradigm might be applied to a set of phenomena other than the one for which it was originally developed. In this instance, they serve a function comparable to the one identified by Herschel, in that they are, in Kuhn's words, "necessary to choose among the alternative ways of applying the paradigm to the new area of interest" (1970:29).

Archaeological experiments have the potential to make contributions in all the areas identified so far. With respect to discriminating among alternative explanations of phenomena and applications of theory, the experiments archaeologists perform are most often used to test beliefs about past cultural behavior; thus they eliminate some and provide support for others. It is worth noting that while experiments undertaken for these purposes may produce quantitative data, their goal is typically qualitative in nature (that is, they are designed to produce a conclusion of the sort: this was possible; this was unlikely; this was not possible). Experiments that have quantitative data as their goal are also common, but archaeology is not physics, so we should not expect to see them used in the development of quantitative laws. Nonetheless, experiments often enable quantification of variables important to specific problems of interest to archaeologists, such as the quantity of chipping debris that results from a particular technique of handaxe manufacture, the person-hours required to complete a unit of construction associated with an ancient monument, and the crop yield per hectare that might be expected from a particular agricultural system. In archaeology, as in sciences such as physics and chemistry, the types of data an experiment is designed to produce are those deemed useful to the solution of problems whose genesis and importance are tied to a particular model or paradigm. For example, Leslie White's (1949) influential arguments on the significance of the relationship between a society's technological level and the amount of energy it can harness provide justification for experimental acquisition of quantitative data on the energetics of prehistoric cultures.

Looked at from the broadest possible perspective, what is most important about archaeological experiments—their true claim to fame—is that they provide a connection between the past and present that facilitates analysis and interpretation of the archaeological record. For this reason they figure prominently, as do ethnoarchaeological studies, in attempts to build what Lewis Binford (1977) has termed "*middle-range*" *theory,* which refers to the gap that separates the actions that created the archaeological record and that record as seen today.[1] Both ethnoarchaeological observations and archaeological experiments provide analogies that can help us link evidence from the past with the actions that produced it. As with any analogs, ones provided by an archaeological experiment or an ethnoarchaeological study must be evaluated for goodness of fit with the actual archaeological evidence at hand. Because experiments typically concern the more mechanical aspects of technology and subsistence activities, application of their results to reconstructions of the past is generally less problematic than is the use of inferences about social behavior drawn from ethnographic and ethnoarchaeological studies (for criticisms of middle-range theory derived from ethnoarchaeology see Hodder 1999:27–29 and Johnson 1999:48–63; see also Raab and Goodyear 1984).

Imitative experiments may also have a certain therapeutic value. They can provide an outlet for the frustrations that some archaeologists experience with the fortuitous and intractable nature of the archaeological record. When archaeologists survey or excavate, they must work with whatever traces of the past they can discover and recover. Excavation in particular is tricky business because it is sometimes difficult, often tedious, and always destructive. With respect to this last point, a chemist who makes a critical mistake in carrying out a research project will certainly have regrets (especially so if a great deal of time and research funds have been expended), but that project can, at least, be redone (and later duplicated by other chemists seeking to verify the results). Archaeologists, of course, don't have the luxury of "do-overs" in most cases. If an excavation is botched, it can't be repeated (although we can excavate similar sites in the region, if any are found). Once room 12 is excavated, it is gone. It can only partially be re-created through photographs, maps, drawings, and the artifacts it once contained. The best procedure is to work with utmost care and attention to detail, make the documentation as complete as possible, and leave part of a site unexcavated for another archaeologist on another day. The perishable nature of the archaeological record makes it all the more precious and is the source of some of its allure, but where excavation is concerned, it would certainly be helpful to be able to do it over and do it better. It would also be nice if we weren't limited to whatever bits of evidence chance has left for us to uncover. With an imitative experiment, we can, in a way, transcend these limitations and make the past repeat itself as many times as we wish. Here we normally have complete control over all variables, and if mistakes are made, no harm is done, except perhaps to egos and professional reputations!

THE LOGIC OF ARCHAEOLOGICAL EXPERIMENTATION: WORKING BACKWARDS AND MOVING FORWARD

After an experiment is performed (or an excavation completed) and before the goal of making edifying statements about the past can be achieved, there are data to be analyzed and interpreted. What kind of logic guides the interpretive process, the process of making inferences about the past? How do we distinguish between a better explanation and a worse one? It should be clear from the discussion of the cultural-historical, processual, and postprocessual approaches that disagreements are common among archaeologists on theoretical and methodological issues, but whatever the approach taken, they all endeavor to construct consistent, coherent, and persuasive arguments. To be taken seriously, an interpretation must be derived in some convincing manner from a clearly specified set of data. The primary sources of these data are, of course, the available material remains of past human behavior along with associated noncultural materials such as pollen, domesticated and nondomesticated animal bones, and soils; secondary sources may come from the results of imitative experiments or ethnoarchaeological investigations. Regardless of the source, the data are in the present while the behavior we're interested in belongs to the past. The primary objective of the archaeologist is to make a meaningful connection between the two.

INDUCTIVE INFERENCE

A good place to start thinking about inference is with what we are most familiar—everyday life. As we grow up we learn to operate according a store of empirically based propositions (rules) that often take the form of $X \rightarrow Y$ (X implies Y). "If I do this (X), I will get that (Y)." Some are given to us outright and others we develop more or less on our own. Think, for instance, about how this sort of reasoning guided you as a child. Think about punishments and rewards, actions that brought pain and pleasure. Perhaps as an inquisitive child you touched a hot woodstove; if so, how many tests did it take for you to learn to avoid contact? After you were punished or rewarded several times for something you did or refused to do, you came to rely on a "rule" substantiated by your repeated experiences: if I do X (raid the forbidden cookie jar, perhaps?), I get Y (scolded, sent to my room, or worse) in return. This process of establishing the rule by experience is an example of inductive inference: the rule (whose possibility may occur to you on the basis of a single event) is validated through repeated observations in which it appears to hold true (I repeatedly see that when X happens, Y is the result, so X really does imply Y).

Induction also figures in the establishment of the archaeology's "rules," that is, the knowledge that it typically presents to the world. When we read about a particular archaeological culture, region, or era, we are being treated to generalizations based on the results of many excavations and analyses. In other words, when many recovered Xs are always (or nearly always) associated with Y, we feel confident in presenting the rule $X \rightarrow Y$, perhaps with some qualifications attached. For example, imagine that in a particular region and during a specified time period called the *Late Archaic,* the houses are all of a certain type (let's say they're round, semi-subterranean structures known as *pithouses*) and associated with them are three types of pottery (plain redware, redware with black painted designs, and black on white). Not surprisingly then, when we consult a book about the prehistory of this region, we are told that "the Late Archaic period is characterized by round pithouses and the following three pottery types: plain redware. . . ." It will no doubt also tell us about tool technology, subsistence patterns, and so on, so that ultimately, at the highest level, the X represents the Late Archaic period and the Y takes on the form of a list of its typical attributes. The confidence to make this type of characterization rests on the many observations in which the specified associations have been found to occur.

Does this then mean that the mode of *discovery* in archaeology is primarily by induction? In other words, do we typically move directly from observation to conclusion? I believe that in most instances the answer is "no." Generalizing statements of the kind in the above example don't explain anything; they merely summarize. And they are certainly not based on "pure" observations, that is, observations made outside the influence of a preexisting model of some kind (remember that paradigms define what is and isn't a fact to be collected—there is no such thing as a value-free fact). In the words of philosopher of science Karl Popper (1962), "the belief that we can start with pure observation alone, without anything in the nature of a theory, is absurd" (46); "inference based on many observations, is a myth" (53). His conclusion that "repeated observations and experiments function in science as tests of our conjectures or hypotheses . . ." (53) gets to the heart of the role most often played by induction. To better understand the kind of reasoning that underlies the discovery phase of science, we must look more closely at how we might first reach the point where we have a conjecture or hypothesis to test.

ABDUCTIVE INFERENCE

Let's move from a situation in which we merely chronicle associations, or otherwise describe, to one in which explanation is our goal. If we want to know about past behavior—what actions and or processes led to what we have discovered—we must, of necessity, work backwards, from results to causes. The archaeological record gives us Y and we have to figure out what contributed to or caused it (X). So now Y may be redware pottery (found, perhaps, exclusively in graves), but the X we're interested in might be the methods and materials that were used to make it (how), the use(s) to which it was put (another how), or the reasons that underlie its manufacture and distribution (why). If, for example, we know that a particular behavior or process, X, will result in Y, do the rules of formal logic allow us to move directly from the observed Y back to X as the cause? Absolutely not! Working backwards here is logically invalid. In more technical jargon, this sort of error is referred to as the *fallacy of affirming the consequent.* Do scientists do this? Yes! And often.

The name given to this type of reasoning by philosopher C. S. Peirce is abduction (he has also referred to it as retroduction).[2] It appears to be quite dangerous—after all, $X \rightarrow Y$ says nothing about Y implying X.[3] In the simple example of pithouses and the Late Archaic, the strong association between the Late Archaic period and pithouses does not mean that it is legitimate to conclude that all pithouses should be placed in the Late Archaic period (they may have been used in other eras as well). Abduction would appear to describe a situation in which one jumps to possibly unwarranted conclusions. If it represented an end point of interpretation rather than a point of departure, we would have to dismiss it as bad practice. But even so, it seems unlikely that we would be able to avoid making abductions, at least in the early phases of our interpretive efforts. Why is this so?

According to Norwood Hanson (another philosopher of science), neither induction nor the hypothetico-deductive approach tells us how explanatory statements come into being:

> Physicists rarely find laws by enumerating and summarizing observables [induction]. There is also something wrong with the H-D [hypothetico-deductive] account, however. If it were construed as an account of physical practice it would be misleading. Physicists do not start from hypotheses; they start from data. By the time a law has been fixed into an H-D system, really original thinking is over. The pedestrian process of deducing observation statements [such as test implications] from hypotheses comes only after the physicist sees that the hypothesis will at least explain the initial data requiring explanation. This H-D account is helpful only when discussing the argument of a finished research report, or for understanding how the experimentalist or the engineer develops the theoretical physicist's hypotheses; the analysis leaves undiscussed the reasoning which often points to the first tentative proposals of laws. (1969:70–71)

According to Peirce, those first tentative explanatory proposals derive from abductive inference: "Deduction proves that something *must* be; Induction shows that something *actually* is operative; abduction merely suggests that something *may be*" (1931:171).

A suggestion that "something may be" is an inference, a hypothesis to be tested. Peirce argues, "Abduction, although it is very little hampered by logical rules, nevertheless is logical inference, asserting its conclusion only problematically, or conjecturally, it is true, but nevertheless having a perfectly definite logical form" (1931:188). What can be said about such a hypothesis? To state the obvious, it wouldn't be offered if it didn't provide an explanation (even a partial one) for the problem at hand. Furthermore, a hypothesis may occur to us after only a single occurrence of whatever it is we feel a need to explain. That hypothesis may subsequently be supported inductively, as it is found to be "operative" in case after case. Hanson summarizes the form of abductive inference as follows:

1. Some surprising phenomenon P is observed.

2. P would be explicable as a matter of course if H were true.

3. Hence there is reason to think that H is true. (1969:86)

Let's consider a simple real-world example. A useful analogy for what archaeologists do in reconstructing the cultural and natural processes that led to the formation of a site can be provided by work of the detective. Enter Sherlock Holmes. The detective, like the archaeologist, typically works from results back to causes. The detective observes Y (a dead body showing signs of trauma, perhaps) and has to figure out what the cause might have been—X[1] (murder), X^2 (suicide), or X^3 (accident). He or she will likely form an initial working hypothesis on the basis of some of the evidence at the scene (data). Both the detective and the archaeologist work with traces of past human behavior that may have been subjected to a variety of cultural and noncultural transformations (e.g., a person deliberately or accidentally moved objects from their original positions, animals picked through the site, some items decayed and left no traces). In each case, the evidence is typically circumstantial, requires interpretation, and may not support a single conclusion, even though one possibility may come to be judged, for reasons that must be specified, more likely than the others. Working abductively requires that corroborative evidence be found. When it comes to crimes, prosecutors prefer to try cases on more than circumstantial evidence (eye-witnesses and videotape of the crime are great to have in court), but for archaeologists that is not possible.

CORROBORATIVE EVIDENCE

Corroborative evidence is central to the development of a persuasive argument in which (ideally) all but one possible interpretation is eliminated. As we have seen, test implications specify what corroborative evidence should be found if the hypothesis is correct (and may also specify what evidence disqualifies the hypothesis). In the case of formal hypotheses designed to guide a research project, the test implications have been carefully established in advance (but flexibility, a nonrigid approach, is key—hypotheses and test implications can, and often are modified during the course of the project). As evidence of the past is discovered, the interpretive process begins. When, for instance, what appears to be a pit is found, I may form a tentative hypothesis (educated hunch) about what it was. The process might go something like this: the pit is adjacent to what appears to have been a habitation structure. I am aware that features classified as storage pits appear in similar contexts at other sites associated with this culture and time period (prior knowledge). As I investigate the apparent storage pits on my site, I discover that the size of the opening is large enough to allow easy access to human arms (physical properties). As I excavate deeper, I find that the shape and depth of the pit are comparable to those of some of the storage pits found in similar sites and a few similar features described in the ethnographic literature (analogy). At this point, the storage pit hypothesis may seem reasonable, but of course, doubts should remain:

> If I interpret an excavated feature as a storage pit, and show that the feature shares five,
> ten, fifteen characteristics in common with ethnographically "known" storage pits, there is
> still a possibility that the feature could be interpreted some other way. (Johnson 1999:60)

Yes, of course there is, and that is why the hypothesis-testing format is useful: it forces me to think hard about what sort of evidence I might be able to collect that would support (or refute) this interpretation. It also encourages formulating alternative (multiple working) hypotheses.

So, what other data might strengthen this conclusion? How can I be as certain as possible that people did store something in this feature? I wonder if traces of what may have been placed in the pit can be found. I use flotation (a process that separates the lighter from the heavier components of the excavated matrix in a water or chemical bath to permit the lighter fraction to be skimmed off) in an attempt to extract organic materials such as seeds, grains, shell, and small bone fragments from the fill. I also have the fill examined for pollen. If those two analyses point to the pit as having once held wheat, my circumstantial argument becomes more persuasive. Imagine further that examination of the walls of the pit reveals plaster or perhaps traces of a type of grass known from ethnoarchaeological studies to be used as a rot-resistant liner in pits used for storage of perishable materials (analogy). Evidence is building in favor of the storage pit hypothesis, and ultimately, I may become convinced that at least once in its life, the pit was used for storage of grain. Could it also have been used for some other purpose? Of course it could. Could it be that at some time in the past this feature, whose original use left no trace of which I am aware, served as a trash pit and that's how the grain and pollen got into it? This could also have happened. Absolute certainty, the elimination of all possibilities but one, is generally impossible in archaeology and in many other disciplines as well.[4] Unlike Sherlock Holmes, we archaeologists have no hope of eventually getting the person who made and used the pit to "confess" and either confirm or correct our interpretation. But circumstantial evidence in a well-reasoned, tightly constructed argument can be very persuasive—in courtrooms and in archaeology. In this example, although I may not have tested a hypothesis in the strictest sense, and was unable to eliminate the possibility that it was used for something other than storage, I did evaluate the goodness of fit between the test implications and the evidence by using a systematic approach that, in my opinion, is more likely to lead us toward the truth than away from it.

TOULMIN'S MODEL

As a final step before looking at the design of archaeological experiments, let's examine the structure of an argument in which data lead to an inference. This will be of value in assessing the coherence, consistency, and persuasiveness of any reconstruction of the past, regardless of the theoretical orientation of its creator. The model that I feel presents a particularly clear schematic is one developed by philosopher Stephen Toulmin (see Figure 2-1).

As with the abduction, we begin with data (D) and end with an inference or claim (C). The justification for the claim is provided by the warrants (W), which are propositions that legitimize the step from D to C; they are "rules, principles, [and] inference-licenses" that "show that, taking these data as a starting point, the step to the original claim or conclusion is an appropriate or legitimate one" (Toulmin 2003:91). In the case of the possible storage pit, the warrants will most likely consist of statements about the characteristics of storage pits derived from studies of other similar-appearing features (from archaeological and/or ethnographic contexts). It is also common to find an assessment of the strength of the claim, that is, an indication of the kind and degree of reliance we may place on the conclusion, in the form of what Toulmin calls a "modal qualifier" (Q). Expressions such as "almost cer-

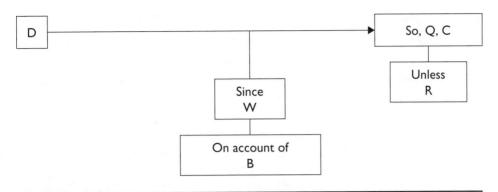

Figure 2-1   Toulmin's model for the form of an argument

tainly," "presumably," and "probably" typically qualify claims when the inference is not absolute. In addition to qualifiers, arguments may also contain conditions for rebuttal (R), when there are known circumstances in which the warrants would not apply.

When we evaluate a claim, we examine the warrants and make a judgment about their suitability; we may question their relevance to the particular argument before us or their value in general. If we are satisfied with the warrants and the "bridge" they provide between data and claim, the matter normally ends there—we accept the assertion. But warrants are not "self-validating" (Toulmin, Rieke, and Janik 1984:62), so if we are skeptical of the ones on which a claim is based, we may legitimately request the "backing" (B) on which they rest (and here things can get a bit messy depending on the level and type of justification we demand). When we speak of the backing of a warrant we are referring to "categorical statements of fact" that, like the data, can be "appealed to in direct support of our conclusions" (Toulmin 2003:98). These statements are "generalizations making explicit the body of experience relied on to establish the trustworthiness of the ways of arguing applied to any particular case" (Toulmin, Rieke, and Janik 1984:61). For instance, if the warrants take the form of statements about the attributes believed to define storage pits, we may ask why those attributes are felt to be diagnostic. The backing of the warrants might be found in ethnographic analogies and/or in archaeological evidence from other pits in which, for reasons we may also feel the need to question, a storage function was inferred. Backing may also come from the results of an experiment in which a variety of materials were successfully stored in a pit similar to the one in question. As an exercise, you might try applying the Toulmin model to the earlier example in which regional abandonment was attributed to climate change. What kinds of statements might serve as warrants and what sort backing would give them legitimacy in this instance?

Ultimately, all archaeologists strive to produce statements about the past that are based on reasonable conclusions drawn from their data. In other words, they all attempt to construct arguments that are consistent, coherent, and convincing. This requires solidly backed warrants that make the proposed connection between data and conclusion defensible. Providing warrants that strengthen arguments about the manufacture and use of artifacts and features and the noncultural processes that transform the archaeological record is the primary job of experimental archaeology. Just how it accomplishes this is what the remainder of this book is about.

THE DESIGN OF THE EXPERIMENT

The obvious first step in the design of an archaeological experiment is a question or idea about some aspect of the past that can be converted into a testable form. When we perform a typical imitative experiment, we are testing whether or not the hypothesized behavior (the X in the section above) *could have* produced an observed result (Y) or, in Peirce's terms, whether or not X *may be* the cause of Y. There are clear limits to the types of questions to which experiments can be applied. For instance, ethnographic analogies may provide us with interesting ideas about the possible meanings and uses of prehistoric cave paintings such as those at Chauvet and Lascaux (France), but no imitative experiment can be performed to support or refute these ideas.[5] We must limit ourselves to the somewhat more mundane aspects of these exotic gifts from the past. We observe the results of past human behavior—paintings on the walls of caves. We wonder how they were produced and this leads us to formulate some hypotheses about the composition and production of the paints and the method of their application to cave walls. Assuming that we proceed to make paints and reproduce the colors, lines, and textures of the ancient artwork perfectly, we have not proved that our methods were used in the past—we have, at best, shown that they could have been used. How do we increase the likelihood that our results of this or any other experiment are relevant? In general, by adhering to the following guidelines:

1. A good experiment begins in the library. Search the relevant archaeological and ethnographic literature. Clues to how something was made and/or used may often be found in evidence obtained from excavations (for example, an unfinished tool or one in association with the materials it was used to process) and observations of similar items in use in living societies. There is, for instance, an abundant and significant ethnographic literature available on the manufacture and use of pottery.

2. Use appropriate materials. In other words, attempt to insure that the "objective" and "effective" materials in the experiment were known to have been used by or were at least available to the people in question. As defined by Ascher (1961:809), the term "objective" refers to the material being studied. For example, in the case of the cave paintings we would need to know if the raw materials we plan to use to make our paints were ever found in the caves or associated habitation sites. If not, were they available in the immediate area? The same holds for the "effective" material, that is,

the material applied to the objective material in order to change it in the desired way. In this case it could refer to the tool(s) used to grind the pigment for the paint and those used to apply it.

3. Work within the limits of the aboriginal situation (Ascher 1961:809–810). In our experiment with cave painting, the method of producing and applying paint must not rely on any technology that exceeded the known, or at least the likely, capabilities of the past people in question. Simplifying the experiment by grinding and mixing materials with modern power-driven equipment is obviously not appropriate, neither is the use of modern paintbrushes or an airbrush to replicate the artwork!

The simple and obvious point of these three guidelines is that the more closely the experiment conforms to what is known about the past culture and environment, the more useful its results are likely to be.

4. Gain experience before performing the experiment. Interpreting the results of an imitative experiment is not always easy. When attempting to replicate what a person may have done in the past, lack of comparable skill and experience on the part of the experimenter can seriously limit the value of the results. A period of informal experimentation and training may be sufficient to master the process being investigated, but in some cases a test subject with special expertise is highly recommended (for instance, an experienced archer in the case of an experiment that tests the performance of replicas of ancient bows and arrows). If an experiment is carried out with the goal of assessing the performance of a tool such as a stone axe, it is not enough either to make a perfect replica of the axe head or (in special circumstances) to use a genuine artifact. The hafting of the axe will be critical and that will constitute a separate experiment in itself. Experience figures significantly in both crafting the tool and using it. In an experiment in which the goal is to assess efficiency of operation, the experimenter must make a determination as to whether or not the tool is functionally equivalent to an original. If chopping with an axe reveals that the head is not being held securely by the haft, it's a safe assumption that the tool's performance will be degraded and test results will have very little if any value. It must also be remembered that since we do not have direct access to the past, we can never be absolutely certain that our technique of using a tool is the same as the one(s) typically employed by the people who made the original version.

5. Perform the experiment more than once whenever possible, because the results of a single experiment can be anomalous. If I apply X (X may be a sequence of steps) and get Y, will it work that way every time? If the experiment failed, was it perhaps because one step was performed incorrectly? Is it likely that someone else would get the same results? Experimental science requires that results be repeatable. Rushing to conclusions on the basis of a single test is inadvisable, as some of the case studies that follow will make clear.

6. Make certain that the report on the experiment is complete and sufficiently detailed to allow another person to critique and, if desired, repeat the experiment.

7. Always keep in mind what you are ultimately attempting to accomplish by performing an experiment. This point was made before, but it is worth repeating: the goal of replicative experiments is typically to learn how something *might* have been made or used in the past, not to prove that it *was* made or used in one particular way. The best that can normally be expected is to narrow the range of possibilities by discarding some entirely and showing others to be more likely than others, either because they fit with independent (corroborative) evidence or just make more sense under the specified circumstances.

8. Finally, remember that these guidelines are only general recommendations. They do not have to be followed slavishly. As we shall see in the case studies that follow, the specific goals of the experiment dictate the details of the replication. Precise replication in terms of materials or scale may or may not be required to provide the desired information.

COMPLEMENTARY APPROACHES

We're now nearly ready to examine a select group of archaeological experiments. But first, the interrelationships among experimental archaeology, ethnoarchaeology, and more conventional approaches (survey and excavation) need to be put into perspective. Just as ethnoarchaeology is used in the development of middle-range theory through its provision of analogs to be tested against the archaeological record, it has also been a valuable source of models to be explored experimentally. As we will see, ethnographic research has proven valuable to studies of the manufacture and use of a variety of implements. It has provided experimenters with processes (Xs) to be applied and tested in their attempts to produce the results (Ys) revealed through conventional fieldwork. In turn, the results of experiments can help in testing the viability of a particular ethnographic analogy as applied to a specific artifact or feature (they may also suggest possibilities that have no contemporary analogs). Another area in which experiments have also been of value is in pointing to the type of corroborative evidence to be searched for in the archaeological record to substantiate an abductive inference. For instance, if an experimentally tested method of manufacture produces some distinctive by-products, a search in the archaeological record for these (perhaps until now) neglected or misunderstood waste materials may result in increased support for the hypothesized manufacturing process actually having been used in the past. This in turn may facilitate interpretation of archaeological evidence obtained from future excavations (for example, a situation in which no tools of a particular type are found at a site, but the likely by-products of their manufacture are recovered).

The examples that follow in the next three chapters have been selected to demonstrate how imitative experiments contribute to the success of modern archaeology in meeting the goals discussed in chapter 1, and how the logic and guidelines discussed above are implemented in their design, execution, and interpretation. They also serve to illustrate the broad range of problems to which experiments may be applied and the unique insight they provide on life in the past.

NOTES

[1] See Kosso 1991 for a discussion of middle-range theories as hermeneutical tools.

[2] The earliest known mention of this type of reasoning is by Aristotle (Hanson 1969:85).

[3] Studies cited by Matthews (1994:88–93) indicate that a surprisingly large number of people, even those well trained in science, do not realize that affirming the consequent constitutes fallacious reasoning. If they are given the rule $X \rightarrow Y$ and are then told that Y is true, they conclude that X is true as well. For further discussion of this issue see "Experiments in Education" in chapter 6.

[4] In spite of all the caveats about the absence of certainty in archaeological reconstructions, sometimes we can come extremely close to what is normally unattainable. Loud and Harrington's study of Lovelock Cave in Nevada (excerpts are reprinted in Heizer's 1959 anthology, pages 238–252) is a case in point. In this particular instance, "storage pits" still contained clear evidence of their lining with grasses and, in one case, a false bottom that concealed a bundle containing decoys for use in hunting waterfowl. Of course, this discovery naturally led to other, less easily answerable questions.

[5] This is not to suggest that investigation of this subject is beyond the scope of archaeological inquiry. See, for example, Conkey 1980, Mithen 1996, Lewis-Williams and Dowson 1988, Rice and Patterson 1985.

CHAPTER 3

EXPERIMENTAL APPROACHES TO ARTIFACTS AND FEATURES

Archaeological interpretation does not begin when the excavation (or experiment, or ethnoarchaeological study) ends. It is a vital part of the data acquisition phase of research, as the archaeologist must attempt to make sense of what is being recovered in "real time." Changes in strategy are often called for by the nature of the evidence coming to light and for other reasons as well. To leave all interpretation until after the fieldwork is completed would be extremely poor practice and an invitation to disaster. At some point, however, the primary activity shifts from data acquisition to interpretation. Answering the questions that were originally posed in the research design as well as those that arose during the course of the investigation requires painstaking examination and analysis of all the available evidence: artifacts, ecofacts, features, and their associations and contexts.

In the case of artifacts, matters of technology and function are always of interest and frequently elusive. If we are fortunate, association may provide some important clues. For example, if we find a sharp, triangularly-shaped, chipped-stone artifact embedded in the rib of a mammoth, a fundamental question about its function has probably been answered. A large ground-stone artifact shaped like an elongated basin and containing traces of corn in its rough surface similarly informs us about its probable use, as does a rectangular wooden box containing a human skeleton. But not all, or even most, circumstances of discovery will be as accommodating to our questions about the past. In those instances, the curiosity that leads us to go to the trouble of digging up buried remnants of days gone by may further motivate us to make and use replicas of artifacts to discover more of their secrets as well as to satisfy a desire for firsthand experience relating to the lives of the people who created them—experience that cannot be obtained through more passive approaches.

Achieving these goals is not always easy. For instance, it is important to keep in mind that making a replica of any tool requires varying amounts of knowledge and skill. Clearly, knowing the steps to be followed in making a copy of a delicate, perfectly symmetrical flint spear point does not guarantee success any more than a serious study of techniques of oil painting confers the ability to create a masterpiece. Knowledge and skill varied in the past as well, and this is clearly reflected in the artifacts ancient people left behind (see discussion of Stafford 1993 below). Some toolmakers were consummate masters and others were less gifted. In addition, certain circumstances may have required a very finely crafted tool, while for others, a much more hastily made and crudely finished version probably served the purpose quite well. Often when archaeologists attempt to replicate a particular type of artifact, the goal is to reproduce a "textbook" example, that is, one on which the type has been based. As significant as these issues are, they have not received nearly as much attention in experiments as have matters of knowledge and skill as they relate to the *use* of ancient implements.

A BRIEF AND VERY SELECTIVE SURVEY

For all the diversity to be found in the many archaeological experiments devoted to artifacts and features, most experiments revolve around the same primary questions: How was it made? What was its function? How was it used? How was this particular result achieved?

STONE ARTIFACTS

Answering such questions for stone tools has proven particularly difficult, as this technology has essentially passed from the scene. Ethnoarchaeological studies, though few in number as a result of the limited survival of stone toolmaking cultures in the era of scientific archaeology, have been quite useful in providing general analogies for techniques of acquisition, core reduction, manufacture, use, and discard (see, for example, Gould 1980; Hayden 1976, 1977; Stout 2002; Toth, Clark, and Ligabue 1992). To transcend the limitations of the ethnographic evidence, archaeologists have had to reinvent a number of flint-knapping techniques in order to determine how specific types of ancient tools might have been made (see Johnson 1978 for a history of knapping experiments; Odell 2000 provides an in-depth overview of stone tool research since the early 1990s in the areas of procurement and technology, while Odell 2001 does the same for research relating to classification, functional analyses, and behavioral processes).

A great deal has been learned about the fundamentals of flint knapping from experiments whose purpose was to determine how the physical properties of materials such as flint, obsidian, and glass affect the fracturing that takes place when a core is struck with a hammer (Dibble and Whittaker 1981, Speth 1977) and how materials such as chert change when subjected to heat treatment (Crabtree and Butler 1964, Purdy and Brooks 1971). Understanding the mechanics and techniques of flaking is clearly critical to our attempts to determine how a particular type of tool may have been made and can provide a basis for attempts to replicate it (see Whittaker 1994 for a clear, detailed, and well-illustrated introduction to the subject of flint knapping, and Odell 2003 for a comprehensive guide to lithic analysis. See also Bordes 1968, Bordes and Crabtree 1969, Crabtree 1972, Flenniken 1978, Newcomer 1971).

When we seek to gain some insight into the functions of particular tool types, we are led to experiments in which we use them to do things we believe the original makers may have done. Since tools recovered from archaeological sites sometimes provide a few precious hints of how they were used—some polish on one surface, a series of striations oriented perpendicularly or parallel to a sharp edge, and so on—we naturally attempt to determine what types of activities produce lasting, diagnostic evidence of their occurrence. And here we enter the realm of experiments involving replication and identification of use-wear (microscopic traces of wear on the working edge of a tool that result from use), such as those done by Sonnenfeld (1962) and Newcomer and Keeley (1979).

Complementing these efforts are ones that explore the operation of stone implements in the performance of specific tasks, such as one by Frison (1989) in which the effectiveness of Clovis (a widespread Paleo-Indian culture of North America) tools as hunting weapons was investigated and those of Jones (1980) and Pitts and Roberts (1998) that evaluated the effectiveness of handaxes and other stone implements as butchery tools.[1] Replicas of handaxes (made of fiberglass and stone) have even been thrown to determine their potential as aerial missiles in the service of hunters (Calvin 1990; O'Brien 1981, 1984; Whittaker and McCall 2001). In a similar vein, archaeologists have also tested the operation of flint sickles (Curwen 1930, Harlan 1967), the use of grooved stones to straighten arrow shafts (Cosner 1951), the uses of projectile points (Evans 1957) as well as the effects on their durability of high thickness:length ratios (Cheshier and Kelly 2006), and the operating characteristics and performance of stone axes (a topic taken up in chapter 4). Experiments conducted by de Beaune (1987) have likewise concerned issues of classification and operation, but on a very different sort of artifact—the stone lamp.

CERAMIC ARTIFACTS

The production and use of ceramic artifacts have been the subject of experiments as well. Although the replication of ancient ceramic technology poses a wide variety of challenges, in contrast to stone tool manufacture there is considerably less mystery surrounding the working of clay (for an excellent introduction, including discussion of experiments and ethnographic studies see Rye 1981). The techniques of modelling, coiling, and throwing on a wheel are all well-known, as all are still in use. Examples of experiments in which particular types of pottery have been replicated include those of Bimson (1956), Griffin and Angell (1935), Lucas (1962), MacIver (1921), and Zuckerman (2000), while ones performed by Liddell (1929) and Quimby (1949) focused on replicating the methods used to create specific types of incised decorations. Some of the fine details of pottery manufacture in the Maya Lowlands were explored in a study by López Varela, van Gijn, and Jacobs (2002). In this experiment, the use of sherds as tools for making pottery was investigated, with microscopic examination being used to compare wear patterns on sherds recovered from archaeological sites with those that developed on replicas used in a simulation of Maya pottery production.

In addition to expanding our knowledge of how ancient pottery was made, experiments have added to our understanding of its use. Although a great deal can sometimes be inferred from attributes related to form, such as a vessel's overall shape and the size of its opening (Berlin 1999), and ethnoarchaeological studies can greatly improve interpretation of use-related alterations resulting from abrasion, absorbed residues, and carbon deposits (Longacre and Skibo 1994, Skibo 1992), testing hypotheses about the use-history of a specific ceramic artifact is ideally approached experimentally; replicas can be made, use-tested, and examined macro- and microscopically for use-wear and other forms of alteration, and so on.

A particularly interesting and unusual experiment centering on wear patterns was carried out by White (1992). In this case, the focus was not on the ceramic vessel itself but instead on its possible use in the processing of human bone. For this experiment, mule deer bones that had been broken into fragments were cooked in a replica of an Anasazi (a prehistoric tradition of the American Southwest that is ancestral to the modern Pueblos) pot to determine if abrasion and polishing seen on the ends of human bone fragments recovered from a site in Colorado might have resulted from contact with the walls of such a vessel as they were boiled. The wear patterns and polish found on the prehistoric human specimens were faithfully replicated on the boiled mule deer bones, thereby providing strong corroborative evidence in support of the hypothesis that the human remains had been cooked in a similar fashion.

Finally, although microscopic and other physical examinations of pottery sherds can tell us a great deal about their properties (for example, tempering materials may be identified) and the conditions under which they were fired (color and porosity being particularly important indicators), experimental techniques allow us to probe deeper. For example, archaeologists have performed experiments on sherds to determine as precisely as possible the temperature to which they were originally fired by reheating them to successively higher temperatures until changes begin to occur (e.g., Kingery and Frierman 1974). They have also used experiments to evaluate water permeability and the effects of different tempering materials and surface treatments on impact and thermal shock resistance (Bronitsky and Hamer 1986; Schiffer et al. 1994; Skibo, Schiffer, and Reid 1989).

BONE AND WOOD ARTIFACTS

Bone and wood artifacts have also been the subject of imitative experiments. One of the bones in White's experiment was converted to a tool when he used it to scrape out a ring of fat adhering to the rough interior wall of the pot; the striations on the bone produced by this action precisely matched those found on a human bone fragment from the site, thus pointing to the use of human bones as tools in food processing. While simple microscopic examination was sufficient in this case, other use-wear studies of organic artifacts have, like their lithic counterparts, benefited from use of the scanning electron microscope, but with some notable differences in technique (see d'Errico, Giacobini, and Puech 1984).

As with lithics, techniques of manufacture of bone and wood artifacts have been investigated experimentally (Clarke and Thompson 1953, Crabtree and Davis 1968, Pokines 1998), and use experiments have been conducted on such items as the atlatl (spear-thrower), the bow and arrow, and the bone projectile point (Browne 1940; Hutchings and Brüchert 1997; Peets 1960; Pope 1923; Miller, McEwen, and Bergman 1986; Pokines 1998; Thompson 1954). In the case of Thompson's experiment we have an example of a preliminary test of an intriguing hypothesis that merited a more realistic replication of ancient circumstances. Thompson reproduced several Upper Palaeolithic harpoon-types of the Spanish Magdalenian (an archaeological culture of the late Upper Palaeolithic in Western Europe) and Azilian (a tool tradition found in France and Spain that dates to the end of the Upper Palaeolithic and the beginning of the succeeding Mesolithic) in order to explore the possible reasons for differences in barb patterns and location of the perforation through which the harpoon line was attached. The experiment was severely limited by the fact that the replicas were not used on an animal but rather on hair-stuffed pillows! Results indicated that the design of the later Azilian uniserially barbed, centrally perforated, small points had the advantage of tending to embed entirely within the animal. They also tended to pivot when tugged by the line and hence were less likely to pull out. This was felt to be significant, as brushwood growing in northern Spain during the Azilian may have tended to snag harpoon shafts as they were dragged over the ground, and this could have resulted in the older-style head being pulled out; the later design would have tended to cause more damage and perhaps even result in the animal being held fast. This may all be true, but Thompson's stationary pillows are insufficiently comparable to the body of a highly animated animal to permit much confidence in the applicability of his findings to hunting in the Upper Palaeolithic. In Pokines' more recent experiment, greater realism was achieved by use of a dressed carcass of a domestic goat as a target for 20 hafted replicas of Lower Magdalenian spear points, which were thrown at it until breakage occurred. The results indicated that these points were strong and flexible, and that translated into much greater durability (longer use-lives) than has been demonstrated for stone projectile points.

ROUNDING OUT THE MARGINS

While experiments with stone, bone, wood, and ceramics comprise the bulk of those that have been performed to answer questions about the what and how of artifacts, these categories are not exhaustive. For example, Coghlan (1940) tested two hypotheses concerning the method by which copper ore was first smelted, while Coles (1962) compared the performance of leather and bronze shields by striking them with bronze swords (the leather shields were far superior, with the bronze ones showing themselves to be of only decorative value). In a very different sort of experiment, Ryder (1966) investigated the plausibility of written evidence and an illustration from the sixteenth century for use of skins suspended over fires as cooking vessels in Ireland and Scotland. His water-filled sheepskin cooking apparatus proved incapable of raising the temperature of a one-pound lambshank over 53 degrees Celsius (57 degrees with an aluminum foil cover that was put in place, in desperation no doubt, after an hour's worth of cooking). Problems were many and varied, and in the end Ryder came to the conclusion that this method of cooking would be difficult at best and perhaps impossible. He then carried out a second, equally memorable experiment in response to ethnographic evidence that referred to cooking in a paunch (the first and largest compartment of a ruminant's stomach.). By heating two water-filled paunches over a fire, and with the addition of hot stones as well as some grain to retain the heat, he was able to achieve temperatures of 90 to 95 degrees Celsius. Ryder concluded that cooking in a paunch would work well for something on the order of porridge, but not for meat (Ryder 1969).

Experiments with features frequently explore possible methods of transporting and assembling building materials. They may also be designed to produce quantitative data on labor and material costs associated with these activities and precisely track the natural transformations of features such as buildings and earthworks over extended periods of time. Multicomponent experiments such as these and ones that investigate the operation of such devices as complex kilns are examined in chapters 4 and 5. Although less common, experiments have been performed to test hypotheses about the possible functions of enigmatic features and improve our ability to recognize ones that leave behind poorly defined remains. Included in the case studies that follow are two examples: one is an experiment that had as its goal improved understanding of the archaeological evidence left behind by ancient Mesoamerican "ephemeral" kilns (Balkansky, Feinman, and Nicholas 1997) and the other features a set of experiments designed to shed light on the function of subterranean chambers created by the ancient Maya (Miksicek et al. 1981, Puleston 1971).

Finally, the artistic endeavors of ancient people have also been the subject of some notable experiments. For example, both Johnson (1957) and Lorblanchet (1991) have investigated cave painting. Johnson's experiment involved replicating the media used to create rock art in southern Africa and then using them in an attempt to reproduce the colors, surface appearance, and lines of the originals. Lorblanchet mastered techniques used by native Australians to duplicate with great success paintings of the type found in Upper Palaeolithic caves in southwestern Europe. His method involved chewing the media in his mouth and then spitting the paint onto the wall of a cave after he had sketched his subject with charcoal. The technique is essentially that of the air brush used by some artists today.

CASE STUDIES

Most experiments designed to test ideas about possible functions and methods of use of artifacts and features follow a similar logic. Although the ideal experiment replicates the item in question as well as the conditions of its presumed creation and/or use in as accurate and complete a manner as possible, sometimes this cannot be done and in other circumstances it may not be necessary. Some compromises aren't necessarily fatal to the validity of the experiment and others are. It's a question of science and art—there is no manual that will teach you how to go about it. Learning by example is probably the best approach. The case studies that follow should provide a good sense of the character of these types of experiment. I recommend critiquing each one according to how clearly its objective was defined and how well it was met. Can you devise a better experiment to answer the same question? What sort of follow-up experiment(s), if any, do you think would be worthwhile performing?

THE EGYPTIAN DRILL

An experiment was performed to determine if an ancient Egyptian drill—known to us only from pictures in tombs (Figure 3-1a), hieroglyphic representations signifying "craftsman" or "drill" (Figure 3-1b), ostensible cutting bits (Figure 3-2) and, more indirectly, objects that were drilled—operated on the principle of the crank (Hartenberg and Schmidt 1969). Richard Hartenberg, a professor of mechanical engineering, had doubts about the prevailing interpretation of the mode of operation of this drill. He noted, "Historians have either positively or diffidently assigned the first appearance of the crank to this tool of antiquity, without, however, giving explanations that ring true" (1969:155). He was particularly troubled by the high position of what appear to be weights. For a device that operated by cranking motion, they were in the wrong place—they should be near the lower end of the tool. Also, if the device operated by cranking, one hand would have to support the shaft at point A in Figure 3-1a. He concluded, "A cranking motion imposed on a top-heavy system whose axis of rotation is supported at only one point is unthinkable" (1969:159). Furthermore, the apparently small radius of rotation of the handle would result in a speed that would not be suitable for long-term use or the drilling of stone, where high speed and low torque would produce much better results.

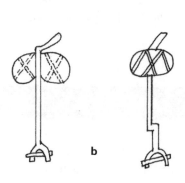

Figure 3-1
(a) Depiction of ancient Egyptian drill based on relief in a tomb dating to 2500 BC and (b) various hieroglyphs representing the drill.

A review of the available evidence from an engineering perspective led to several preliminary conclusions about the drill's design. Although the ancient illustrations did not allow a determination of whether or not the central component of the tool was a single piece with a curved end or of two-piece construction with an attached handle, Hartenberg felt that the former was much more likely, given the difficulty of making a strong connection between two pieces. Furthermore, he agreed with the prevailing assumption that the fork at the lower end of the device was meant to hold one of the many crescent-shaped "drill points" that have been recovered from a number of sites. Hartenberg surmised that the crossbar that appears in the hieroglyphs most likely functioned as a wear-pin (an easily replaceable part that prevented the drill bit from wearing away the lower part of the drill). In addition, he concluded that the notch in the bit would articulate with the wear-pin in such a way as to center itself in the fork (Figure 3-2). This all seems quite reasonable.

Seeking to do more than simply add opinions to the existing mix, Hartenberg enlisted the assistance of John Schmidt, Jr., an instrument-maker in his department, to produce a working replica of the tool. In this instance, it was not felt necessary to produce a model suitable for a museum exhibit—that is, one that replicated the details in the ancient drawings and was made of materials available to the Egyptians. The key requirement was to reproduce the approximate size, proportions, and configuration of the tool depicted in the ancient representations (see Figure 3-3):

Figure 3-2 Possible arrangement of Egyptian drill wear-pin and flint bit.

The body is bent from a length of electrical conduit, a 5/8 inch twist drill substitutes for flint bit as a matter of convenience, and two common bricks serve as weights, secured to the body with brazing-rod and wooden clamp. The principal as-built dimensions are: over-all height 43 inches; hand off-set 5 inches; . . . and weight 10 pounds. (1969:161)

Attempts to operate the drill with one hand failed and, in fact, the results were deemed "frightening" because of the wobbling induced by the rise and drop of the eccentric center of gravity. In the process of attempting to maintain the drill in a vertical position, "the left hand soon discovered what to do, namely, move back and forth with respect to the operator's body after the right hand had given the bricks a slight push before hurriedly joining the left hand in holding onto the handle" (1969:161). Once this back and forth operation was used, the drill proved easy to manipulate and it rapidly bored a hole in a wooden block. The conclusion: the Egyptian drill was not a crank-driven device but one whose design was considerably more complex. The "wobble-drive" would be especially effective in drilling stone, as it would act as an impact hammer of sorts, spalling off chips at a rapid rate.

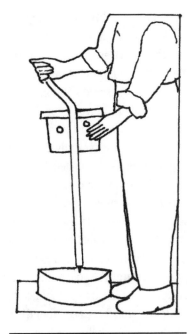

Figure 3-3 Model of Egyptian drill constructed by Hartenberg and Schmidt.

Discussion

I had the opportunity to work with a full-size replica of the tool created by Hartenberg and Schmidt and can easily agree with their conclusions. The device will not operate effectively by means of a 360-degree cranking motion, but once the weights are given an initial push to make the shaft rotate, moving the handle back and forth in a straight line (toward and then away from the body) causes it to revolve rapidly; the tool is stable and easy to control. In spite of these rather dramatic results, it would certainly have been preferable to build a model that more closely approximated a hypothetical original. Had that been done, additional aspects of the drill's operation could have been investigated.

For instance, Hartenberg's and Schmidt's drill could not be used to investigate the efficiency of the original, as it clearly did not satisfy the guidelines provided in chapter 2 concerning appropriate materials and technology. If they had wanted to answer questions about the rate at which the drill bored into in the various types of stone drilled by the Egyptians, the use-life of the flint bits, the value of the wear-pin, and so on, they would have had to build a replica from suitable materials known to have been available in the original setting and do this using appropriate techniques of manufacture. And, of course, the same types of stone known to have been drilled in ancient Egypt would have been required as well. The model produced by Hartenberg and Schmidt was minimally appropriate to the question of *modus operandi* in that it reproduced the geometry and overall configuration of the original, which allowed investigation of its basic mechanics. In spite of its very obvious limitations, the experiment provided useful knowledge concerning the potential of a device of this kind to spin at high speed with only a back-and-forth movement of the operator's arm.[2]

Although the results of this experiment were impressive, caution is in order. The fact that a device with the geometry of the Egyptian drill can be made to spin rapidly does not prove that it was typically used that way. Experiments with a variety of carefully replicated Egyptian tools conducted by Denys Stocks (1993, 1999, 2001, 2003) have, among their many important findings, pointed to an alternative method of operation for this device. Stocks has demonstrated how the drill may have figured in a two-step process used to hollow out stone vessels. First, a coring drill, featuring a hollow copper tube on its working end, is used to cut a cylinder in the solid vessel. This is then removed by chiseling. The drill of interest to Hartenberg and Schmidt is fitted not with a flint bit but with a stone borer and is used to enlarge the hole to the desired size. It is this component that Stocks believes is represented in the hieroglyphs rather than a wear-pin (as with the flint bits, numerous examples of stone borers have been found). The drill's mode of operation does not involve high-speed rotation or a back-and-forth movement of the operator's arm. Instead, it is rotated a quarter-turn clockwise, followed by a quarter-turn counterclockwise (Stocks refers to this as the "twist/reverse twist" drilling method [1993:599]). Hollowing out the interior of a stone vessel that could easily be broken would require slow speed and no wobble, which is exactly what this method provides.

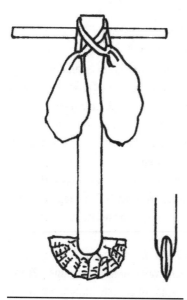

Figure 3-4   Egyptian boring tool.

Some questions remain, of course. Stocks' approach involved placing one hand on the curved handle and the other on the drill shaft, which would suggest that positioning the weights closer to the forked end would make the tool easier to use, as argued by Hartenberg and Schmidt. When it comes to precision boring, a configuration such as that shown in Figure 3-4, with a straight handle to be grasped with both hands would seem to make more sense, especially in light of the many repetitions of the twist-reverse-twist sequence that would be required to complete the job. I am left to wonder if the device that sparked these experiments might have been used with flint bits to drill holes at high speed in soft stone (such as gypsum), when less precision and delicacy was required, and with stone borers and the twist-reverse-twist method when hollowing out the interior of a fragile, thin-walled vessel. There is clearly more to be learned about this interesting example of ancient Egyptian engineering prowess. As Stocks notes: "We do not know, with reasonable certainty, how particular materials were worked in any given situation. . . . The precise construction and use of the stone vessel drilling and boring tool is only partly perceived" (2003:2). We can, at least, hope that a complete original will someday be discovered. When it comes to future experiments with the drill, it should be clear that replicas that are as close in all details to what we believe the originals were like must be used if the results are to have any value.

BRAIN REMOVAL IN MUMMIFICATION

Let's have a look at another interesting, if rather gruesome, problem solved by the ancient Egyptians: how to remove the brain as part of the process of mummification without disfiguring the corpse. The documentation for this procedure differs from that of the drill, in that no illustrations in tombs or hieroglyphs provide insight into the process. In this case, we have embalming tools and the words of the historian Herodotus, who wrote in the fifth century BC, "First they [the embalmers] drew out the brain through the nostrils with an iron hook, taking part of it out this way, and the rest by pouring in drugs" (Leek 1969:112).

LEEK'S SHEEP EXPERIMENT

F. Filce Leek sought to learn more about this process through examination of Egyptian skulls, followed by experiment. Inspection of a collection of 500 skulls showed that 56 percent had a hole (made postmortem) through the cribriform plate of the ethmoid bone (a fragile bone located at the base of cranium and between the eyes). In most cases the nasal septum (a vertical piece of cartilage and bone that separates the right and left nasal airway) had been partially or completely removed, whereas in 8 percent of the specimens the hole had been made through one of the nostrils.

Leek's initial impression was that extraction of the brain through such small openings would not be possible. The ideal test of his hypothesis would involve experimentation on a human cadaver, but with none available for his investigation, he obtained two sheeps' heads. Stainless steel replicas of ancient tools were used; in Leek's opinion, the design of the tool was significant and the material not. In spite of the relatively long passage from the nose to the braincase in a sheep, extracting brain tissue proved easy. Breaking through the ethmoid bone was accomplished with a surgical hammer and chisel, and when an instrument— straight or coiled at its end—was inserted, it had brain tissue adhering to it when withdrawn. Leek concluded that by repeating the process enough times, most of the brain tissue would be removed. Hypothesis 1 (extraction through a small hole not possible)—rejected. Hypothesis 2 (the design of the tool was important)—also rejected. In spite of Herodotus' description of the brain being drawn out with a "hook," the observed process was different. Leek concluded that it was the "glutinous and viscid" quality of the tissue that caused it to adhere to the instrument. The only significant variable he found was the size of the instrument's end—the larger it was, the greater the damage to the brain and the more rapid its extraction from the skull. Leek noted, "Had this process been continued and the head turned face downwards, much or all of the tissue would eventually have drained away" (1969:113). No explanation was provided as to why this last supposition was left untested.

From here, Leek moved on to test the effectiveness of natron, a combination of salts used by the Egyptians to desiccate and preserve the body. He filled the nose and partially empty braincase of one sheep with natron. The brain was not removed from the second sheep's head; instead, an opening was made in the parietal bone to allow natron to be put in contact with the intact brain tissue. Both heads were then fully covered with the salts. The purpose of this part of the experiment was to determine whether or not the natron had any antibacterial properties. The conclusion reached was that natron retarded, but did not stop decomposition of the brain tissue; neither did it preserve the eyes. These results, according to Leek, help explain the Egyptian practice of removing those organs.

In an appendix, Leek included a comment provided by pathologist Mark Patterson who, in response to Leek's experiment, was able to replicate the process of brain removal on a human specimen. Working through the right nostril, entry into the brain case was easily effected. The brain was macerated by slowly rotating the inserted rod. Its removal was then accomplished in three ways: by positioning the body properly, it simply drained out (albeit very slowly); it was speedily aspirated using a catheter and syringe; it was evacuated by irrigation with water, which flushed the tissue through the opening in the ethmoid bone. Interestingly, no mention is made of removing tissue by adhesion to the rod.

Discussion

In this example much closer attention was paid to replicating the original materials and circumstances than in the Egyptian drill experiment. The tools used by the ancient embalmers were carefully replicated, the only significant difference being in the choice of metal. It should be noted that although Herodotus specifies iron, copper and bronze implements were likely more widely used. Although it seems unlikely that brain tissue would adhere more or less effectively to iron or copper than to stainless steel, this could also have been tested. Nonetheless, the compromise made for convenience here doesn't seem significant.

Potentially more serious is the difference in anatomy of the skull between sheep and humans. Again, the most significant variables are in the experiment's favor. Brain tissue is comparable between the species. If a sheep's brain is easily macerated with the extraction tool, the same would hold true for that of a human being (as, of course, the follow-up experiment by Patterson demonstrated). Further, we would reasonably expect that human brain tissue would also adhere to the tools. What effect, if any, the difference in length and configuration of the nasal passage in a sheep might have on the complete process would require a comparative experiment, which Leek was unable to perform. In addition, the action of natron on the skin, eyes, and brain of the sheep should be comparable to its effects on their human counterparts.

The experiment's key achievement, of course, is its demonstration that brain tissue can be extracted through a very small opening without disfiguring the corpse in any way. But it also informs us on the need for brain removal to prevent putrefaction that natron alone cannot eliminate. Unfortunately, Leek did not completely remove the brain tissue and the amount he was able to extract was not specified. Patterson's follow-up experiment provided more solid support for the primary hypothesis in that he used a human subject and completely removed the brain, apparently by a combination of three methods he believed would have been available to ancient embalmers (the use of the catheter and syringe is problematic). Despite some serious limitations, Leek's and Patterson's experiments do, at least, shed light on how ancient Egyptians prepared their dead for the afterlife.

BRAIN REMOVAL REVISITED

More recently, Bob Brier and Ronn Wade performed an experiment in which they used ancient Egyptian practices to mummify an entire person (Brier 2001, Brier and Wade 2001). Of interest here is the approach they took to removing the brain:

> Egyptology journals occasionally contain articles theorizing how the brain was removed through the nose. They describe a cadaver lying on its back while a long hooked tool is inserted into the nose and pushed through the cribiform [sic] plate . . . and into the cranium. A small piece of the brain adheres to the end of the tool and can be pulled out. The process is repeated until the entire brain is removed. . . . Ronn and I tested this process on two heads obtained from body-donors, but could not get the brains out—they weren't viscous enough to stick to the tool. We finally hypothesized that if we used the tool much like a kitchen whisk inside the cranium, the brain would liquefy and then, if we inverted the cadaver, would run out through the nose. We would try this method on the donated body waiting to be mummified. We inserted a long bronze instrument, shaped like a miniature harpoon, inside the nasal passage and hammered it through the cribiform [sic] plate into the cranium with a wooden block. (Brier 2001:47)

> To macerate the brain, we used a bronze wire, very much like a coat hanger with one end coiled so that it would be just smaller than the opening made in the cranial floor of the skull. . . . With the coiled end extended into the right hemisphere of the brain, the wire was rotated for approximately twenty minutes to reduce the brain to a semi-liquid state. Periodic removal of the wire brought out residue of the dura and aerated brain tissue. Attempts to remove larger pieces of dura mater or tissue were done without success due to tearing and maceration. . . . We then repeated the same procedures to the left hemisphere of the brain.

> The brain cavity was irrigated, filled to capacity with water using a hollow reed connected to a leather bladder type flask. This method used only the force of gravity pressure and thus the force did not distend the soft outlying tissue of the face. The body was

repositioned so that it was lying on its abdomen. The head was placed on a downward slope to enhance drainage from the frontal lobe of the brain cavity, through the openings created and out the nasal passages. Inserting the wire with its coiled end permitted the initial and easy removal of a significant amount of brain dura mater. (Brier and Wade 2001:paragraphs 26–29)

To be certain that the cranium had been evacuated completely, Brier and Wade used the wire tool to force long strips of linen into the cranium and used them as swabs. After repeating this process several times, they came out clean.

Discussion

In their report, Brier and Wade noted the problems with Leek's experiment and the lack of details in the very short account of Patterson's trial that was appended to it. Although their experiment essentially confirms several of the key findings of those earlier investigations, they found it impossible to remove anything more that a small amount of the brain's outer membrane (meninges) by repeated insertion and removal of a hooked tool. Although Patterson is silent on this matter, his failure to include this approach among the three techniques he described suggests that it was not viable. The relative ease with which a brain can be liquefied by inserting and rotating a rod with a coiled end, combined with the simplicity of irrigating the interior of the skull and then draining it using only gravity and repeated insertions/removals of a coiled instrument, argues for the use of that approach in ancient times. In sum, this set of experiments confirms both the feasibility of the process and, when combined with the type of damage to the cribriform plate seen in ancient skulls, its likely use as well.

PALAEOLITHIC LAMPS

The thought of Upper Palaeolithic people creating works of art on the walls of caves by the light of torches and small lamps as long as 36,000 years ago is a captivating and inspiring one. Gazing at photographs of the painted and engraved walls and ceilings of places such as Chauvet and Lascaux in France and Altamira in Spain can be enough to induce a mental journey to a world far removed in time and space from the one we inhabit today. But what about the mundane-looking artifacts found in those caves that have been assumed to be lamps? Were they lamps? If so, how did they work and how much light did they produce? Here is fertile ground for both ethno- and experimental archaeology.

Sophie de Beaune (1987) devoted considerable effort to answering these very questions. The primary aims of her investigations were to come up with a proper definition of the Palaeolithic lamp, establish a typology, and discover how it worked. Her approach was multifaceted and well conceived. She began by inventorying all known objects that might have been used as lamps by Upper Palaeolithic people. She then compared the objects' technical, morphological, and functional attributes as well as their distribution in time and space. Analytical techniques such as mass spectrometry and gas chromatography were used to identify, where possible, the types of fat used as fuel and the materials from which the wicks were made. The lamps were then replicated and tested. She compared her results to evidence provided by studies of the fat-burning lamps used by the Inuit and Aleut.

Phase I: Definition and Analysis. In order to qualify as a lamp, an artifact must provide evidence of having had what de Beaune defined as an "active" zone, consisting of the area where fuel is burned and a wick, and a "passive" zone, which provides support and a means of holding the device (see Figure 3-5). She rejected any classification of an object as a lamp on the basis of raw material, size, and shape alone; instead, she insisted that evidence of use or residues produced by burning must be present before such a designation can be made. Further, the indications of burning should be numerous, located in and around the active zone, and absent elsewhere. Only 169 of the 302 "lamps" that she examined met her stan-

Figure 3-5 A simple open-circuit lamp made by the author using a piece of unmodified shale. After allowing the stone to warm in the sun (to facilitate melting of the beef-kidney fat used as fuel), a wick made from a piece of moss and saturated with fat was placed on the sloping surface. Note the pieces of fat placed on the wick to insure a supply of fuel and the liquefied fat running off at the lower (passive) end.

dards for inclusion in a group termed "certain, probable and possible." Of these, 85 merited the designation "certain." Analysis of residues on some of the lamps showed the presence of fatty acids with compositions similar to those found in *Suidae* (swine) and *Bovidae* (cattle). Wick residues proved more difficult to identify, but conifer and nonwoody wicks were found to have been used.

The spatial distribution of known lamps revealed that they were apparently not common outside France. Further, their distribution by site was not what might logically be expected: only 19.5 percent were found in deep caves (1987:571). Although provenience data were not available for many lamps overall, the spot where a lamp was abandoned was known for a large number of specimens recovered from dark caves. De Beaune conjectured that the lamps were placed at "strategic" points where people passed (such as entrances and intersections of galleries) so that they would be easy to find and reuse (1987:571).

Phase II: Formulating and Testing the Hypothesis. On the basis of her examination of the lamps, de Beaune was able to hypothesize that they were of three distinct types: open-circuit, closed-circuit, and closed-circuit with carved handles. Open-circuit lamps were the simplest, consisting of small flat or slightly concave slabs or naturally formed bowls with cavities that open to the side (liquid fuel runs off). Closed-circuit lamps have (closed) bowls that are generally circular or oval and that may be naturally formed with some retouch of the cavity or entirely fabricated (liquid fuel accumulates in the bowl). These are the most common form. Rarest are the closed-circuit lamps with carved handles, about a third of which were decorated and half of which were made of sandstone.

Experimentation was key to understanding how these lamps operated and pointed to why certain materials and types were preferred in particular circumstances. Some of the major findings were:

1. Open-circuit lamps lost fuel rapidly, as the fat drained away as soon as it melted. Those made on slabs with concave surfaces were easiest to handle, as the fat drained toward the lower end, leaving the opposite, "passive," end dry.

2. Any stone base will work, but limestone tends to occur in shapes that require little modification. Sandstone conducts heat much better, making a handle on a lamp of this material a practical attribute.

3. The size and shape of the cavity are important. Sloping sides permit good contact to be made between the fat and the wick. It was found that the preferable arrangement has the fat placed partially on the wick, to provide saturation as it melts.

4. Fuel must melt at low temperatures and must not contain much adipose tissue. The most efficient, in order, is fat obtained from *Phocidae* (seal), *Equidae* (horse), and *Bovidae*. Although analysis of residues pointed to *Suidae* and *Bovidae*, de Beaune noted that a direct link cannot be established with certainty, as the composition of certain fats in animals from the Upper Palaeolithic is unknown.

5. A wick must, of course, be able to absorb fat and transport it (by capillary action) to the free end. The fuel must burn without the wick itself being consumed too rapidly. The form and structure of the wick have an important effect on efficiency. Of the various wicks tested, lichen and moss, followed by juniper, proved easiest to use. Analysis of remains from ancient lamps revealed conifers, juniper, a grass (in one instance), and some nonwoody residues. De Beaune noted that there is probably a sampling bias here, as juniper is never completely consumed and so is probably better represented.

6. The traces of use that developed on replicated lamps were enlightening. De Beaune noted that their nature and appearance are determined by the functional zone of the lamp—"the position of fat and of the wick, drainage zone for the melted fat, storage of 'oil,' etc." (1987:575). In addition, she discovered that identical stains may result from different causes. For example, blackening can result from the wick being carbonized, soot from the flame, or the charring of adipose tissue. Also, reuse of a lamp gradually expands the blackened area, which may eventually extend completely around the bowl. Further, scorching and blackening on the outside of a lamp, which would suggest that it was heated in a hearth, may be the result of other processes (1987:576).

7. The experiments suggested that the ideal lamp represents a compromise between open- and closed-circuit design. Such a lamp is easy to empty simply by tipping it up (to prevent the wick from being covered in melted fuel); sloping sides or a gap in the rim were found to make this partial emptying easy to accomplish. The sloping-side approach is seen in 80 percent of the lamps examined by de Beaune.

8. The most common Upper Palaeolithic lamps and those that were the simplest and most efficient in the experiment were similar in key respects to ones often used by southern Inuit and Aleut. These lamps were used in circumstances in which there was "an absence of good raw material, such as steatite, the use of hearths for cooking, heating, etc., . . . scarcity of fat from marine animals and . . . [a] specialized function of the lamp, for lighting only. These four conditions are strangely reminiscent of Palaeolithic times" (1987:576).

9. Light output (measured by a photometer) was low, less than that produced by a typical candle. But it was found sufficient for navigating about a cave or doing precision work, provided the lamp was nearby.

Discussion

De Beaune's study shows very nicely how experiments may permit us to turn conjectures into testable hypotheses. There is clearly no substitute for replicating and lighting Palaeolithic lamps if we wish to know how they worked and why they were designed the way they were. Not only does this lead to better understanding of traces of use on original specimens, it provides us with a means of experiencing and measuring the light such lamps produce. The operational requirements of open- and closed-circuit lamps became clear through the experimentation as well, leading to better understanding of finer details of base material selection and modification. Again we see the process of moving from results back to causes. The experiments conducted by de Beaune provided clues to the type of corroborative evidence needed to increase the reliability of any hypothetical designation of a stone object as a "lamp." In this experiment, close attention was paid, of necessity, to authentic replication of the prehistoric implement as well as the subsidiary materials (type of fat and wick) required to make it work.

HANDAXE MANUFACTURE

The systematic investigation of stone tool manufacture by means of imitative experiments was largely pioneered by François Bordes and Don Crabtree. They both became experts at replicating ancient tools and we may credit them with the rediscovery of some of the techniques of ancient flint knappers. An experiment by Mark Newcomer (1971) attempted to add a "new dimension" to this kind of replicative experiment by undertaking a quantitative study of handaxe manufacture (see Figures 3-6 and 3-7).

Newcomer began with two quartzite hammerstones and three red deer antler soft hammers of varying sizes and weights. His raw material was nodular black flint. He conducted two experiments and in each one the manufacture of the handaxes took place in three discrete stages:

- The first was "roughing-out" (10–20 blows). This involved flaking the nodule bifacially around its edges by direct percussion with the larger of the two hammerstones. The flakes produced were consistently thick and had varying amounts of cortex on their dorsal surfaces.

- The second involved thinning and shaping, using the large and medium soft hammers (10–20 blows). Newcomer noted that the flakes produced in this stage were "very characteristic," with many similar examples known from sites in which the Acheulian (a stone toolmaking tradition of the Lower Palaeolithic in Africa and Europe) and Mousterian of Acheulian (a stone toolmaking tradition of the European Middle Palaeolithic) traditions were present (1971:88). He then proceeded to analyze the flakes produced to that point, to discover diagnostic differences in the characteristics of flakes produced with hard and soft hammers and in the flake scars on the handaxe itself.

- The third stage was "finishing" (15–30 blows). The medium and small soft hammers were used for final shaping and straightening of edges. Newcomer noted that small thin flakes were produced at this stage and that the handaxe could be thinned, if necessary, by making a striking platform and then removing a long thin flake with a medium or large soft hammer. He also noted that the latter process produced flakes

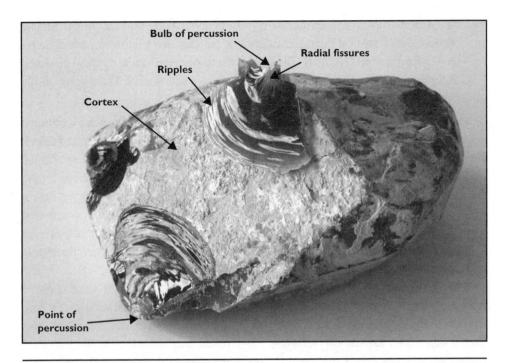

Figure 3-6 An obsidian core from which a small, shallow flake has been detached with a hard (stone) hammer.

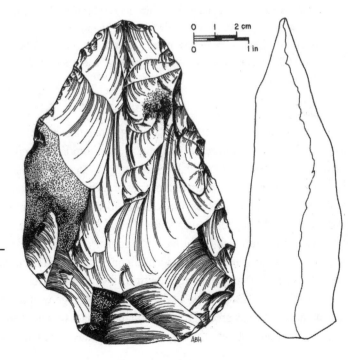

Figure 3-7
Acheulian hand-axe
from Amiens, France.
Most likely made with
hard-hammer
percussion.

that superficially resembled Levallois (a stone toolmaking tradition of the Middle Palaeolithic) flakes on their dorsal surfaces, but they were thinner and had flatter bulbs of percussion (1971:90). The bulk of the flakes were similar to those produced from thinning and shaping, but they were shorter and thinner. Flake scars on the handaxe were very shallow.

In Newcomer's first experiment, a nodule weighing nearly 3,000 grams was transformed into a handaxe weighing 30 grams. Flakes were numbered as they were removed and associated with the appropriate hammer. All debitage (chipping debris) was recovered and the nodule reconstructed. Unnumbered chips were dry sieved through a 1-mm screen. Those that did not pass through were counted, giving a total of 4,618. On the basis of this experiment, Newcomer reached the tentative conclusion that careful sieving of material recovered from living floors of sites from which Acheulian or Mousterian of Acheulian materials are found should point clearly to handaxe manufacture by virtue of the large number of tiny flint chips (1971:93).

The second experiment involved making three handaxes. As flakes were removed (excluding those that resulted from platform preparation), they were numbered in sequence and later weighed. For each handaxe, Newcomer produced a graph on which each flake was plotted with respect to these two variables. This revealed three distinct areas corresponding roughly to the three stages of manufacture. Newcomer concluded:

> Thus the experimental manufacture of handaxes can be expressed in two ways: firstly as the use of different flaking tools to perform distinct operations on the nodule/rough-out/handaxe, and secondly as the incremental decrease in size of the flakes removed. While we may never know exactly which techniques were used in the making of palae-olithic handaxes, it seems possible that we may be able to define *stages* in the manufacture of these tools by studying the morphology and weight of flakes from reconstructed nodules. (1971:93)

Discussion

This experiment enhances our understanding of handaxe manufacture and offers potentially valuable clues to the interpretation of lithic debris from Lower and Middle Palaeolithic sites. It can serve as a source of external, corroborative evidence of the sort discussed in chapter 2, as Newcomer's characterization of the types of waste flakes produced by the combination of hard and soft hammer percussion facilitates identification of similar methods used in the past. Likewise, the quantitative data he collected provide a further basis for identification of handaxe manufacture and could facilitate informed estimates of the number of such tools made at a particular location, provided of course that the ancient knappers left their chipping debris largely in place and did not tread upon it excessively (Newcomer was careful to avoid stepping on waste flakes, as the resulting breakage would have arbitrarily increased their numbers). This is precisely the middle-range data that we need to help us connect the archaeological present with the behavioral past because it provides a direct link between an interrelated set of actions (the knapping techniques used by Newcomer to produce hand-axes) and the material evidence that would potentially be left behind for an archaeologist to interpret (the specific kinds and quantities of debitage that result from those actions).

This experiment is one in which the guidelines presented in chapter 1 were, of necessity, followed closely. Appropriate objective and effective materials were selected and used in a manner consistent with existing experimentally and ethnographically known techniques of flint knapping. In addition, the characteristics of the flake scars and striking platforms produced corresponded closely to those on lithics recovered from archaeological sites, thus adding to our confidence in the results. Unlike the previous experiments with the Egyptian drill, brain removal, and Palaeolithic lamps, the experience and skill of the experimenter was critically important in this experiment. Newcomer had extensive experience making handaxes before he attempted this quantitative study, and confidence may be placed in his ability to make handaxes with the sort of efficiency expected of at least some ancient toolmakers.

Experiments of this kind continue to be performed and with increasing sophistication. For example, a more recent and especially ambitious experiment along the same general lines as Newcomer's was carried out by Michael Stafford (2003). It required skills beyond those of most contemporary knappers and, in Stafford's opinion, beyond those of most knappers in the society responsible for the original artifacts. The goal of this experiment was to investigate the "production technology" and "associated archaeological implications" of the beautifully crafted parallel-flaked, bifacial flint daggers that appear suddenly in Neolithic Denmark around 2350 BC (2003:1537). Beginning with careful study of finished specimens, preforms, and production debitage, Stafford succeeded in adding significantly to our understanding of how the daggers were probably made, how much time would have been expended on each stage of production (bifacial reduction and preform development, surface grinding and polishing, platform preparation and parallel pressure-flaking, and final-stage parallel pressure-flaking and pressure retouch), the level of skill required, the tools that might have been used, and the characteristics of the debitage produced (2003:1540). He also assessed their likely role as high-status items—"objects whose value was defined in ideological rather than functional terms" (2003:1548) and offered some thoughts on the organization of the society responsible for creating them and how archaeological evidence yet to be discovered may help to clarify such issues.

THE FUNCTIONS OF STONE TOOLS

Inferences about the utilitarian (as opposed to ideological) functions of tools have sometimes been relatively easy to make—many lithics that are popularly called *arrowheads* probably were just that. And of course, as noted earlier, association may point the way. But how can we determine function when, as is much more often the case, we lack such clues? As early as the 1930s experiments were performed involving the production of polish on what had up until then been assumed to be sickle blades. Increased confidence in that functional designation as well as valuable information on their operation and efficiency as harvesting tools resulted from experiments, such as those by Curwen (1930, 1935), Steensberg (1943), and Harlan (1967). A systematic approach to this problem was developed in the late 1950s and early 1960s by Russian archaeologist Sergei Semenov. Semenov (1964) used microscopic traces of wear on the surfaces of stone tools as clues to the ways in which they had been used. For example, the orientation of fine striations along a working edge were used to distinguish a sawing motion (parallel orientation, as shown on Figure 3-8) from a chopping motion (perpendicular orientation). Experiments performed by Sonnenfeld (1962) and Newcomer and Keeley (1979) followed this general approach, and their work provides us with two good examples of how experiments involving replication and identification of use-wear can put interpretation of function on a sounder footing than would otherwise be possible.

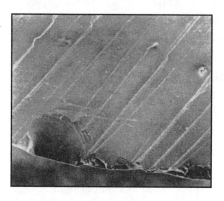

Figure 3-8 Striations on obsidian microblade used to saw fresh wood. Scanning electron microscope, magnification 145x.

WERE CELTS USED AS HOES?

J. Sonnenfeld's research provides an example of an early experiment involving use-wear analysis. He began by carefully examining 300 celts obtained from a collection belonging to the University of Delaware and the Archaeological Society of Delaware:

> The celts proved ideal for the purposes of this study, since they had had ascribed to them multifarious functions as hafted and unhafted axes, adzes, hatchets, choppers, chisels, wedges, scrapers, hoes, spades, picks, and flakers for use, according to classifications, as weapons for hunting or war, as tools for work in stone, wood, leather, or for use in butchering, digging, grubbing, or mining. (1962:56)

Given the high degree of variability in celts with respect to size, thickness, and other form attributes, Sonnenfeld acknowledged that as a group, they could have been used for the many different functions ascribed to them: "The problem then, was to determine if there was a relationship between form and function which could yield to form a determining role as a criterion of function" (1962:56).

Most of the celts Sonnenfeld examined could be placed in two major categories: bifacially asymmetrical—suggesting use as scrapers, adzes, or gouges—and bilaterally asymmetrical—suggesting hafting and use as axes or hatchets. Examination of the edges with a stereomicroscope at powers between 10 and 30 revealed a variety of modifications and equally varied scratch-and-groove patterns. But what did these signify—methods of manufacture, patterns of use, or postdepositional damage? Sonnenfeld was particularly concerned with precisely measuring the edge angle and the taper of the working edge faces. A system was devised that incorporated a template that allowed quantification of taper. This, combined with measurement of the edge angle, allowed Sonnenfeld to compute a "bluntness index" (edge angle/taper radius). To be able to infer function from variation in dimension, two approaches were identified: (1) association of wear with artifacts whose function was known, and (2) using artifacts to produce wear of the kind seen on artifacts. Of interest here is Sonnenfeld's attempt to establish, by means of an imitative experiment, criteria that would permit identification of a celt's use as a hoe.

The difficult issue of the precise methods of hafting was skirted; emphasis was placed on hafting in a way that simply permitted the celt to be used as a hoe. Three types of haft were used, two modern (an adaptation of one from a garden hoe and another from a grub hoe) and the third representing something felt to be more "aboriginal" (a forked tree branch with one arm trimmed and modified so that it would hold the celt). A variety of celts were obtained from collections; each specimen was either unworn or reworked to produce a fresh edge. Eight hoes were taken to the field and three were used in the laboratory. Usage ranged from "less than an hour to several hours spread over several days, weeks, and even months" (1962:61). Most worked well, with ease of use affected by hafting method, taper, and soil condition.

Wear of various types developed on all the celts. The most characteristic damage produced by hoeing proved to be "wear-scoured grooves" that were extensive on the edge faces and sides of the tools. These grooves varied in form from tool to tool, with the differences being attributed to "the form of the implement, the nature of the original manufacture marks appearing on the working surface, the stone texture . . . and the quality of the soil" (1962:61). Examination of 300 celts revealed only a few that had this sort of wear; most had none at all, with only a few showing wear that extended more than ½ inch from the edge (where present, indications of wear typically extended less than ¼ inch from the edge), despite other indications of substantial use, such as smoothed and battered edges. This contrasted sharply with the hoes used in the experiment, all of which "had scour-grooves that extended—continuously on ground stone blades, discontinuously on chipped blades—from one to two inches or more from the edge" (1962:61). Beveling and polishing were also found to occur, but were not, in themselves, sufficiently diagnostic of hoeing. Sonnenfeld concluded that the "scour-grooves would appear to constitute, by the extent of their penetration onto the edge faces, as well as by their character, an excellent, if not unique criterion of function" (1962:61).

Discussion

The goal of Sonnenfeld's experiment was simple: he wished to determine if using a celt as a hoe would produce diagnostic wear patterns. Although it is unfortunate that prehistoric tools were used instead of replicas, care was taken to select specimens showing no wear or to resurface those that did show the effects of ancient use or subsequent damage. The method of hafting was also less than ideal, but at least one of the three types of haft appears to have been a reasonable approximation of a type that would have been used in prehistoric situations (I shall have more to say about the matter of hafting tools in chapter 4). Longer trials on a variety of soils would have been desirable, with more attention paid as well to ethnographic descriptions of technique. However, the results of the experiment are clearly of some value. Regardless of the type of stone, distinctive wear patterns were formed. The "scour-grooving" is quite dissimilar from the wear produced by use as an axe or adze. The fact that very few of the celts in the large collection examined by Sonnenfeld showed wear of this type, argues against their having been used as hoes. Also significant was the fact that the wear was produced quickly—the total number of hours that each tool was used was not great. Stone hoes would be expected to have a long use-life, so again, the absence of scour-grooving on an artifact should be sufficient to exclude hoeing as a possibility for its use (unless, of course, its surface was subsequently reworked in antiquity or otherwise abraded). We end up with a conclusion here of the sort, if X (where X is use of a celt as a hoe), then Y (where Y is scour-grooving). We may thus be fairly confident asserting that in situations where Y is not true (~Y), then not X (~X), with the possibilities of edges being reworked, the tool subsequently being used for another purpose, or the occurrence of post-depositional abrasion of the surface providing conditions of rebuttal (R). But of course we cannot say if Y, then X, unless we can be absolutely certain that no other activity but hoeing will produce the particular wear patterns recorded by Sonnenfeld.

TESTING MICROWEAR ANALYSIS WITH EXPERIMENTAL TOOLS

An experiment performed by Mark Newcomer and Lawrence Keeley (1979) was the first one designed to provide a test of the diagnostic value of microwear analysis by having one person make and use a set of stone tools and a second person, working in isolation, attempt to identify the uses to which they had been put (see also Keeley 1980). This protocol, known as *blind testing,* has the obvious benefit of eliminating the possible bias that might figure into the identification of tool use if the person making that determination knew what the uses were. This simulates the actual situation faced by archaeologists when they perform microwear analysis of genuine artifacts and thus can provide an excellent test of the reliability of the approach.

The tools made for this experiment were simple—a set of 15 unretouched flakes and simple unifacially flaked tools of the sort that are found in Lower and Middle Palaeolithic assemblages. All were made from a single block of homogeneous black flint. Percussion and retouch were accomplished with a quartzite hammerstone and red deer antler hammer. The materials worked included hard and soft woods (ash and pine), bracken, ox bone and hide, rabbit skin and bone, pork fat, and raw and frozen lamb (1979:198). Seven of the 15 tools were used to work the animal materials and seven were applied to the vegetal materials. One tool was left unused. All were unhafted. The basic actions included "scraping, slicing, boring, chipping, and whittling" (1979:198). Multiple uses were avoided, as Newcomer and Keeley considered this to have been an uncommon practice in the past. They were led to this conclusion by the large numbers of tools discarded at many sites, which argued for short use-lives. Furthermore, the simplicity of the tools appeared to limit the range of uses to which they could be put.

When Keeley received the used implements from Newcomer, he cleaned them and then examined them under a microscope with scanning at 100x and identification at 200x. His first goal was to locate a used edge. This involved looking for microwear polish, striations, and edge damage. Used edges generally have at least two of these attributes, with microwear polish the most reliable indicator of use. The process of identifying the use of each tool required several pieces of evidence: "(1) the general shape and size of the tool, (2) the type and placement of the utilization damage, (3) the distribution and particularly the orientation of linear wear features like striations, and (4) the location and extent of the areas of microwear polish" (1979:199). Identification was based primarily on microwear polishes, because Keeley had found through previous experimentation that materials such as wood, bone, hide, meat, and antler produced distinctive polishes that he could distinguish from each other under the microscope.

The results of the experiment were impressive.[3] Easiest to determine was the specific area of the tool that was used, with 14 out of 16 assessments correct (one tool had two areas that were used, hence the total of 16 rather than 15). One error appeared to be solely the result of carelessness on Keeley's part. Reconstruction of the movement of the tool (chopping, sawing, drilling, scraping, etc.) was correctly assessed in 12 of 16 cases. Most difficult, as one would expect, was identification of material worked. Yet, 10 out of 16 of Keeley's determinations proved correct. It was noted that Newcomer's use of a wooden cutting board as well as aged or seasoned materials in the wood- and bone-working experiments complicated identification in ways unlikely to present themselves when Palaeolithic specimens are analyzed.

Discussion

The experiment performed by Keeley and Newcomer differs in several ways from the previous examples in that it did not attempt to determine the function of a particular tool-type or replicate the process by which a specific task was performed. Instead, it used an experimental approach to test a method of identifying the materials the tools were used to work and the type of motion associated with that activity. The results suggested that identification of the used area of a tool is possible in many instances and, of even greater significance, the material that was worked may be determined with a fair degree of certainty. It involved both the replication of simple tools comparable to many found in prehistoric sites and the types of uses to which they may have been put. It was clearly geared toward the "middle-range," as it provided a means to link archaeological evidence to past human behavior. In terms of Toulmin's model (discussed in chapter 2), the goal of this experiment was to establish warrants for an argument linking data (microwear on stone tools) to conclusions (identification of working area and material worked).

In a case such as this one, we may start with the possibility that any one of several actions/uses (X^1, X^2, X^3, etc.) might have produced the observed result Y, where Y represents a particular type of edge damage and/or microwear polish. Newcomer and Keeley established that some actions leave seemingly diagnostic Ys, thus making it possible to infer with some confidence that a particular tool was used to cut bone, wood, or whatever. Think again about corroborative evidence in the way any detective (archaeological or otherwise) would. Imagine that a tool is found in proximity to a piece of wood that has been sharpened to a point. We might hypothesize that the tool has an edge suitable for whittling wood. But was this tool used to make the point? If we could demonstrate that the edge damage and polish on the working edge of the tool are consistent with woodworking, the connection between the two artifacts would be strengthened.[4] Being able to identify the likely uses to which stone tools were put is extremely valuable—not only do we gain insight into the probable functions of at least some of these otherwise enigmatic objects, we may also be able to learn about the activities that were performed at a specific site when all other evidence (the wooden point, for instance) has vanished.

EXTENSIONS AND ENHANCEMENTS IN LITHICS RESEARCH

One of the most important aspects of the scientific process is the way that ideas are examined, reexamined, refined, rethought, extended, and yes, even rejected. In the best tradition of science, the line of experimental research typified by the work of Semenov, Sonnenfeld, Keeley, and Newcomer has led to questions about its application and reliability, attempts to expand its usefulness, and searches for new ways to enhance our understanding of stone tool use through close examination and analysis of clues left on working surfaces (see Odell 2003:136–173 for descriptions and critical evaluations of the various techniques currently in use).

After archaeologists recognized that using a stone tool to cut, chop, and scrape could create recognizable traces of the activity on its surface in the forms of wear and polish and that those traces could be used to infer something about function, it was only logical to investigate the factors affecting the preservation and modification of those traces. Stone tools in archaeological sites have obviously been subjected to a variety of postdepositional, natural, and human-induced transformation processes. For instance, tools that have been discarded may be trampled by humans and animals and they are also subjected to abrasion and breakage from freeze-thaw cycles, compaction of sediments, and so on. The issue of trampling as it affects the three-dimensional patterning of artifacts as well as their physical condition has been examined by a number of investigators. An experiment carried out by Gifford-Gonzalez et al. (1985) investigated the effects of human trampling on the horizontal and vertical dispersal of two sets of obsidian debitage that had been screen-segregated into three size fractions, with sizes ranging from 3.0 mm to 13.0 mm. The effects of trampling on loamy and sandy soil were evaluated by placing the artifacts on 2 m × 2 m plots and having two people (wearing soft-soled moccasins and rubber sandals) walk over the scatters and adjacent areas at a "normal pace" for two hours (1985:807). Of significance to microwear analysis was the finding that the most common damage on the larger pieces was along the edge. In a complementary study by Nielsen (1991), materials were laid out in 1 m × 1 m squares and the number of crossings over each square by people shod with tennis shoes was recorded. Nielsen carefully examined vertical and horizontal displacement (migration) of items of various sizes and assessed damage (breakage, microflaking, and abrasion) using bones, obsidian flakes, sherds, and fragments of brick and wood on hard-packed sediments (when dry and after a rain).

As to the special challenges trampling creates for the microwear analyst, Shea and Klenck (1993) state the problem clearly:

> There are a wide variety of behavioural and geological factors that affect the microwear traces on the edges of prehistoric tools. . . . Trampling by humans or by livestock can cause significant abrasion and microfracturing of stone tools lying on the surface or suspended in a substrate. Trampling is also likely to have been a factor in the formation of wear on the edges of stone tools at most localities in which stone artefacts have accumulated. The effect of trampling on the preservation of microwear traces is clearly an issue that needs to be investigated if the results of microwear analysis are to be used in reconstructing archaeological site and assemblage formation processes. (1993:175)

The experiment that they performed took the form of a blind test in which "four sets of 15 tools, an untrampled control sample and three sets of tools that had been subjected to concentrated trampling for different lengths of time" were given to Shea in four discrete sets (1993:177). He was asked to rank the sets "in order of greater or lesser amount of trampling damage, identify the use-worn edges of the tools, characterize the motions involved, and describe the worked materials" (1993:177). The flint flakes that formed the subject of this study were used by Klenck in four activities: woodworking, cutting soft plant matter, hide-working, and carving antler. Thick hemp rope, soaked in water, was used as a substitute for soft plant matter because of the absence of such material in winter at Klenck's location in New England. Each tool was used for no less than 20 minutes. After information on the attributes of each tool was recorded, it was placed in one of four groups: one was a control and the other three corresponded to trampling times of 15, 30, and 45 minutes. Trampling was accomplished by wrapping Klenck's rubber-soled shoes with leather pads after which he "delivered between 40–60 two-step loading episodes per minute" on a wet, sandy soil placed in a wooden box in which the tools were 2–5 cm below the surface. Once removed from the matrix, the tools were washed and treated to remove any organic residues that may have adhered to them.

The results of this experiment were sobering: they demonstrated that the preservation and interpretability of use-wear traces can be significantly affected in as little as 15 minutes, when trampling occurs in moist silt. Most affected were use-wear traces produced by working softer materials. The combined error-rate (where errors were of three types: use-wear entirely overlooked, use-wear recognized but misinterpreted, use inferred for unutilized edges) was 150–200 percent greater than the rate for the control sample (1993:190). The wear caused by trampling, not surprisingly, was apt to be confused with that produced from cutting more rigid materials. However, Shea and Klenck rightly note that many lithic assemblages have not been subjected to significant trampling. And they point the way forward: more objective methods of microwear description and analysis based in part on the results of careful mechanical studies of wear formation. Trampling, of course, is one of several ways in which the record of the past may be partially erased from the surfaces of stone tools— microwear analysts are wisely advised to work with soil scientists to determine the degree to which soils have been compacted by human activity and otherwise disturbed (1993:192).

More recently, new approaches to inferring use of stone tools have been explored. For instance, Jahren et al. (1997) performed an experiment in which flakes were made from a chert nodule and then used to split bamboo and scrape and splinter bone. When examined by light microscopy and a scanning electron microscope (SEM) equipped with energy dispersive spectroscopic capability (EDS provides a qualitative chemical analysis), the used flakes were found to exhibit bone and bamboo residues that were chemically and morphologically distinct. Chemical treatment of the flakes that simulated the effects of burial slightly altered the residues but did not inhibit the ability to distinguish them; it also suggested that the residues might well be sufficiently durable to be retained on ancient specimens.

In a somewhat similar vein, Hardy and Garufi (1997) performed a series of 100 trials in an investigation of the value of residues on tools as indicators of their use in woodworking. Using unmodified flint flakes, they whittled, sliced, and incised; unifacially retouched flakes with steep working edges were used for scraping and polishing actions, and boring was accomplished with flakes that were bifacially retouched into an elongated point (1977:180). The woods that were worked comprised six species—three hardwoods and three softwoods. Each individual "use-action" was performed for five minutes on a fresh piece of wood without resharpening. Much like the earlier experiment by Keeley and Newcomer, 50 additional trials were carried out for blind testing by Hardy.

The results of this study showed that "microscopic examination of the experimental tools yielded clear patterning of use-wear and residues associated with different use-actions" (1997:180). In line with earlier research, Hardy and Garufi concluded that the presence of multiple kinds of evidence (residue, polish, striations, and edge damage) increases the strength of an interpretation of wood processing. As to the blind tests, Hardy was able to correctly determine the presence of wood residue on all 50 tools, 49 of which he correctly identified with respect to use-action. He also attempted to identify the type of wood worked at the class level on 15 tools and was successful in 13 cases; two of the 15 specimens contained microscopic structures that permitted attempts at species identification (one correct, the other not, with the latter error possibly the result of Hardy's lack of expertise in botany).

THE DISCOVERY OF SMELTING

In this experiment, H. H. Coghlan (like Hartenberg, an engineer) sought to test two possible scenarios for a most remarkable and important discovery: that copper may be obtained from ore. But before he did that, he investigated the use of native copper, which in contrast to copper ore, is metallic and malleable. As one would expect, the first copper implements were crafted from this "ready-made" metal. After reviewing evidence for the prehistoric use of native copper in the Old and New Worlds and the methods by which it was worked to manufacture items such as beads, needles, awls, and small arm and hair rings, Coghlan performed an experiment in which he attempted to work a lump of native copper weighing approximately 1½ lbs. It was not a success. The copper proved to be "most intractable to work" because it was not malleable enough to be hammered into shape (1940:50). Too much hammering was detrimental, as the copper cracked and became so tough that it proved more difficult to cut with a hacksaw than mild steel. Coghlan noted an earlier experiment by another investigator in which a nugget of copper from near Lake Superior was hammered in an attempt to make a small ornament after the fashion of ancient Native Americans in the region. Success in that case was achieved when hammering was followed by annealing (softening by heating the metal to approximately 500°C and then allowing it to cool). This process clearly had to date after the earliest use of copper, which led Coghlan to conclude that light forging and grinding most likely preceded the use of heat as a cure for its brittleness. Casting molten copper had come later still, as it required furnaces that did not come into being until after people had learned to smelt the ore.

But how might smelting have first been achieved? There is nothing in the character of an ore as examined by the eye or felt by the hand to suggest that it can be made into a metal. Somehow, the discovery had to be accidental. At the time of Coghlan's study, the prevailing belief was in what may be termed the "camp fire" theory, which posited that a piece of ore protruding from the ground at the bottom of a fire pit could have been converted (reduced) to metallic copper. Coghlan wondered if this was a realistic possibility. An experiment was clearly in order.

Coghlan's first consideration was of the requirements for the reduction of ore to metallic copper. For this to happen, two conditions had to occur:

> (a) The temperature of the fire would have to be sufficiently high to reduce the ore without the aid of forced or induced draught.

> (b) The fire would have to be sufficiently large to exclude excess air from the ore, so that the latter would be in a reducing zone of the fire, i.e. the ore would have to be well surrounded and covered by the hot fuel. The fuel could only have been wood or charcoal. (1940:55)

Coghlan noted that for the first requirement, an open, hot wood fire would have a temperature of 600 to 700 degrees Celsius, with the carbonate copper ores requiring a temperature of

700 to 800 degrees Celsius for reduction. He reasoned that if there were a strong wind, there might barely be enough heat for reduction to occur. The second requirement suggested a larger fire than would be the norm in most instances. And, of course, the ore had either to be thrown into the fire or have been present in the ground adjacent to the pit's bottom. Finally, if reduction did take place, the metallic copper would have had to have been noticed under the ashes.

Much like the experiment with the Egyptian drill, this one began with a serious doubt, namely that a small "hole in the ground" furnace would be capable of smelting ore without the use of a bellows to create a draft. For his experiment, Coghlan selected malachite (see Figure 3-9), because it was quite likely to have been the first ore smelted. It is often of high purity, as is much of the earliest copper from Mesopotamia and Egypt, and it occurs in surface deposits in the areas where the earliest smelting was carried out. In Coghlan's words (1940:58):

> Primitive conditions were simulated as far as possible, and the fuel was charcoal. A hole of about 1 ft. diam. was made in the ground, the hole was well dried out by means of a wood fire and then a good hot charcoal fire was started in the hole. To give the experiment every chance of success, a ring of stone was made round the hole, and concentric with it; the inside diameter of this ring was about 3 ft. A cone of charcoal was then built up and the ore was well embedded in the centre of the cone; small pieces of malachite were placed in two layers in the cone, each layer being separated from the other by charcoal. A March day when there was a strong wind blowing was selected for the experiment, and after an hour the fire reached a very bright red heat; it could certainly not have attained any greater temperature without the aid of forced draught created by the use of bellows or other means. Fresh fuel was added and the fire was kept going at full heat for several hours and was then allowed to burn down slowly.

Figure 3-9 Malachite (copper carbonate ore) in unmodified, polished and ground forms [left]; native copper nugget and irregular mass [right].

When the fire burned out and the malachite was recovered, a change had occurred, but not the one desired: the black oxide of copper had been formed. This reduction occurs at a temperature of only about 140°C. As a further check, the experiment was repeated using cuprite, the red oxide of copper, in place of malachite. It too, failed. For reasons associated with the depth at which they occur and other technical challenges to ancient people that they would have presented, no need was felt to try the experiment with sulphide ores. Coghlan concluded (1940:59):

> The failure of these experiments to obtain metallic copper from the ore seemed to be clearly due to the fact that in spite of the careful surrounding and packing of the ore in the fire, an excess of air was present so that the necessary reducing atmosphere was not attained. Later experiments proved that low temperature of the fire was not the cause of failure. . . . Since the failure of the experiments indicated that the camp fire or "hole-in-the-ground" fire was very unlikely to have been the first metallurgical hearth, the only suitable remaining source of heat would seem to have been the pottery kiln or furnace.

A second experiment with a simple kiln made good sense, as kilns were used for firing pottery prior to the earliest smelting. The conditions in a kiln should be favorable for reduction of ore, as the requisite temperatures and reducing atmosphere would have been produced. Coghlan sought to replicate an early type of kiln that consisted simply of a dome of brick or clay, with a fire under and around the dome. He chose to invert a redware pot and set it over a flat ceramic plate, on which he had placed a small piece of malachite. This miniature kiln was then set on a bed of hot charcoal and fully covered with a "cone" of burning charcoal. After several hours of exposure to red heat, a spongy lump of copper was found to have formed on the plate. Further experimentation with malachite that had been ground into small particles succeeded in producing a "compact and close-grained bead of copper which could have been forged into any shape required" (1940:61). Coghlan concluded:

> If a piece of malachite, or ground malachite, were left accidentally in the baking chamber of a . . . pottery kiln, it would become reduced, and since the baking chamber would not contain any fuel, the resulting copper would be easily noticed. (1940:61)

This begged a final question: how likely was it that malachite would get into a pottery kiln? Two reasons for its presence in a kiln were suggested. The first was that it may have been a primary ingredient in a slip (a mixture of clay and water applied to the surface of an unfired clay vessel used to create a desired texture or to add color) or was painted on a vessel to create a black decoration. Coghlan made a paste using ground malachite, painted it on some redware and produced a smooth black surface. The second possibility was that it was a component of a glaze. Coghlan noted the use of blue and green glazes in ancient Egypt and an analysis of one example that showed copper oxide to be a significant constituent.

Discussion
In some respects this study can be seen as part experiment, part demonstration. Coghlan first performed a convincing test of the "camp fire" hypothesis and rejected it. In his second test,

he demonstrated that under more controlled firing conditions, smelting could occur; he then provided a quite reasonable scenario that would account for the ore's making its way into a kiln in ancient times. Given our extensive and precise knowledge of the conditions required to smelt the various copper ores, it can be taken as a given that if small pieces of malachite are heated to a high enough temperature in a reducing atmosphere, metallic copper will be produced. Ideally, an experiment would test the ability of a kiln comparable to those in use in Mesopotamia at the time of the earliest known smelting to produce the requisite conditions to reduce ore. An inverted flower pot embedded in burning charcoal is not a close replica of such kilns, but it is technologically simpler and it did achieve the desired result.

It should also be noted that this experiment had chronology in its favor: pottery was being made before copper was first smelted. As to the possibility that native copper was melted and cast before the discovery of smelting, Coghlan pointed out that prior to the smelting of copper, furnaces capable of producing the required temperature of 1085°C did not exist. He also noted that sophisticated ancient kilns capable of producing very high temperatures, such as those at Tel Halaf and Susa (Mesopotamia), were clearly not used to melt copper.

In recent years new ideas have been advanced on the circumstances surrounding the earliest smelting of ores and more sophisticated experiments have been performed. I will return to this subject in my discussion of the research program at the Butser Ancient Farm in chapter 5.

CLUES TO THE IDENTIFICATION OF ANCIENT MESOAMERICAN KILNS

The motivation for an experiment carried out by Andrew Balkansky came from frustration with the difficult process of tracing back in time the diverse methods of ceramic production in contemporary Mesoamerica. This experiment was part of a larger study undertaken with Gary Feinman and Linda Nicholas on ancient pottery kilns in Ejutla, Oaxaca, Mexico. After reviewing pottery-making practices in the region today and evidence from a number of archaeological sites, Balkansky, Feinman, and Nicholas offered the possibility that "the scarcity of archeological kilns and the past variability of ceramic production would be more explicable if production contexts were less formal" than at the few sites where kilns have been found and more like the open-firings employed by contemporary potters at San Marcos Tlapazola (Balkansky, Feinman, and Nicholas 1997:142). The major empirical difficulty was felt to lie in "the identification of production sites, especially kilns and other firing features, in archaeological contexts" (1997:139). It was the discovery and excavation of "relatively ephemeral ceramic firing features" at the site of Ejutla that led directly to an experiment whose goal was to provide an understanding of "how these firing features worked and the nature of the remains that they would have left" (1997:139).

The excavations at Ejutla provided a wealth of valuable evidence concerning pottery production in the form of "large numbers of figurines and figurine wasters [items that cracked or were otherwise damaged during firing], figurine molds, and hundreds of wasters from a variety of ceramic vessels [that] were found to overlie shallow features that the pre-hispanic inhabitants had dug into the soft bedrock" (1997:142). The investigators report that the use of these bedrock features for firing did not fit their expectations, which were derived from their familiarity with the formal production methods and kilns at larger sites in the region such as Atzompa and Monte Albán.

To increase understanding of the firing features at Ejutla, Balkansky constructed and then fired a pit kiln at the University of Wisconsin in Madison. Lacking an analog for pit firing in Oaxaca, he relied on ethnographically described techniques used in India, Pakistan, and the southwestern United States. To construct his experimental kiln,

> a shallow depression was dug into the ground surface, and its contours defined by a layer of sand as a referent for the post-firing excavation. To improve the draft, the kiln floor was slightly inclined, with the open end or "mouth" at a greater depth than the rear of the firing chamber. The chamber was filled with a mixture of pottery . . . kiln furniture (to separate the vessels and improve airflow), and fuel (cow dung, grasses, and fallen tree branches). The mixture of pottery and fuel was then covered with straw to form a matrix upon which to construct a mud plaster roof. The mud plaster provides structure to minimize the damage caused by the shifting of pots as the fuel is consumed, and insulation, to conserve fuel and better control temperature and atmosphere. The atmospheric conditions can be modified throughout the firing. Openings in the mud-plaster dome maintain an oxidizing atmosphere; alternatively, smothering the fire yields reduced wares. Four thermocouples were placed at different locations inside and beneath this feature, and temperature readings were taken at 15-minute intervals over an eight-hour period. (1997:146)

The results were useful and sobering. The firing left little in the way of diagnostic evidence of what had occurred at the site; remains were limited to some broken vessels, a thin layer of ash and charcoal, and a discolored and partially baked (to a depth of 1 cm) ground surface. Consequently, it seemed likely that unless the deposits were sealed soon after firing, little evidence of the event would remain intact. More encouraging was the fact that the fired fragments of the mud plaster covering were found to strongly resemble clay concretions found at Ejutla and other sites where pottery was made. Balkansky concluded that in the presence of other evidence suggesting pottery manufacture, such concretion-like materials would most likely point to an approach involving impermanent roofing (1997:148).

The temperature data he collected indicated that the kiln reached a maximum temperature of 768°C, which was high enough to fire most ancient Mesoamerican pottery. It was also noted that this temperature was within 100°C of sherds that were refired to determine the original firing temperature, thus suggesting that a kiln of this type could have been used in the past.

Discussion

This experiment provided evidence that should help explain some important aspects of the archaeological record for prehispanic Mesoamerica and lead to revised approaches to excavation and interpretation. It demonstrated that the expectation that significant ceramic production would be associated with substantial kilns was probably unjustified. It also provided an interesting and valuable lesson on overreliance on ethnographic analogy. Balkansky, Feinman, and Nicholas pointed to the possibility that absence of pit-kiln firing in contemporary Mesoamerica (and hence the absence of an analog for this ceramic technology) may be at least partly responsible for the failure of many archeologists to recognize the evidence it leaves behind. They also noted that the "tyranny of ethnographic analogy" may not be the only reason for this failure, as the type of field methods typically used (e.g., narrow test trenches and isolated 2 m × 2 m units) may work against the recovery of impermanent features such as pit kilns (1997:153). Further, "inattention" to midden deposits has most likely led to some of these kilns being misidentified as "burnt areas within middens" or "as the ubiquitous 'ash-filled pit'" (1997:154). It should be noted that this experiment did not have as part of its design the duplication of a particular type of pottery (although it is noted in the report that the pit kiln would work well in producing the reduced grayware common to the Oaxaca Valley [1997:147]). Therefore, the lack of information in the report on the vessels that were fired is understandable.

In sum, the results of this experiment not only contribute significantly to our knowledge of the manufacture of ancient Mesoamerican pottery and the performance characteristics of ephemeral kilns, they also provide valuable diagnostic clues that will facilitate proper identification of that technology in the archaeological record. Now that archaeologists have greater understanding of the results (the "Ys") produced by pit-kiln firing, they should be able to do a better job of identifying it as the cause (the "X") of that evidence and, consequently, documenting the distribution of ephemeral firing sites throughout Mesoamerica.

SEEKING THE LONG-VANISHED CONTENTS OF MAYA CHULTUNS

In contrast to ephemeral kilns, underground chambers ("chultuns") constructed by the ancient Maya are well-defined and less likely to escape detection. These features, which are often lined with plaster and cut into rock, are typically dated to the period between approximately 300 BC to AD 900 (see Figure 3-10). They have no counterpart in the ethnographic record. Some of the ideas advanced between the 1840s and 1960s about their possible function include: cisterns, food storage, burial chambers, ceremonial chambers, chambers in which weaving was done, sweat baths, mines, drains, refuse pits, latrines, and naturally produced holes resulting from uprooted palm trees, which were sometimes modified by the Maya (Puleston 1971:326).

PULESTON'S DISCOVERIES

Dennis Puleston decided to perform an experiment to determine the purpose of chultuns "after it became obvious that excavation was not going to produce the information needed to evaluate a whole range of possibilities suggested by the archaeological data" (1971:322). Puleston took note of an experiment conducted in 1930 in which several chultuns were replastered and allowed to fill with rainwater (1971:324). Water from one of these chultuns was subsequently used to supply water for an archeological field crew, thus strengthening the cistern hypothesis, which dated back to the 1840s. After citing some ethnohistorical evidence from the southern Maya lowlands that appears to support this use, Puleston stated the issue:

> The problem which concerns us now is the unintentional amplification of the designation "chultun" in the nineteenth century to include superficially similar holes-in-the-ground found only in certain parts of the southern Maya lowlands. (1971:324)

He then went on to point out significant differences between the chultuns found in sites of the southern region and those of northern sites in Yucatan and Campeche. The small, lateral-chambered chultuns of the southern lowlands are significantly different in form and lack the plaster lining that is characteristic of the larger cistern chultuns of the north; aspects of their siting and design also argued against their having been used for water storage, as did the results of a simple experiment in 1965 in which he poured 400 gallons of water into a chultun at Tikal, only to see it rapidly disappear through the porous limestone into which the chamber had been cut. Puleston's investigations at Tikal provided him with a variety of clues that pointed to a food storage function rather than use as cisterns, latrines, or burial chambers. His next step was to construct a replica.

The value of constructing a chultun rather than using an ancient one lay in what could be learned about its construction with stone tools and the elimination of any "uncontrolled variables accruing from the age of Maya chultuns" (1971:328). The result of the first phase of his experiment led Puleston to conclude that:

1. Flint tools were entirely adequate for the job.
2. Adze-hafted tools were needed for most of the work, with a long-handled bit-ended tool being used to dig out the deeper areas.

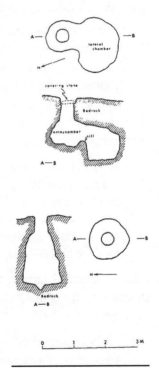

Figure 3-10 Chultuns from Tikal. Section and plan of a lateral-chambered chultun [top]; section and plan of pit chultun [bottom].

3. Tool marks on the walls of the chultun corresponded closely with those seen on the walls of ancient chultuns.

4. The time and labor required were not great (30 hours, with the assistance of a person to carry away baskets of excavated material when the inner chamber was excavated).

To test the value of using a chultun for food storage, a variety of vegetables, including maize, beans, squash, cassava (manioc), sweet potato (camote), macal (cocoyam), and potato were used. The potato was for comparative purposes, as it was not an ancient Maya food. Several varieties of some of the vegetables were used and the maize in the test included fresh on the cob, dried on the cob, and dried kernel forms. Samples were placed in the chultun, with controls stored above ground. All samples were observed, weighed, and photographed every two weeks for a period of eight weeks and again at the end of eleven weeks. None of the samples fared well. In the following year one more test with maize was performed, this time using samples that had been parched in a fire, following the practice used by Navajo before they store maize underground. The parched maize began to mildew well before the unparched samples showed any signs of decay.

At about the same time as the experiment with parched maize was being carried out, Puleston noticed a very strong correlation between the distribution of ramon trees and the remains of Maya home sites. When he came to realize the high nutritional value of the ramon nut and the "staggering" productivity of the trees, ramon's potential significance as a food crop seemed obvious. The following year another experiment was performed, with ramon being added to a group of fruits and vegetables in the chultun. Results were much as in the original experiment, with one exception:

> the ramon seed . . . after nine weeks gave every appearance of being as fresh as when it had been put in. Though some of the seeds had produced short sprouts, they were unaffected by fungi or mites. The seeds remained hard and did not soften up as the beans . . . had. These seeds were left in the chultun at the end of the summer, and . . . after thirteen months of underground storage, they were still in excellent condition and completely edible. (1971:332)

Puleston attributed the performance of the ramon in the chultun to its low water content as compared to that of dried maize and beans. At the end of his report he offered the following conclusion:

> I wish to point out the key role that experimentation can play in the construction and testing of hypotheses when dealing with problems of function. It offers a potent means of getting beyond what would otherwise be dead ends in archeological research if only archaeological data were used as evidence. (1971:333)

Discussion

Puleston's work nicely illustrates the experimental approach. He first reviewed the ethnographic evidence relating to chultuns as well as the various opinions of archaeologists concerning their function. He was left with sincere doubts about the common assumption that the chultuns in the southern Maya lowlands served the same function as their larger counterparts in the north. He then tested the hypothesis that chultuns of the kind found at Tikal could have served as cisterns. A simple test showed that the porous limestone into which a Tikal chultun had been cut allowed water to drain away, thereby falsifying that hypothesis. Food storage appeared to be a much more likely possibility. A second experiment was thus required. To eliminate any possibility that over time the characteristics of an original chultun had changed in a way that might affect its performance, a replica was created in fresh limestone. The results of the second experiment falsified multiple hypotheses (that chultuns could be used to store maize; chultuns could be used to store sweet potato; etc.). One final possibility then presented itself to Puleston: chultuns could be used to store ramon. That hypothesis was supported, leading to the conclusion that ramon seeds were the only perishable foodstuffs known to have been used by the ancient Maya that would store well in chultuns. How likely was it that they were used for this purpose? That possibility was strengthened not only by the negative evidence provided by maize and the other vegetables but by the high nutritional value of ramon and the clustering of ramon trees around ancient Maya house platforms.

A SHORT-TERM EXPERIMENT IN BELIZE

In the best traditions of science, Puleston's data and conclusions raised doubts in the minds of other Maya specialists. Yes, ramon trees often clustered around Maya residential sites and ramon seeds could be stored in the small chultuns of the southern lowlands. But did the distribution of those trees point to the location of ancient orchards? In the opinions of Miksicek and his colleagues "this association could simply reflect the ecological pre-adaptation of ramón to disturbed habitat" (Miksicek et al. 1981:917). They offered evidence to support this characteristic of ramon, including the conclusions of a study by Lambert and Arnason (1978) that linked the distribution of ramon to "purely edaphic" factors (i.e., factors associated with the soils, such as organic matter and mineral content, water retention characteristics, etc.). They also found it troubling that to their knowledge, "no remains of ramón with secure archaeological context have ever been recovered from any site in Mesoamerica" (1981:917), thus calling into question the degree to which it figured in the ancient Maya diet.

If chultuns weren't used to store ramon, what might they have held? Inexplicably, Miksicek and his associates claim that "Puleston failed to include any root crop" (1981:918) in his trials when clearly he included several (see above). They then performed an experiment in which a recently excavated chultun at the Cuello site (Belize) was stocked with camote, jicama, manioc, yam, cocoyam, as well as unhusked and shelled maize (with the latter stored in an open container), ramon, and (to test a suggestion made by Reina and Hill 1980) smoked maize. After sixteen weeks of storage, the squash, camote, one manioc rhizome, the ramón with pericarp (outer covering), both types of beans, the unhusked maize, and the maize smoked for one or two days were essentially completely decomposed. The ears of corn smoked for five and ten days were fairly moldy. The yam and ramón kernels (without pericarp) had sprouted . . . but were firm and completely usable. The maize kernels stored in a container had some fungal growth but would have still been edible after they were washed. The cocoyam, jicama, and one manioc rhizome survived the four-month storage period in pristine condition. (1981:918)

Discussion

The short term of this experiment (sixteen weeks) makes a comparison with Puleston's results (based on a thirteen-month trial) difficult. Taken together, these experiments leave us with the possibility that chultuns may have served for storage of some root crops (but for how long?) and ramon.

DAHLING AND LITZINGER'S REEVALUATION

A final note on chultuns is in order. The work of Puleston, Reina and Hill, and Miksicek et al. led to an interesting and compelling reevaluation of the use of these features by Dahling and Litzinger (1986). They did not perform an experiment, but on the basis of the inter- and intrasite distributions of chultuns they argue against the hypothesis that chultuns served for household storage of foodstuffs. They note that chultuns are not found in a number of sites where ramon is prevalent and that where they are found, their numbers seem to have no positive correlation with population size (1986:725). This is followed by a close examination of chultun distribution at Tikal. Dahling and Litzinger formulate three hypotheses that should be supported if the chultuns at that site were used for crop storage:

> (I) All, or almost all house mound groups, which are thought to have been inhabited by farmers in nuclear or extended families, should have chultuns to store their crops.
>
> (II) Residential groups containing larger numbers of structures, and presumably more inhabitants, should have more or larger chultuns and thus more storage capacity, than groups containing smaller numbers of structures.
>
> (III) The more land available to residential structures, with obvious limits in extremely underdeveloped rural areas, the more chultuns there should be to store crops. (1986:726)

All three hypotheses are said to be falsified (the validity of this conclusion depends, of course, on the reliability of chultun detection in the archaeological record). While this could be taken as support for Puleston's ramon storage hypothesis (the present-day low status of ramon, which is considered a famine food, suggests that it might have been associated in the past with smaller, presumably poorer households lacking sufficient land to produce an adequate maize crop), Dahling and Litzinger instead provide an intriguing argument based on ethnographic and archaeological evidence in favor of a specialized function associated with a cottage industry: fermentation of maize and a variety of fruits and other botanical materials for the production of alcoholic beverages (1986:728–733). This last possibility provides yet another hypothesis for testing by experiment.

CHAPTER SUMMARY

The primary goal of this chapter has been to provide concrete illustrations of the means by which imitative experiments can enable us to move from the primary evidence of the past recovered from the archaeological record to reconstructions of the behaviors that led to its formation. In each example, a question about how an artifact or feature was made, or the function it served, or how a particular result was achieved was converted into a testable hypothesis. In addition, whether explicitly stated or not, decisions were necessarily made on how broad the scope of the experiment would be and what compromises for the sake of economy (with respect to both time and money) could be made without jeopardizing the validity of the results. Although it would be easy to conclude that an elaborate reconstruction that produces data no more useful and reliable than those obtainable from a "barer bones" design makes little sense from a scientific perspective, more elaborate experiments typically permit more hypotheses to be tested and hence allow more thorough exploration of the problem being investigated (as the example of the Egyptian drill should make clear). In addition, the greater expenditure of time, money, and effort that a more complete reconstruction requires may also be justified when humanistic and esthetic issues are given weight (this matter will be touched upon in chapter 6). The issue of compromise will assume greater importance as the scale, complexity, and cost of the experiment increases, as we will see in the following two chapters. The guiding principle, of course, will always be the appropriateness of the experiment to the specific questions to which the archaeologist seeks answers.

NOTES

[1] Although no stone points were involved, a related experiment with a slightly different objective than that of the others discussed here was more recently performed by Schmitt, Churchill, and Hylander (2003). I describe it briefly to further illustrate the flexibility of the experimental approach. In this case an experiment was used to answer a question about prehistoric human anatomy: could the habitual use of a thrusting spear in hunting produce the bilateral asymmetries in upper limb strength seen in Neanderthals and early modern humans? As with the experiment by Hartenberg and Schmidt, it wasn't necessary to produce an implement that looked like something a Neanderthal might actually have made and used. The key here was to replicate the physical activity of using a spear in a thrusting motion, so a hollow, un-tipped, aluminum rod fitted with strain gauges was used to "attack" a padded cushion. The justification was that the "goals were to determine the contribution made by each limb to propelling the spear, to determine forces operating along the spear shaft that are imparted to the limbs, and to determine the limb positions of the subjects during and after peak impact" (2003:108). One significant result of the experiment was that the trailing limb applied as much as 6.6 times more force than the leading limb during the strike. With a stone point affixed to the end of the spear and a

large, and undoubtedly unhappy, herbivore as a target, I suspect that the disparity might have been even greater. Although, the investigators argue that asymmetry in the robusticity of the humerus of the trailing limb in Neanderthals resulted primarily from the habitual use of thrusting spears (2003:111), the potential contributions of other commonplace activities to the morphology of Neanderthal upper limbs require investigation.

[2] It is possible to experience the operation of the drill yourself with minimal materials and effort. Hartenberg and Schmidt suggest rebending a paper clip into the form of the drill shaft in Figure 3-1a and then using a suitably large eraser to simulate the weights (simply impale the eraser on the shaft). With an elbow on a tabletop and a finger on the top of the drill, give the eraser a push and then move your arm back and forth, with as little downward pressure as possible so that the drill can rotate. If you place this little device on a piece of chalk, it will actually bore a hole.

[3] Although Holly and Del Bene (1981) are critical of the results, Keeley (1981) offers a solid rebuttal. Gonzalez-Urquijo and Ibáñez-Estévez (2003) have recently sought to make the identification of use-wear polish less subjective by using image analysis to facilitate its quantification.

[4] An experiment to determine whether or not a set of prehistoric tools had been used for woodworking was performed by Binneman and Deacon (1985). The evidence obtained from using replicas and then examining their working surfaces under a microscope led to the conclusion that all the prehistoric adzes from Boomplaas Cave, South Africa, had wood polish and some had been used on wood that had been charred first (charring makes shaping hard wood easier).

CHAPTER 4

BUILDING ON THE BASICS
REPLICATING COMPLEX EVENTS AND PROCESSES

The experiments in this chapter do not differ in any fundamental way from the ones in chapter 3. Their distinctions lie primarily in the number of discrete imitative steps required, the number of variables involved, and/or the overall scale or complexity of the project; several of them also illustrate the shift in focus in many recent experiments from answering "what" and "how" questions to modeling processes composed of a number of tightly integrated sets of behaviors and, in many cases, to acquiring quantitative measures of key behavioral variables. In some instances, the activities associated with the primary behaviors imitated or the technology replicated provide the source material for distinctive, subsidiary experiments that greatly expand the scope of the study. In other cases the primary focus is not on human behavior but rather on the transformations of archaeological materials that result from natural processes. The guidelines and the logic that have already been established apply to all imitative experiments, of course, and this means that our standards of evaluation are the same for this group as well. As in the previous chapter, the case studies that follow were selected to give a sense of the range of problems that have been addressed and by no means exhaust the subject matter of this level of experimentation.

OVERVIEW

As might be expected, experimenters often build on the results of previous investigations and in the process break some new ground of their own. For instance, once archaeologists were reasonably confident in classifying certain types of stone artifacts as axe heads, the next logical step was to experiment with them to gain a better sense of how (and how well) they worked. After having attained some facility with their operation, experiments such as one by Iversen (1956), in which the time taken to clear small areas of forest was measured, led to increased understanding of and appreciation for the effectiveness of these tools. Those experiments were followed by ones that sought to compare the performance of a stone axe and a steel axe in terms of both time and energy expenditure (Saraydar and Shimada 1971, 1973) and, more recently, by comparisons of the cutting performance of stone, bronze, and steel axes on a variety of hard and soft woods (Mathieu and Meyer 1997). Experiments such as these, in which the capabilities of implements are evaluated in a variety of real-world scenarios, can be combined in a set of interrelated activities, such as forest clearance, plowing, planting, and harvesting, to enable modeling complex processes such as farming with far greater precision than would otherwise be possible. This sort of concatenation of experiments will be explored in the case studies in chapter 5.

The investigation of advanced ceramic technology and metallurgy has likewise often required multicomponent experiments. For example, the construction and firing of large, updraft kilns (e.g., Brightwell et al. 1972; Mayes 1961, 1962) requires more discrete imitative steps (and hence more decisions to be made) and presents the experimenter with greater technical challenges as well as a larger set of variables to be controlled than did the experiment examined in the previous chapter in which Balkansky constructed and fired a simple pit kiln (this doesn't make experiments with complex kilns any more valuable than ones that replicate simpler technologies, as each explores different aspects of the past). Similarly, when we move from an experiment such as Coghlan's, in which the earliest smelting of copper was explored, to ones that replicate evolved metalworking, the complexity of the experiments must, of necessity, increase. Examples include testing the operation of particular types of furnaces (Hansen 1977, Schmidt and Avery 1978, Shimada and Merkel 1991) and replicating ancient metalworking techniques and the artifacts that were used to create them (Lechtman, Erlij, and Barry 1982; Long 1964; Tylecote 1973, 1986).

Some experiments feature an additional layer of complexity by virtue of their impressive scale. For example, experimenters have taken on the difficult and sometimes dangerous task of replicating the methods by which ancient monuments, such as the famous statues *(moai)* of Easter Island (ca. AD 500 to 1500) and the megaliths (large monuments made of stone) of Europe and Britain (ca. 4,000 to 2000 BC), were transported and set in place (Atkinson 1956; Love 1990, 2000; MacIntyre 1999; Osenton 2001; Pavel 1990, 1992, 1995). Experiments like these typically require a set of interrelated problems to be solved and thus tend to have the form of experiments within experiments (e.g., if the goal is to test the use of a sledge to move a 15-ton stone, one must first experiment with sledge design and construction and only then investigate the various means by which it may be used to transport its cargo). Equally challenging, and in some instances more perilous, are experiments in which ancient sailing vessels have been replicated and then actually put to the test (Finney 1979; Heyerdahl 1950, 1971; Horvath and Finney 1969; McGrail 1974; McKee 1974; Severin 1978).

Still other experiments have taken on the task of learning about ancient dwellings. While one has investigated the potential to learn from scale models (Saraydar 1981), most efforts in this area have featured construction of life-size replicas for the purposes of increasing our knowledge of the time, skills, and materials required to build them; evaluating the living conditions they provided; and improving our ability to decipher the evidence left behind when they either decayed in place or burned (Coles 1979:131–158; Hansen 1964, 1977; Reynolds 1979, 1993, 1995a). Buildings have also been replicated to serve as centerpieces of exhibits for the general public. The research and educational value of full-scale replicas of ancient dwellings and associated experiments in agriculture will be discussed in chapters 5 and 6.

Sometimes an experimenter's primary motivation for replicating the past is to learn about the effects of noncultural processes on the archaeological record itself and how they might be interpreted more accurately. It is obvious that in the time between the creation of a site and its recovery by archaeologists, a variety of transformations resulting from natural processes—decay, movement caused by phenomena such as subsidence, frost heaving, flow of water, earthworm activity, burrowing and scavenging by animals, and so on—have conspired to leave us with a distorted picture of what was originally there. Working backwards from the archaeological evidence—that is, the results of both the human behavior that created a particular site and the changes brought about by natural processes prior to and after its abandonment—to reasonable reconstructions of what it was like during the period of occupation requires that we be able to compensate for such distortions. To this end, the ways in which various materials such as bone, textiles, and leather change in character with exposure to the elements or after burial have been investigated by means of experiments (Ascher 1970, Brain 1967) as have the transformations over time of carefully replicated structures such as Neolithic British earthworks (Ashbee and Cornwall 1961; Ashbee and Jewell 1998; Bell, Fowler, and Hillson 1996; Jewell 1963; Jewell and Dimbleby 1966).

In the examples that follow, the focus is on key aspects of the experimental design, pointing out strengths and weaknesses, and evaluating what has been gained from the effort.

CASE STUDIES

WORKING WITH AXES OF METAL AND STONE

Experiments with stone axes nicely demonstrate the ways in which an experiment may be elaborated upon to answer a variety of interrelated questions about past behavior.

Unlike esoteric tools that go by unfamiliar names such as burin, notch, and denticulate, "axe" requires no explanation. Many people have used axes and those who haven't are almost certainly aware of their function and method of operation. Stone and bronze axes also look quite similar to their steel counterparts and that makes them seem all the more familiar. Although imitative experiments with axes necessarily address their utilitarian functions, it is worth noting that in some cultures an axe may be much more than a utilitarian implement, as ethnographic studies of their social and economic significance in several small-scale societies have clearly demonstrated (see, for example, Salisbury 1962 and Sharp 1952). What these studies have shown is that Western attitudes toward material culture in general and technology in particular are not shared by all people. It is worth keeping in mind that when we study an axe or any other item of material culture from technological and functional standpoints, we see only a part of the picture—a matter to which I will return briefly at the end of this book.

When we examine stone axes, we see that many different types have been produced. A primary classification is based on technology: chipped-stone versus ground-stone. Within each category, axe heads vary considerably in size and shape. In each instance, however, there must be a cutting edge and a body sufficiently large to permit the axe head to be hafted with its blade parallel to the long axis of the handle. Not surprisingly, there are a variety of options for the handle's design, hence a number of ways to secure the axe head. Assuming that we are in possession of some suitably hafted axes, the case studies in the previous chapter would suggest that, at a minimum, we may profitably perform experiments to learn about how they were operated, their effectiveness as cutting implements, and the types of wear patterns that may develop on them. We could then apply this knowledge to improve our understanding of how ancient specimens were actually used (e.g., was this particular artifact used as an axe, an adze, or a hoe?). But what else is possible?

MOVING BEYOND THE BASICS: A FIRSTHAND ACCOUNT

As a teenager I never suspected that cutting firewood would be preparation for an archaeological experiment, but it was. As an undergraduate I became interested in prehistoric technology and decided to compare the relative efficiencies of a stone axe and a steel axe. With the encouragement of Professor Robert Ascher and some borrowed equipment, I set out to measure not just the time required to complete a comparable task with each tool but also the energy expended. I needed a partner and was fortunate that a fellow student, Izumi Shimada, was interested in working with me. Together we hafted a small stone axe and set out to learn how to use it. I quickly discovered that the stone axe required a different chopping technique than the over-the-shoulder swing I was accustomed to from my experience with steel axes. That approach tended to cause the stone axe to bounce back from the tree, with the result that the tool's effectiveness was reduced. Much as Hartenberg and Schmidt reported that their hands quickly learned how best to operate the Egyptian drill, Izumi and I soon found that a short swing worked best for this particular axe (Saraydar and Shimada 1971). With practice, the stone axe became as easy to wield as the steel version. Once we were satisfied that the stone was properly hafted and our technique was sound, we set out to measure the energy expended when cutting with stone and steel axes. To do this, we used an instrument known as a Kofranyi-Michaelis meter. This device measures the volume of air expired by a test subject and also permits a sample of that air to be collected in an attached butyl rubber bag. The sampled air can then be analyzed with an oxygen analyzer, and from the oxygen consumption and the total amount of air expired during the sampling period, the energy expended by the test subject can be computed.

Our test consisted of chopping on a 5.6-inch-diameter maple that had recently been cut down and was supported about 2 inches off the ground. We attempted to chop at a constant rate for about 24 strokes per minute over a period of 16 minutes. When the log was cut ¾ of the way through, a new cutting was begun. The results of our experiment showed the steel axe to be 6.4 times faster than the stone axe and to require 5.1 times less energy per inch of cut.

This experiment was followed up by another, somewhat more ambitious one in which two 30 ft. × 30 ft. plots of land were cleared, one with a stone axe and the other with a steel axe, and then planted with corn (Saraydar and Shimada 1973). Here I discuss only the part relating to felling the trees; comment on the other aspects of this experiment is reserved for chapter 5. The results of this chopping exercise—one in which small trees were actually cut down—showed the stone axe to be considerably more efficient than in the first experiment, in which it was 3.6 times slower and required 3.3 times more energy to do the same amount of work as the same steel axe used. Rather than simply measure the depth of cut, an attempt was made to base calculations on the actual surface area through which each axe cut. A simple "wood index" was computed, which equaled the sum of the squares of the radii of the trees cut down by each axe, with measurements made on the cut surfaces (each tree was completely cut through). The wood index allowed us to correct for the differences in the actual amount of surface through which each axe cut, thus normalizing the results.

Discussion
The first experiment succeeded in that it introduced a new way of analyzing the performance of ancient tools. It was less successful in the results of its comparison of two technologies. One difficulty appears to have been the hafting of the stone axe. By the time the

second experiment was conducted, we were able to attach the axe head more securely and thus prevent it from gradually loosening and moving on impact (see comments on hafting that follow the discussion of the next case study). Although we didn't investigate this possibility, the swing used when cutting on a horizontal log may have placed the stone axe at a greater disadvantage than when felling standing timber. A variety of trials would have made for a better experiment; information on the profile of each axe head, including the angle of the cutting edge, should have been included.

The second experiment built upon the results of the first. It featured more chopping and the felling of small trees. With an improved haft, greater overall experience, and a more typical scenario, the data provided a sounder basis for comparison.[1] Since each axe was used on a unique group of trees, it was necessary to estimate the total surface area through which each had cut. Our "wood index" was probably adequate under the circumstances of this experiment, since none of the trees was very large in diameter. However, if trees of greater diameter had been felled, the larger notch that the thicker stone axe head would have cut would have meant that it had removed more wood than a steel axe in felling a tree of equal diameter (why this would be so is discussed in the following experiment). Although the variety of types of trees cut on each plot was more or less the same, data on species (and hence hardness or softness) would have been desirable. Nonetheless, the data acquired on performance provide some insight into the differences between stone and steel axe technology.

REFINING THE APPROACH

Seeking to expand upon the results of earlier studies, James Mathieu and Daniel Meyer (1997) performed an experiment designed to compare the time-efficiency of stone, bronze, and steel axes and investigate the effect on tree-felling efficiency of the hardness of the tree being cut, haft length, blade width, axe weight, axe shape, and tree size. Here we look at a few key results that provide some insight into the thought processes that guide archaeological experiments.

As in all prior studies, metal axes proved superior to stone axes in felling trees, and their advantage with respect to time-efficiency was comparable to that recorded by other investigators. This was not a surprise. More interesting was the observation that steel did not hold an advantage over bronze. As Mathieu and Meyer pointed out, on the basis of difference in hardness between the two metals, "one would suppose that the bronze axes would be inferior to the steel axes" (1997:340). The results did not support this hypothesis. Why? In essence, the hardness of the bronze axe was sufficient for it to cut into wood as effectively as the steel axe. Also not a surprise was the steel axe's ability to hold a sharp edge longer, although this didn't turn out to be quite as advantageous as one might expect, since the steel axe took longer to sharpen (power sharpening equipment was not used).

Another interesting conclusion concerned the variation in advantage of metal over stone as tree diameter increased. All of the axes tested were quite efficient in felling small trees (under 10 cm in diameter). The shape of the stone axes (they were, of necessity, thicker in profile than the metal axes and thus had greater edge angles) was disadvantageous on large trees because they required more wood to be cut away. To visualize this, think of a large-diameter tree being cut and try to imagine the vertical dimension of the notch a thick axe must make in order to reach the center and compare that with the size of the notch a thin blade would have to make to reach in as far—the thin blade of the metal axe allows for a narrower notch. With this in mind, it is easy to understand the advantage that thinner (and sharper) polished flint axes have over their ground-stone counterparts (but, of course, thinner stone is more likely to break).

Discussion

Mathieu and Meyer controlled for more variables than was done in previous experiments. Although they did not use an authentic haft for the bronze axe, they felt that all that really mattered was for the axe head to be securely attached and the length of the haft to be appropriate. The value of the experiment involving the stone axes was increased by the testing of four polished flint and four ground stone axe heads; all were actual Neolithic-period specimens.[2] A deliberate attempt was made to have large and small axe heads, but each with approximately the same blade length. Hafts were of ash leaf maple and were fabricated by chiseling an opening for the axe head (assembled this way, the tool is technically a celt), which was further secured with cotton rope. Mathieu and Meyer admitted that their hafts did not replicate Neolithic examples, but as they met the primary requirements that the heads be securely held in place and the handles be comfortable to swing, the researchers concluded that efficiency was not reduced. This may be so, but it needs to be tested. Replicating a haft is, of course, an experiment unto itself (see below).

The relative efficiencies of the various axes were presented in a series of graphs in which the time taken to cut each tree is plotted against that tree's diameter (see Figure 4-1. Note the increasing disparity between the performance of stone and metal axes as the diameter of the tree increases).

Beyond this, testing was sufficient to allow conclusions to be reached concerning the effects on efficiency of metal hardness, tree species and diameter, haft length, blade width, axe weight, and head shape. In spite of the compromises, the results added greatly to our understanding of these implements in a way that will facilitate the modeling of forest clearance as a component of Neolithic farming (more on this in chapter 5).

A Note on Hafting. When performing an experiment, we must assume that the performance of a tool such as an axe will vary with the style of haft (to what degree we do not know in advance of a comparative test). Examples of suitable haft types for replication are provided by specimens recovered archaeologically and from ethnographic descriptions and collections. Duplicating an authentic haft requires some skill and can be time-consuming. For example, after a suitable wood is selected, a straight tree branch or trunk of appropriate length must be cut. If a J-shaped haft for a grooved axe head is desired, a section must be carefully whittled

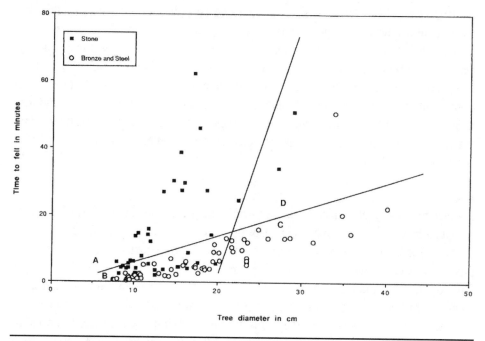

Figure 4-1 Stone, bronze and steel axe performance.

to fit the groove as precisely as possible. Next, that section must be formed into a J-shape by bending it to fit into the groove (soaking in hot water will facilitate bending) and holding it tightly in place by wrapping with rope or hide strips. Although conventional wisdom suggests that wet hide strips are preferable because they will shrink when they dry and hence hold more tightly, I have not found this to be of benefit. If the fit between haft and groove is poor or the wrappings do not hold the head and haft together tightly enough, the tool's efficiency will be reduced (in part because of operator fatigue, as anyone who has worked with a defective tool of any kind can probably attest). There are other issues to be considered, including the how much cushioning the haft provides to the head and how that affects breakage rates and so on (see comments on this matter by Woods and Titmus 1996:483)

COPPER CASTING IN MEXICO

The goal of this experiment by Stanley Long (1964) was to test a sixteenth-century ethnographic description of Mexican *cire perdue* (lost wax) casting recorded in Bernardino de Sahagún's *General History of the Things of New Spain*. Although Sahagún's text mentions copper and gold casting, he provides details only for the latter. Nonetheless, Long was confident that the method described for casting gold would work equally well with copper, in spite of the difference in melting temperatures (1083°C for gold and 1063°C for copper). He proceeded to test that hypothesis by attempting to cast several copper bells.

In his experiment, Long used native materials as much as possible and modeled his bells on examples of known chemical composition recovered from the site of Amapa (located in western Mexico). Sahagún indicates that the materials used for molds were potter's clay, charcoal, beeswax, and white copal (a tree resin); in the experiment, white dammar, which is comparable to white copal, was substituted. The purpose of mixing charcoal with the clay was to reduce shrinkage and insure that the mold would be able to withstand sudden temperature change. Beeswax is easy to mold as a result of its low melting point, and when heated in a furnace the wax quickly vaporizes; the addition of white copal or white dammar makes the wax firmer and easier to form into the desired shape (1964:191).

Long's approach to replicating this process was as follows. His mold material consisted of a mixture of charcoal and clay in a ratio of 2:1. For the core of his bell, a small ball of this same mixture was formed around a pebble to serve as a clapper. After the core had dried, wax was pressed around it and shaped into the form of a bell. A rolled "rope" of wax was formed into a ring and fitted to the wax bell; when later replaced by copper it would serve as an attachment ring. The purpose of the reservoir (see Figure 4-2) was to provide a source of additional molten metal as the outer region of copper began to cool and harden.

Long acknowledged that it is not known if such a reservoir was used aboriginally but considered it "a minor casting technique used only to make the most of the available heat supply" (1964:191). He also had to hypothesize as to how the mold was vented, as Sahagún is silent on this point (venting is required to allow air

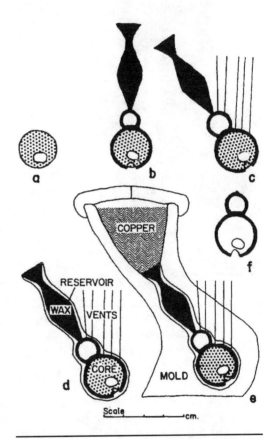

Figure 4-2 Cross-section of mold used in Long's experiments: (a) charcoal and clay bell core containing pebble; (b) bell core with wax bell and stem; (c) wax bell with straw vents; (d) vented wax bell with coating of fine charcoal and clay plaster; (e) coated bell with outer charcoal and clay covering, crucible, and top; (f) copper bell with stem and core removed.

to escape as the molten metal is poured into the mold and thus helps to eliminate air pockets in the finished piece). The lack of "venting flash" (excess metal at the site of the vents) on the body of the bells recovered from Amapa suggested fine venting holes, which would have allowed air to escape while being small enough to prevent the entrance of copper. This contrasted with the significant amount of flash found on the ring attachments. Long's use of fine straw to form the channels for the vents was thus justified by the attributes of the artifacts themselves. To create a smooth surface, several applications of charcoal and water, with sufficient clay to act as a binder, were brushed on the wax form and allowed to dry. The next step was to cover it with the crushed charcoal and clay mold, with the tops of the straw vents left exposed. A crucible made of the same mixture was placed on the top of the stem, thereby making the mold and crucible a single piece.

After working through two possible translations of Sahagún's description of the actual casting (and opting in favor of the one that more closely agreed with an illustration in his book), Long settled on a process in which the vaporizing of the wax, the melting of the metal, and the casting took place in a single step. After carefully orienting the mold to make sure that the vents were not closed prematurely, he placed pieces of copper in the crucible and then capped it with clay and charcoal, leaving a small hole to allow for the escape of gas. Once dry, the crucible mold was placed in a wind furnace containing charcoal and heated to 2200°C. When the cooled cast was broken, he extracted a fully formed bell, complete with a clapper (see Figure 4-3). Long concluded:

Figure 4-3 Cast copper bells: (a and b) replicated bells; (c) copper bell from the site of Amapa, Nayarit.

> While the above casting method is based on a 16th-century description of Mexican gold casting, it is not implied that precisely this design or these mixtures were originally used. It is inferred, however, that a similar technique was employed aboriginally. It is likewise inferred that Sahagún's description of gold casting also constitutes a valid description of copper casting. (1964:192)

Discussion

This experiment made excellent use of the ethnographic record. Long meticulously replicated the technique of lost-wax casting used in ancient Mexico as described by Sahagún and succeeded in producing a bell closely resembling original examples.[3] The wind furnace was not a duplicate of an ancient device but nonetheless involved no exotic technology and operated on similar principles. Its use was entirely acceptable given the objective of the experiment. There was no question about whether or not the Mexican bells were cast, hence no doubts about their makers' ability to melt copper; therefore the ability of an ancient furnace to reach a high enough temperature for lost-wax casting was not an issue. Replication of aboriginal furnaces would provide the basis for a worthy complementary experiment and would further enhance our knowledge of ancient Mexican metallurgy.

FIRING ROMANO-BRITISH KILNS

Philip Mayes performed two experiments with replicas of kilns dating from the Romano-British period (AD 43–410). His primary purpose was to increase understanding of techniques of construction and firing. He was also able to "observe the effect of firing on several types of clay, [investigate] the reasons for the occurrence of certain types of pottery wasters . . . [and obtain] a continuous record of kiln temperatures, gas conditions and the magnetic anomaly . . . for both firing and cooling" (1961:4).

THE FIRST EXPERIMENT: A REPLICA FROM THE NENE VALLEY

The kiln Mayes constructed for his initial experiment was modeled closely on two Romano-British originals recovered in the Nene Valley (see Figure 4-4 below). He quickly learned that the flue roof was not only difficult to construct, but it was also one of the weakest parts of the kiln and prone to cracking as it dried. Furthermore, the kiln's overall rate of drying was very slow, the result primarily of the high water content of the local clay that was used and the inclusion of fresh grass clippings in the fabric to improve its refractory qualities. To reduce the likelihood of an explosion due to moisture during firing, sand was mixed with the clay used to construct the floor; this also allowed for more rapid drying, a process aided by small fires that were built in the flue. These fires also revealed that the draft would be adequate regardless of wind direction. The excessive amount of time required to dry the kiln suggested to Mayes the reason why prefabricated blocks were used in some ancient kilns. He also estimated that with sufficient clay readily available, construction by two men could be accomplished in three days.

To complete the kiln in preparation for an initial test, a dome was constructed using a mat of sticks covered by a mound of grass. Clay plates covered the grass and were molded together. A central vent was then formed. This dome was allowed to dry for a week and during that time all cracks that appeared were filled. The prefiring lasted 12 hours. Pottery cones of the kind used by contemporary potters were placed in the kiln to monitor temperature. A peak of 750°C was reached in six hours and held at that level for six hours. The type of wood and its condition (wet or dry) had no effect on the temperature. The kiln was allowed to cool with the vent and flue open, thus creating oxidizing conditions. When the kiln was inspected it was discovered that two firebars (supports for the floor of the kiln) had cracked badly, but overall damage was minimal.

Properly testing a kiln requires pots to be fired, so Mayes had 182 made that imitated Romano-British coarse ware types. Most were jars, with a few pots weighing up to nine pounds (wet), and the smallest weighing in at a few ounces. The average was three pounds. Each pot was given an individual serial number and stamped to indicate the source of its clay. Additional information concerning slips and other treatments of the clay were scratched into the base.

In preparation for the firing, nine thermocouples were placed in the pottery chamber to allow precise tracking of internal temperatures. Loading the pottery proved to be a difficult

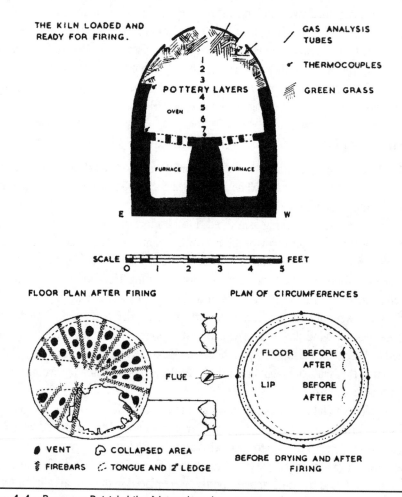

Figure 4-4 Romano-British kiln. Note that the pots are placed in the upper chamber and are not in direct contact with the burning fuel in the furnace.

process; as Mayes noted, "loading was obviously a skilled technique of which we had no experience" (1961:10). The position of each pot within the kiln was recorded. A central vent six inches in diameter was formed, with four-inch vents later added on the east, west, and south sides of the dome. Four thermocouples were inserted along with three gas extraction tubes and a two-inch-square silica window. The kiln was then fired for 13 hours and reached a maximum temperature of 1000°C.

When the pots were ready to be removed (after very carefully disassembling the dome piece by piece), the position of each one was recorded. The fabric of the kiln was found to be "extremely friable." Although the oven floor and firebars were fully fired through ("bricked"), the walls of the kiln were found to be bricked to a depth of from one to two inches, with the area just outside of that region having had the grass burned away and the outermost part of the kiln wall still retaining its original plasticity.

All of the pottery was oxidized, the result of oxygen in the kiln as it cooled. Of the 182 pots that were fired, 79 were classified as wasters. Examination of cracked pots suggested that only three had cracked during firing, with 30 showing cracks or chips resulting from the effects of the collapse of part of the floor and possibly by too rapid cooling. Mayes drew seven primary conclusions from his experiment:

1. The difficulty of moving pottery to the kiln for firing suggested that pots would be made close to the kiln site, but not within 30 feet because of smoke and heat.

2. Kilns would probably be located near a good road or navigable river to facilitate bringing clay and wood to the site.

3. The wood was easier to transport than the clay, and the equivalent of only a single cartload was required. This suggested that kilns might be situated closer to clay sources than timber.

4. A well-drained site is important for the kiln to dry out easily (flooding was a problem for the experimental kiln). A hill slope and permeable soil would be desirable.

5. Special care should be taken to distinguish between construction and relining of ancient kilns. Examination of some areas of the experimental kiln gave the erroneous impression of having been relined. Also, if the gas seal of a kiln was tested by means of a preliminary firing and found inadequate, relining would be necessary and would thus not be an indicator of reuse, but rather it would be associated with construction. Also, clays that have high shrinkage rates are unsuitable for a reducing kiln.

6. Although the time to prepare the clay and make the pots was not recorded, a reasonable estimate for one potter and an assistant was one week, thus making weekly firings possible.

7. If the experimental kiln had to be refired, a considerable amount of repair and reconstruction of the floor, flue walls, roof, furnace, and tongue would have been required. Nonetheless, this would be easier than constructing a new kiln.

Appendices to the report provided detailed information on temperatures by time and location within the kiln, gas analysis (oxygen and carbon dioxide) for the primary purpose of detecting and locating leaks, sampling for directions of thermoremanent magnetism, and measurement of the magnetic anomaly (discussed below).

THE SECOND EXPERIMENT: A REPLICA FROM DONCASTER

The purpose of Mayes' second experiment

> was to consolidate the knowledge gained from Kiln 1 . . . and to compare the difference in efficiency of a kiln with twin pedestals with that of the previous tongue pedestal type. Additional tests to elucidate the cause of the variation of the magnetic vectors about the mean direction in samples taken from the fired structure were incorporated into the experiment. (1962:80)

This time the kiln was based on a Romano-British example excavated in Doncaster. To eliminate some of the problems encountered with the strength of the fabric of the first kiln, all of the alluvial clay used for the second example was mixed ("grogged") with sand. To allow for precise evaluation of the direction of thermoremanent magnetism, asbestos rods were driven vertically around the lip of the chamber so that movement of the kiln walls could be precisely measured. When the kiln dried, cracking was less severe than in the first kiln and nearly absent in the grogged firebars. The bulk of the pottery was made from a commercial potter's clay, with some local clays being used as well.

Eleven thermocouples were placed inside the kiln, with four more embedded in the kiln wall. Prefiring eventually proceeded without a dome after two domes collapsed when the supporting material had burned away. As a result, the fabric of the kiln was fired but it was clearly not possible to test for a gas seal. Prefiring lasted 14 hours, with the maximum temperature reaching 800°C. Afterwards, a cooling period of 17 hours was allowed prior to loading. The lowest layer of pots placed in the kiln consisted mostly of wasters from the first experiment. A total of 205 green pots formed the rest of the load.

When the kiln was fired, a temperature of 900°C was reached after 12 hours and was held, with some fluctuation, for five hours. During that five-hour period water was sprayed into the flue and green vegetation was placed in the flue and furnace chamber in attempts to produce a reducing atmosphere prior to sealing the kiln. It proved impossible to maintain a reducing atmosphere while allowing the kiln to cool. As a precautionary measure against ruining the pots because of rapid temperature change, the kiln was reheated and then sealed with clay and earth as in the previous experiment.

Unlike the results of that first experiment, only about 10 percent of the pottery suffered either distortion or breakage. Most was reduced as well, with some oxidized pots appearing adjacent to cracks in the kiln wall over the flue. Only minor structural repairs would be necessary in preparation for a second firing, but a complete relining would be required for a reduction firing. Mayes reached the following conclusions:

1. Fuel consumption was remarkably low, especially in light of the temperature being held at maximum for five hours longer than was required.

2. Difficulty in drying the kiln suggested that kiln construction may have been a seasonal activity.

3. Reducing conditions occur immediately after the kiln is sealed. Retention of these conditions for an extended period of time is extremely difficult with this type of kiln. This suggests the importance of allowing the temperature to drop after sealing to a point where any air leaks will not be able to reoxidize the pottery.

4. Using standardized pottery forms and sizes and "saggers" made of wet clay to separate and balance green pots resulted in low wastage.

5. Complete bricking (which did not occur in the experimental kiln) may be the result of heat accumulation resulting from situations in which the kiln was reused before it had a chance to cool completely.

As in the report on the first experiment, Mayes provided appendices featuring in-depth discussion of the thermal performance of the kiln, the results of the gas analysis, and an evaluation of the archaeomagnetic measurements.

Discussion of Experiments 1 and 2

Lacking ethnographic evidence, Mayes relied on the results of excavations of Romano-British kilns to guide construction of his replicas. The experience gained from the first experiment enabled a more successful firing to be carried out in the second. The results provided an estimate of time and materials required to construct and fire Romano-British kilns as well as a wealth of quantitative and qualitative evidence relating to their operation and performance. Once fired, the remains of the kilns yielded valuable clues to the proper interpretation of the use-history of ancient kilns (e.g., relining does not necessarily indicate reuse) and their potential as sources of thermoremanent magnetism.

The careful measurement of thermoremanent magnetism constituted a separate investigation unrelated to the behavioral variables associated with pottery production. The interest in the magnetic properties of kilns lies in the fact that these structures may contain within their fabric a record of the direction of the earth's magnetic field at the time that they were last heated to high temperature. This information can be used to increase our understanding of the movement of the earth's magnetic poles and also serve as a means of dating features such as kilns, furnaces, and firepits (for a discussion of "archaeomagnetic" dating see Eighmy and Sternberg 1990, Michels 1973:130–147, Renfrew and Bahn 2004:163–165). Unfortunately, use of this method is not without problems, as "samples taken from ancient structures show considerable dispersion of their magnetic vectors about the mean direction" (Mayes 1961:23). The aim of the investigation associated with the experimental kiln was to find out why this should be so. One hypothesis was that kiln wall "fallout" (a systematic outward tilting of the walls), had occurred after the thermoremanent magnetism had formed. The data obtained from the experimental kiln showed dispersion comparable to that observed in some ancient kilns and consistent with fallout of the walls. But the walls did not appear to have moved.

The second kiln provided the opportunity to monitor the kiln walls closely to detect any possible movements. A combination of eight vertical rods were embedded around the lip of the kiln at equal intervals, and nine horizontal rods fitted into asbestos tubes and equipped with pistons were placed against the kiln wall in three horizontal planes and at three azimuths. The results indicated that tilt during cooling did not exceed 1½ inches, and that it was not uniform with azimuth. The thermoremanent magnetism results were consistent with a four-inch fallout (which, of course, did not occur); they also showed a dispersion that was random with respect to azimuth (Mayes 1962:107). The conclusion, not surprisingly, was that wall fallout made no significant contribution to the dispersion in thermoremanent magnetism. Why the systematic error would occur in the absence of significant fallout was unexplained.

The time and effort required for multifaceted experiments like the ones Mayes carried out are considerable, but the potential yield in knowledge they provide combined with their value in bringing the past to life make the investment worthwhile. Experiments of this kind might be fundable through the sale of the replicas of Roman pots that they can produce and are just the sort of enterprise that would serve as an interesting and educational demonstration for the public. More will be said about this sort of enterprise in chapters 5 and 6.

MONUMENTAL UNDERTAKINGS

One of the most impressive achievements of ancient people was the transport of very heavy objects and the construction of monumental structures. People today often marvel (and rightly so) at what was accomplished in the absence of modern technology. If the popularity of the *Secrets of Lost Empires* series and other television programs devoted to this subject is any indication, this is an area of archaeological inquiry in which there is considerable public interest. For some people, such feats as making and transporting the statues on Easter Island and constructing the Egyptian pyramids are sufficiently mind-boggling that they've been quite willing to believe that extraterrestrial help or magical powers were required! Catering to this ignorance, Erich von Däniken has written a series of ludicrous (but highly profitable) books in which he ignores scientific evidence of the sort that experimental archaeology and other serious research into the past have provided, in favor of the totally unsubstantiated claim that "alien astronauts" were responsible for just about every great achievement of ancient people (for an excellent discussion of von Däniken's work and "pseudoarcheology" see Feder 2008). The case studies presented below were selected to provide a sense of how archaeologists use experiments to figure out how ancient transport of heavy materials and construction of large monuments may have been accomplished without help from other worlds or antigravity spells.

THE MOAI OF EASTER ISLAND

The huge stone statues on Easter Island, the moai, are among the most famous monuments of the ancient world. They are immediately impressive for their size: some that were transported a considerable distance from the quarry exceed 30 feet in length, with the largest ever carved measuring a staggering 65 feet. Their haunting appearance and sculptural beauty also work to captivate everyone who has seen them in person, in photographs, or on television. Mystery has surrounded their manufacture, transport, placement on equally impressive stone platforms *(ahu)* that ring the island, and their meaning (see Figure 4-5).[4] For a brief but interesting and beautifully illustrated book on the island's history, culture, and statues, *Easter Island: Mystery of the Stone Giants*, by Orliac and Orliac (1988) is worth a look. *The Enigmas of Easter Island*, by Flenley and Bahn (2003) offers considerably more information on the Island's settlement and early history and features an excellent discussion of experimental attempts at transporting and erecting the statues. It also provides an overview of the island's cultural ecology in conjunction with a sobering discussion of the deleterious effects on the environment and ultimately the civilization itself brought about by factors such as population growth, agricultural intensification, deforestation, and overharvesting of resources.

Figure 4-5 Moai with pukao on platform (ahu).

Moai on the Move. As you might expect, there are more ways than one to move a giant piece of sculpture and this is clearly reflected in the variety of methods that have been proposed to explain how the Easter Island statues were transported from the quarry high up on the steep slope of an ancient volcano to their intended places of display—a journey in some instances of over six miles. Rather than examine a single experiment in detail, I discuss key points from several of them to better convey a sense of how this type of problem has been approached.

The carving of moai apparently ended sometime around AD 1500, when civilization on the island went into decline. Although this was over 200 years prior to the arrival of Europeans (whose presence proved disastrous for the islanders; see Orliac and Orliac 1988:11–27 for a moving account; see also Fischer 2005), the era of statue carving and transport was near enough to the period in which oral tradition was first recorded to have some potential value as a guide to how statues might have been moved. That tradition says, in essence, that the moai, which probably represented powerful ancestors, "walked" to the platforms. What significance, if any, might this statement have for archaeologists?

There are two obvious possibilities for the orientation of the statues as they were moved: vertical or horizontal. Statues at the base of the volcano from which they were quarried have been found in upright positions in pits. It appears that finishing of their backs was done here prior to transport. If we assume that they were typically upright at the quarry site, then moving them in a horizontal position required a difficult and dangerous operation—laying them down (see Love 2000:117). And of course, movement in a horizontal position does not suggest walking. So, let's assume, as many experts do, that the statues were moved in a standing position. They could, as the experiments of Love and others have demonstrated, be moved on sledges. Sledges running over a track of logs lubricated with mashed sweet potatoes have been shown to work quite well on level ground (Love 1990; see also figure 35 in Flenley and Bahn 2003:128). But does this sort of movement convey walking? It could, but is there another alternative that more realistically resembles walking, makes sense from an engineering perspective and is appropriate for prehistoric Easter Island?

Czech engineer and avid archaeological experimenter Pavel Pavel devoted some serious thought to this problem and visualized a tilting and twisting movement that most resembled a strolling motion:

> The results of my research surprised me. My calculations have told me that the islanders could be correct. I estimated that the transport of the moai statues by this method could be ten times easier than pulling the moai on a sledge. (1995:69)

He noted that some variation of this technique has widespread use around the world when tall, heavy objects must be moved (think about moving a refrigerator that lacks wheels). Pavel saw two possibilities: simply pulling alternate sides of the statue forward or, accomplishing the same movement but with less effort, tilting the statue to the side, to reduce the surface area in contact with the ground and hence lessen the friction, and then twisting it forward. He decided to test his calculations with an experiment involving a full-size replica of a moai.

Using a clay mold, Pavel and his associates cast a concrete replica measuring 4.5 m in height and weighing 12 tons. By fastening one set of ropes around the base for twisting and a second set of ropes around the head for tilting, two groups of men, nine on the former set and eight on the latter, were able to "walk" the moai replica forward. Pavel noted that as a result of a recent rain, the ground was muddy and the statue tended to act like a "bulldozer." A second experiment took place four years later on Easter Island and involved authentic moai. A small statue was used for the first trial (2.8 m high and weighing between 4 and 5 tons). Three men tilted and five twisted. This successful effort was followed by moving a 4-m-high, 9-ton moai (this method as well as a method for moving moai in a horizontal position are nicely illustrated in Pavel 1990:142–145).

Pavel next devoted some consideration to making the process easier and thus reducing the number of people required. He reasoned that attaching a horizontal beam to the moai's back and using it as a lever might reduce the number of laborers needed by one-half to as much as one-third. An experiment in which ropes were attached to the ends of the beam was also carried out successfully (reported in Love 2000:117).

Another experimenter who has taken the oral tradition as a source of inspiration is Ferren MacIntyre (1999). After providing a useful summary of seven experimental approaches to moving moai and their results, he provides a number of examples of history remembered in the form of oral tradition. For MacIntyre,

> the point is that one should not automatically dismiss traditional oral information. If legends say moai "walked" to their ahu, there is a good chance that they did just that. . . . There is always the chance that the "problem" with walking moai lies in our own failure of imagination. (1999:72)

MacIntyre's imagination led him to a modification of the approaches taken by Pavel. He noted that Pavel's experimental work has demonstrated that walking a flat-bottomed moai causes damage to the base in the form of spalls coming off the corners (see discussion below). His solution to this problem was a curved "rocking foot" (see Figure 4-6). The rocking foot may be detachable and made of wood or integral to the base of the moai (use of the latter would lead to damage and would require retouching of the base before it was placed in position on the ahu).

To move the moai, MacIntyre proposed the use of a walking rig that incorporated a lever much like Pavel's. This device would require using 12 tree trunks, with two of them needing to be approximately 10 m in length. Cross-bracing would be required as would rope to lash the rig together. MacIntyre noted:

> The timbers are reusable and formed a structure which could have been pegged together for added rigidity; the many short ropes probably wear out. Transport is incremental in small steps, interruptible at any time, and can cope gracefully with small gradients. It would be described as "walking" by anyone who participated in it. (1999:74)

Figure 4-6 Moai with rocking foot, tilted 10°.

To facilitate movement up a gradient, MacIntyre suggested that one can climb onto the lever. Rotating the moai was found, not surprisingly, to consume the most energy because of the friction between the rocking foot and the ground. As model building proceeded, the rig was improved in its design. MacIntyre assumed that a similar evolutionary process occurred on Easter Island as the islanders gained experience moving moai. He felt that with a rig such as the one he designed "any terrain that can be negotiated (however awkwardly) on a bicycle with high-pressure tires can be traversed by a walking moai" (1999:75). The motion would in most cases be "rhythmical" and could be sustained for "minutes on end," with walking speed over level ground possibly exceeding 150 m/hr.

At the end of his report, MacIntyre raises a point near and dear to all scientists: that of how a hypothesis such as his might be falsified. He notes that "a hypothesis which cannot be falsified is not very helpful" (1999:76). As experience has proven, we can devise a considerable number of different methods of moving moai and other large stone objects, all using materials that would have been available to ancient people, but this does not mean that any one of them was actually used. In the absence of any direct evidence on Easter Island of a detachable rocking foot, all that would appear to support the possibility of movement by the tilting and rocking method is indirect evidence from the wear and retouching seen on the bottom of some moai (MacIntyre 1999:73–74). What other evidence might potentially be found that would increase the likelihood that methods such as Pavel's and MacIntyre's were actually used? In other words, can any test implications be derived from the hypothesis? MacIntyre offers the following:

> There are field marks which would support the idea of walking a moai. (1) Most convincing would be . . . a moai at the quarry with a rocking base, but this would not exist if the rocker had been a wooden cradle; (2) Abrasion tracks. (1999:76)

Although the abrasion tracks would most likely be erased quickly by weathering, MacIntyre holds out the possibility that some might have been preserved under soil. To get a sense of what they might look like, he fitted the base of a model moai with coarse sandpaper and "walked" it over a scratch board.

Discussion

These experiments have helped to remove some of the mystery surrounding the moai in particular, and all ancient transport of very heavy objects in general. The popularity of explanations based on magic or the assistance of extraterrestrials has served to illustrate not only how gullible many people are but also, and more importantly, how often the abilities of ancient people are underestimated. The use of materials and techniques available to the ancient Easter Islanders in the statue-moving experiments performed by Pavel and Love was crucial to the integrity of their results, which have demonstrated the feasibility of transporting moai using timber, rope, a relatively small labor force and, of course, human ingenuity, while clearly falsifying the ridiculous hypothesis that something beyond ordinary human capabilities was necessary to do the job.[5]

MacIntyre's experiment is more problematic. His walking rig appears not to have been tested on a statue comparable in size and weight to an actual moai. In fact, he does not provide any information on his apparently small model but does indicate that he would like to test his walking rig on a 9-ton replica created at the University of California at Los Angeles (1999:75). His estimates of the size of the requisite labor force and the rate of movement appear to be based primarily on calculations derived from the dimensions of an average moai and the results of previous experiments. With objects as large as moai, problems typically arise when actually attempting to implement a promising hypothetical method of transport, as many investigators have learned. In any case, MacIntyre's model was not fully tested and his experiment (in contrast to his ideas) is thus of limited value. However, in MacIntyre's favor is the overall similarity of his approach to one by Pavel in which the latter successfully tested a tilt-swivel method in which a long wooden lever was attached near the base and ropes were tied to the head. MacIntyre's walking rig also included the lever and differed from Pavel's approach primarily in the use of wooden props in place of the ropes (and, of course, in the addition of the detachable walking foot).

At the very least, the experiments carried out to date have demonstrated several methods by which statues *might* have been moved. Circumstantial evidence in support of an upright mode of transportation comes in the form of the damage present on the bases of many moai (Pavel 1990:144). Chipping debris associated with retouching the bases of moai set on ahu has also been discovered (in one case wear was sufficient to have required the statue's hands, which are always located near the base of these legless statues, to be recarved by the Islanders). Furthermore, there are a number of broken statues that appear to have fallen during transport (Pavel 1990:144, MacIntyre 1999:74). As a cautionary note and a reminder that successful experiments neither prove our hypotheses nor eliminate the need for new ones, consider these reflections by Pavel and Love:

> My study about transport of the moai took 12 years. All those attempting to solve the problem made the same mistake as I did. We took the questions of the moai transport as one problem. There was simply the question, "How were the statues transported?"

and nothing more. There are many sorts of statues on Easter Island. Their shape is very similar but their proportions are different. The weight depends on the proportions, and weight is the most important problem for transport. . . . The similar problem is with the analysis of transport routes. The transportation from the quarry of Rano Raraku was probably different from the route crossing the island or from the finished transport road direct to an ahu platform. When we determine the statue and part of its trail we can start with the discussion of "How was this moai transported to this place." (Pavel 1995:72)

Excavations were carried out in the summer of 2000 which uncovered a total of 210 linear meters of the prehistoric southern coastal roadway over which the statues were moved, including an area entirely surrounding the fallen road statue at Ahu Hanga Hahave. The road was cut and fill style. The cut portions are extensive, and were excavated to the rotten bedrock (regolith) level in the form of a shallow V, or broad U shape some 30 cm deep and 5.5 meters wide. Curbstones line portions of the roadway, and large numbers of post holes were discovered outside the curbstones, suggesting whatever contraption held the statue in place was somehow pried along. The cut parts of the road are not conducive to rollers or skids or tilting a statue along. It would appear that all of our experimental methods of moving moai are not yet correct. Until some roadways are constructed and methods devised to move statues along them either vertically or horizontally, the mystery of Easter Island remains. . . . Whatever contraptions are built for the moai moving processes, they will have to be able to accommodate both the flat fill surfaces as well as surfaces that are V-shaped. (Love 2000:118)

A CROWNING ACHIEVEMENT

After having transported a moai and set it in place on an ahu, the Easter Islanders sometimes presented themselves with one further challenge by fitting the statue with a *pukao,* which probably represented a topknot or feathered headdress worn by warriors. Although there is some disagreement, most experts feel that these adornments were not in place when the statue was raised and maneuvered onto the platform (for discussions of this issue see Flenley and Bahn 2003:135–146, Love 2000). How might this have been accomplished? Once again, a very reasonable and elegant solution has been provided by Pavel (1995). His initial test of the method took place in 1990 as part of an investigation of another famous monument from antiquity—Stonehenge. In his experiment he successfully raised a 6-ton replica of one of the lintels that were fitted to pairs of upright stones to form the sarsen trilithons (see Figure 4-7). He later demonstrated that the same technique would work equally well for raising a pukao and placing it in position on top of a moai (see Figure 4-8). In that case, the technique involved setting two beams in a sloping position in front of a moai, with their upper ends supported by sturdy vertical poles. A long lever arm was placed on top of the moai, with the greater part extending to the rear of the statue. With a rope attached to the forward end and connected to the pukao, it was possible to move the pukao up the sloping beams by pulling the lever down. A crossbeam located just behind the pukao, and held in place with loops of rope, prevented the pukao from sliding backward when the pull rope and lever were adjusted for the next upward move.

A FEW REFLECTIONS ON MOVING MEGALITHS

While transport of moai in a standing position may make the most sense, both from the standpoint of their upright orientation at the quarry and an oral tradition in which these sacred objects are said to have "walked" to the ahu, horizontal transport of large stone objects was probably more common in other locales, such as ancient Europe. A number of

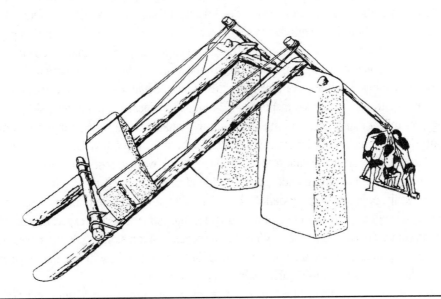

Figure 4-7 Pavel's approach to raising lintels at Stonehenge.

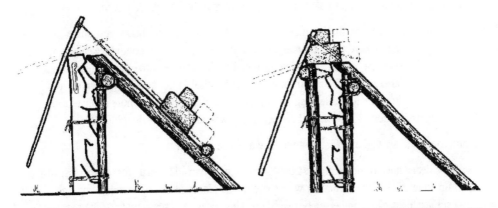

Figure 4-8 Pavel's method applied to moving a pukao into position on a moai.

experiments involving the movement and erection of megaliths have been carried out in Britain and on the European continent over the last 80 or so years. Whatever oral traditions may once have existed concerning the process of creating monuments of stone in the Neolithic and Bronze Ages have, of course, long been forgotten (assuming we dismiss tales of Merlin the magician, fairies, and giants!). However, evidence from quarries as well as other considerations point to horizontal transport as being the most reasonable possibility. Accordingly, experimenters have taken that approach in their tests and have focused on the use of wooden sledges. They have also investigated methods of erecting the stones to create such structures as dolmens and the trilithons of Stonehenge (ca. 3000–1500 BC; see Richards and Whitby 1997 for a clearly illustrated discussion of experiments involving the transport and erection of the stones of Stonehenge. See Price and Feinman 2008:515–522 for illustrations and descriptions of the primary types of megalithic monuments in Western Europe).

In a recent experiment, Osenton (2001) attempted to replicate megalithic engineering methods using only stone axe–based technology and working "by eye" rather than with the aid of calculations. I will not examine this experiment in detail but feel it is worth pointing out that Osenton had success transporting a 2-ton load by means of a 4-m-long sledge running over rollers that were 2 m long and 5 cm in diameter. He also experimented with a "short sledge," which proved ineffective, as the weight of the stone was sufficiently concentrated to cause the sledge to sink into the wooden slats it was supposed to move over. The combination of a 4-m sledge and rollers was found to be "very effective, with the sledge moving easily, even over softer ground" (2001:295). Osenton also noted that the sledge was capable of handling gradients of up to one in seven. Interestingly, he also experimented with moving stones directly over rollers. With this approach, a 4-ton stone could be moved, but one weighing 10 tons caused the rollers to jam against each other; in addition, the rough surface of the stones added considerable resistance to movement.

Osenton's experiments included the use of levers in the construction of three replica dolmens with 5-ton capstones and the erection of a 3-ton bluestone that had been transported on a 7-m-long sledge with a total weight of approximately 5 tons. He noted:

> With 28 members of the hauling crew, who were anticipating heavy resistance, the sledge moved forward faster than expected and it was possible to continue easily at an estimated speed of 5 k.p.h. This demonstrated the advantage of the longer sledge running over large rollers [30–50 cm in diameter] by displacing its weight, allowing it to cross soft ground without leaving an impression. It was also much more efficient than using smaller rollers between a short sledge and wooden-ground rails. (2001:297)

When the stone arrived at the site where it was to be erected,

> the sledge now formed a high, stable platform, with two additional cross beams lashed on either side of the stone and with spare rollers placed behind the stone providing a surface for stacking timbers to be placed on. This produced a strong, safe structure from which to lever the 3-m long stone upright. (2001:298)

Considered together, all of these experiments with moving heavy objects demonstrate that a variety of effective methods were available to ancient people. Still to be determined are the limits of the experimental methods tested so far (e.g., will a method that works well for a 9-ton stone work as well with a 20-ton load?).

MODELING ANCIENT BUILDINGS

Studies of ancient architecture may be undertaken to answer a wide variety of questions. In the next chapter, replication of component activities associated with the construction of ancient Maya ceremonial architecture will be used to estimate the time and the size of the labor force required to create the site of Uxmal (Yucatan, Mexico). A different sort of interest might prompt an experiment in which the goal is to learn something about the type of environment an ancient building provided. For example, several experiments I performed (Saraydar 1981) were designed to investigate the potential of scale models to provide information on the thermal performance of ancient houses. Today, with the sophisticated modeling of complex processes that powerful microcomputers make possible, investigations into the thermal characteristics of "virtual" houses have undoubtedly become much easier for architects and within the grasp of archaeologists wishing to explore this aspect of ancient technology. Hypotheses may be tested in a virtual environment by varying numerical values associated with key parameters such as solar angle and intensity, output of internal heat sources (hearths, occupants, etc.), composition and thickness of roofs and walls, wind speed and direction, and so on. But hardware models will always have some advantages—they can be touched and otherwise "experienced," and we learn a great deal about the many attributes of the structures they are designed to replicate through the acts of acquiring building materials and constructing and then observing them. Once built, they also serve as valuable instructional aids and exhibits for the benefit of students and the general public.

Regardless of the type of model used, investigating the performance of any building requires evaluating the thermal resistance (R-value) of its shell and measuring the rates at which it gains and loses heat. With the steadily rising cost of energy for heating and cooling, R-value has become a familiar term to many people seeking to increase their home's energy efficiency by adding insulation. To determine the R-value of a particular building material, measurements of heat transmission are required (typically expressed in Btu's per hour per square foot for a 1°F differential in temperature between the exposed surfaces); this sort of testing is conducted in specially equipped laboratories and the results are affixed to most commercially available building products. To model the thermal behavior of a building mathematically, one needs to know not only the R values of the materials from which it is made but also the various angles at which the sun strikes its surfaces during the course of an entire year; ambient temperatures; wind directions and velocities; the amount of air infiltration through walls, windows, and doors; output of internal heat sources; and more. If we build a replica of an ancient structure, we can avoid having to quantify all of these and other variables and simply evaluate its performance under various conditions directly by means of inexpensive instruments that measure temperature and humidity levels. I decided to pursue the latter approach.

After some preliminary experimentation with several simple structures constructed of plywood, I decided to carry out a more formal experiment with pithouses (see Figure 4-9). I selected the pithouse because I believed that its combination of above- and below-grade surfaces would provide a rigorous test. I had also acquired an interest in this type of house while conducting fieldwork in eastern Arizona in the early 1970s. I decided to perform an experiment in which the thermal behavior of a scale model would be tested against the behavior of a full-size replica. I was not attempting to model a specific type of ancient pithouse, but rather I was attempting to determine if the scale-model approach had any merit.

My large house wasn't as large as an actual dwelling—its base was seven feet in diameter and the pit was excavated to a depth of 20–22 inches. The roof was supported by a central post about six inches in diameter and seven feet long (see Figure 4-9). The roof itself was built on radial supports that ran from the fork at the top of the centerpost to the ground just outside the edges of the pit. Wooden cross-pieces were attached at regular intervals to the radial supports to increase strength and stability. Thatch material was provided by bundles of goldenrod stems lashed to the supports and crossbraces. The entire structure was then covered with sod, with an additional layer of soil about two inches thick around the base to improve sealing against drafts and rain. The smaller pithouse measured three feet in diameter, which made it a .43 scale model. The thickness of the thatching and the sod were the same as in the larger model, as I wanted the same thermal performance from those materials. If I had reduced the thickness of the roof to scale, the critical time lag associated with the transmission of heat through it would have been significantly shorter than in the larger model. And of course, overall heat transmission through any material increases with decreasing thickness (see Olgyay 1963:115–119 for a discussion of these variables).

The thermal performance of the two pithouses was measured with a telethermometer (a meter to which thermistor probes were attached). Three probes were attached to each pithouse, as shown in Figure 4-9, and internal temperatures were plotted against the outside temperature. In addition, relative humidity inside each house was measured using an electric psychrometer. A series of tests over a four-month period revealed that the two structures were within ½°C of each other 85 percent of the time. Only one measurement showed a discrepancy as great as 1½°C. Relative humidity levels were identical. The structures were not heated artificially. I had expected that the smaller structure's higher ratio of external surface area to internal volume would result in significant discrepancies between the internal temperatures of the two structures, but this did not prove to be the case. Most likely this happy circumstance was the result of the scaling factor not being extreme (see Olgyay 1963:182–184).

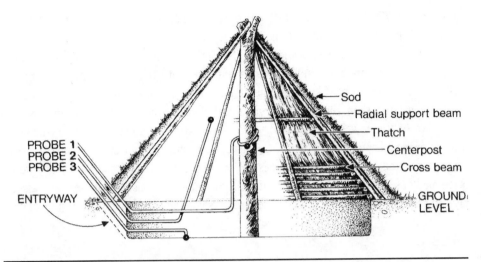

Figure 4-9 Schematic showing principal features of pit houses and probe locations (not to scale). Thatch has been cut away to reveal crossbeams.

Discussion

Although the results of my limited experiments were promising, considerably more testing of the approach is needed to determine how accurately the thermal performance of a small model tracks that of a full-size structure. With increasing interest in energy-efficient buildings, further study of the thermal characteristics and heating "costs" of ancient houses should be in order. And, as noted above, hardware models have value beyond what they may tell us about thermal behavior: we learn about their construction firsthand and they make fine exhibits. Full-size models obviously have the most to offer. They permit many more attributes of the structures being modeled to be explored and will more closely approximate the behavior and internal environment of the originals. Furthermore, nothing quite compares to spending some time in a replica of an ancient dwelling and simply experiencing its ambiance. It's important to keep in mind that numbers can't tell us everything we might wish to know (see the discussion of Neolithic and Iron Age houses in chapters 5 and 6).

PADDLING ABOUT THE OCEANS BLUE

Ancient sailing vessels have provided the subject matter for some of the most ambitious experiments that have been attempted—both in the replication process and in performance testing. The best known have featured replicas of a South American balsa raft (Heyerdahl 1950), a Polynesian double-hull canoe (Finney 1979), and two Egyptian reed boats (Heyerdahl 1971). But equally interesting and ambitious efforts have involved replicas of Viking ships (Coles 1979:74–79, McKee 1974), one of which made a successful trans-Atlantic journey in 1893. In the summer of 2007, the largest replica ever made of a Viking warship (a vessel measuring 30 meters in length and named *Sea Stallion*), began a series of trials that took it from Roskilde, Denmark, to Dublin, Ireland, a distance of 1,000 nautical miles (see Figure 4-10). Information on boat building, the ship, and its journey may be found at http://www.vikingshipmuseum.dk.) Clearly, a great deal of skill is required to construct a seaworthy replica of a large vessel, and sailing across vast expanses of ocean is not for the faint-hearted or the inexperienced mariner. Construction of small craft such as birchbark canoes for use on inland waterways also requires considerable skill, even if testing the final product is less perilous. In all cases, the details of construction—materials, preparation, and assembly—must be tightly controlled. Once the replica is completed, one must learn how to pad-

Figure 4-10 *Sea Stallion*, a reconstructed Viking sailing vessel on its way from Denmark to Ireland.

dle or sail it correctly just as one must learn how to use a stone axe in order to make a fair assessment of its capabilities.

The matter of experience and skill in sailing figured prominently in an unusual experiment by Horvath and Finney (1969), whose purpose was not to investigate ship construction but rather to evaluate a controversial aspect of Polynesian voyaging—whether the ancient Polynesians used "planned colonizing expeditions and long-distance two-way voyaging" as a major strategy in their expansion and settlement in the Eastern Pacific or, as others contended, reached new islands through "random drift voyages or one-way exile voyaging" (1969:271). To investigate this issue, Horvath and Finney conducted experiments to determine the degree to which paddling could be used in long-distance voyaging.

They chose to use a Hawaiian double-canoe for their trials because of the availability of plans and other materials necessary for its duplication; in addition, it was the "modern" vessel (eighteenth century) that was the most like earlier sailing vessels. The completed canoe measured 40 feet long and over 11 feet in overall beam. The hulls had a maximum beam of 2 feet and a maximum depth of nearly 3 feet (1969:271). They were lashed together with six wooden crosspieces, which also supported the central platform that carried the mast. The paddling crew of 12 had a mean of 10 years paddling experience with outrigger canoes.

The primary tests took place in Hawaii. The first involved a round-trip voyage off the shore of Oahu that took two days, covered 52 nautical miles, and consisted of two 8-hour excursions, while the second involved a 4-hour run (1969:272). Horvath and Finney reported that in the first voyage a variety of conditions were encountered, ranging from calm to strong winds and currents, with moderate seas; conditions for the second experiment were described as "light." Loss of body weight was measured by weighing the men before and after paddling and was corrected for fluid intake and urine output. Body temperatures were measured, as were heart rates. An instrument comparable to the Kofranyi-Michaelis meter used in the experiments with axes discussed at the beginning of this chapter measured the volume of expired air of two paddlers. Samples of expired air were collected during the last two minutes of the collection period and analyzed for oxygen content. To provide a basis for comparison of the level of energy expenditure, 6 of the subjects were tested to determine their maximum capacity by means of an adjustable treadmill.

The results of the paddling experiments showed that speeds of 6 to 7 knots (one knot is equal to approximately 1.15 statute miles per hour) were attainable but could not be sustained for more than a few minutes (1969:273). A speed of just over 3 knots was felt to be reasonable for long periods of time. A mean speed for the two-day voyage was 3.15 knots, with a range of 1 to 4.5 knots, depending on conditions. It was felt that if strong headwinds were accompanied by the heavy headseas that would be encountered in the open ocean, no forward progress would have been possible. The physiological tests indicated that the subjects, whose maximal capacities had been measured, had to work at 57 percent of their limits (1969:273). Horvath and Finney also reported considerable variation in energy expenditure during a single day and day to day. Loss of body weight was also significant, with a mean loss of 2.45 kg per crew member in spite of adequate food and water.

In a discussion of their results Horvath and Finney offered the following:

1. The average energy expenditures of the most experienced and physically fit paddlers were within the range that they could be expected to maintain for 8 hours. The paddlers themselves felt that they could maintain this pace for several days.

2. The weight losses that occurred despite adequate food and water suggest that availability of adequate water supplies may have been a major limiting factor to long-distance voyaging.

3. A rough estimate of the caloric intake for each paddler indicated that 4,000 to 4,500 calories per day were needed, which would also restrict the distance that this type of vessel could travel.

4. It was also felt that high ambient heat stresses might pose a problem.

From these points Hovarth and Finney came to the overall conclusion:

> The results of the present experiments suggest that padding, as the sole propulsive force of a double-canoe, would have been of extremely limited value for long-range voyaging. . . . Paddling as an auxiliary source of power may, however, have been a significant factor in long-range voyaging. Polynesian voyaging canoes were combination sailing and paddling craft. . . . When the winds failed, the strategic option could have been to paddle until a favorable wind zone was reached rather than to wait out the calm. (1969:275)

Discussion

This experiment added considerably to our understanding of the means by which ancient Polynesians traversed great distances in their canoes and provided useful data on the energetics of paddling. The ability to paddle at about 3 knots for an extended period of time would clearly have been significant when winds were insufficient to carry a vessel forward on its course. As a supplementary method of propulsion it may well have proved critically important on long-distance voyages. Paddling would always have been very important as land was approached.

An actual long-distance voyage in an authentic double-canoe would provide an even better test of theories concerning the travels of the ancient Polynesians. Such an experiment would evaluate considerably more than the vessel, as it would require use of the complex and highly sophisticated navigation methods for which the Polynesians are famous. With this in mind, Finney went on to conduct one of the most ambitious experiments ever performed (Finney 1979). With a dedicated group of colleagues, including expert Polynesian navigators and sailors, he constructed a 60-foot replica of an ancient Polynesian double canoe—named "Hokule'a"—which was sailed from Hawaii to Tahiti and back, a voyage of nearly 6,000 miles.[6] This experiment has helped to put to rest the once popular notion that the people who colonized the Pacific did so essentially by accident (Finney 1979:10–16; see also Flenley and Bahn 2003:66–74).

Experiments such as these obviously require detailed knowledge of the materials from which an original vessel was made, the methods used to construct it, and money (in the case of the Hokule'a, quite a bit of it). They also require considerable seafaring skill in order to fairly assess the craft's performance (as well as live to tell about the experience). Replicating smaller, technologically simpler vessels is a more manageable task, and one that a single individual may reasonably attempt. But anyone who has tried to build a common-variety canoe, for instance, will appreciate the knowledge and ability required to make a good one. Though few in number, the experiments that have been performed with replicas of watercraft have given us an appreciation of the boatbuilding skills of ancient people and their ability to sail the great distances, when that was what they desired.

REPLICATING NONCULTURAL PROCESSES: NEOLITHIC EARTHWORK

As noted in chapter 1, experiments need not be limited to replicating past behavioral processes. The study of thermoremanent magnetism and kiln-wall fallout in Mayes' experiments with Romano-British kilns (discussed earlier in this chapter) provides one example of why it is important for archaeologists to improve their ability to recognize and then control for the transformations that take place in the interval between the time that an artifact enters the archaeological record or a feature is constructed and the time of recovery. Experiments have been carried out both to increase understanding of these transformations as they may have affected specific types of sites, as the following case study on Neolithic earthworks will illustrate, and to develop precise methods of investigating in a more general way the effects of natural agents and time on a wide variety of materials associated with archaeological sites, such as bone, leather, pottery, and textiles (Ascher 1970).

In 1960 a Research Committee of the British Association for the Advancement of Science that included Paul Ashbee, Ian W. Cornwall, Geoffrey W. Dimbleby, and Peter Jewell set out to increase knowledge of how ancient monuments are modified by nature over time. In particular, they sought to learn how processes such as "weathering, denudation and silting" take place and to quantify their effects (Ashbee and Cornwall 1961:129; see also Jewell 1963 and Jewell and Dimbleby 1966). To do this, they first had to construct a replica of a ditch and bank of the type common to many Neolithic sites in Britain, and that exercise provided an opportunity to increase understanding of how these features were created (see Figure 4-11). The work was entirely carried out with hand tools, with authentic implements— antler picks, shovels made of equine and bovine scapulae, and wicker baskets for carrying soil and the underlying chalk—being used to construct one portion of the bank. These efforts produced valuable data on the efficiencies of the various tools, and it was observed that the picks left characteristic marks in the chalk that matched those found in Neolithic sites. Time and motion studies were performed to show the relative performance of steel tools and their primitive counterparts; modern methods were found to be three to four times more efficient. It was noted that steel shovels held the greatest responsibility for that discrepancy as they were significantly easier to use and more efficient than ones made of scapulae. This result led Ashbee and Cornwall to speculate that wooden shovels of a type recovered from a West Country barrow might have been used for this type of activity (the scapulae were found to be better suited for use as scraping tools).[7]

The results of this part of the experiment were then used as the basis for estimates of the number of "man/hours" required to construct barrows of various sizes and shapes as well as the ditch at Avebury (diameter 347 m) and the Dorset Cursus (a 10-km-long monument consisting of two parallel banks with adjoining ditches). Consideration was also given to the difficulties associated with applying the figures from the Overton Down experiment to considerably larger-scale monuments such as the one at Avebury, the need to take into account the time expended by supervisory staff (at Overton Down, 388 man/hours versus 1,167 man/hours by the diggers), and the social organization that made these constructions possible (Ashbee and Cornwall 1961:133–134).

Figure 4-11 Overton Down, 1960: the finished ditch and bank.

Although the construction of the earthwork has added greatly to our understanding of this type of activity in antiquity, the primary purpose of the experiment was to investigate the noncultural transformation processes associated with ditch and bank features. To that end, the research design called for examining the construction for changes by means of excavation of sections at intervals of 2, 4, 8, 16, 32, 64 and possibly 128 years. Jewell and Dimbleby (1966) report that examinations at the two- and four-year marks showed that changes in the ditch and bank developed independently from each other (see Figure 4-12).

In the 1962 and 1964 sections, the scree (detritus) that formed in the ditch was measured in terms of its depth, angles, and content, and the morphological and textural changes in the bank were documented. The effects of time on organic materials such as textiles, leather, and wood billets buried in the bank were investigated as were the effects of earthworms on the movement of Lycopodium spores that had been dusted over the ground in an attempt to simulate pollen rain at the time of construction. In addition, movement of artifacts (flower pots and pottery discs) that had been seeded in the bank was recorded. On the basis of the observations, measurements, and analyses derived from the first two sections, Jewell and Dimbleby offered a number of "archaeological implications" concerning such matters as reconstructions of the original profiles of ancient ditches, calculation of the original width of the berm, the activity of moles and earthworms, the potential of seasonal alternations of fine and coarse rubble layers of fill in the ditch to provide precise chronological information concerning the early stages of silting, and the use of finds contained in the ditch for dating purposes (1966:339–341).

A detailed presentation of subsequent investigations and a summary of all key results were published in 1996 by Bell, Fowler, and Hillson. This report led to some reflection by

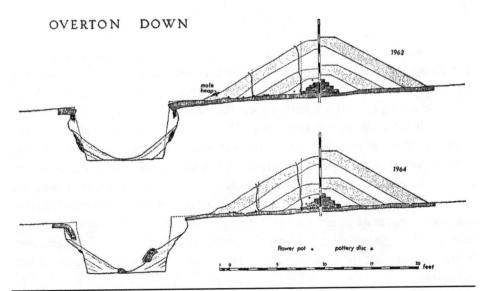

Figure 4-12   Sections of the Overton Down experimental earthwork, 1962 and 1964.

Ashbee and Jewell (1998) on their experiences with the Overton experimental earthwork since its inception. One important issue they discuss concerns the difficulties associated with maintaining a proper commitment to a long-term research project in terms of personnel and financial support, a subject discussed in the following chapter. They also remark on the sometimes surprising developments brought to light by the most recent excavations. For example:

> We had not fully anticipated that what was seen in the initial sections was not of itself static and thus a basis for the interpretation of subsequent sections. It happened that we were surprised, if not shocked, to see the beautiful, unambiguous banding seen at the corners of the ditch-fill in early sections to be indistinct and obscured in later sections. . . . Also remarkable was the erratic degradation of certain of the buried materials. (1998:499)

In addition, they comment on the greatly expanded scope of the investigations at Overton made possible by the remarkable advances the have occurred in archaeological science since 1960.

Finally, it should be noted that in 1963 another experimental earthwork similar to the one at Overton Down was constructed at Wareham, Dorset (Ashbee and Jewell 1998; Bell, Fowler, and Hillson 1996; Evans and Limbrey 1974). It was designed as a complementary effort in that it replicated monuments located on acid heathland soils (podzols), whereas Overton Down was situated on nonacid soils (chalk rendzinas). A report on the project provides an in-depth analysis on the micromorphology, chemistry, and magnetic susceptibility of the topsoil buried beneath the bank and illustrates the highly specialized nature of some of the research problems that may be associated with this type of experiment (Macphail et al. 2003).

Discussion

A few comments on these complex experiments will have to suffice. Each has two major time frames associated with it—short (the construction itself) and long (documenting changes that occur as a result of natural processes over time). In the cases of Overton Down and Wareham a great deal was learned about the construction of earthworks through the use of authentic implements in timed trials. The trials at Overton Down also illustrate a method of estimating such things as the time and workforce required to construct specific archaeological features by means of extrapolations from measurements of the component activities that went into their creation. In both cases great care was taken to incorporate into the design and construction of the site means by which changes could be precisely tracked (reference poles, numbered artifacts with precise provenience data, etc.). Finally, a commitment to a long-term experiment presents the investigator with a number of problems unrelated to the replication itself, not the least of which is protection from unwanted disturbance by human activity.

CHAPTER SUMMARY

Each step in an experiment typically requires a decision to be made about how best to replicate an ancient behavior. The examples in this chapter have shown that with explorations of more complex technology (e.g., pre-Columbian copper casting and Romano-British pottery production) the number of steps that must be successfully integrated in an experiment to produce a worthwhile result increases considerably. The same is true with the attempts to demonstrate how societies lacking draft animals and mechanical devices such as cranes accomplished physically demanding and difficult tasks like moving and raising very large and heavy objects such as moai and megaliths. In these instances the experimenters had to give careful consideration to issues such as the orientation of the object, the device(s) used to manipulate it, the labor force required, and the adjustments that had to have been made as terrain and other conditions varied during transport. And of course, as the number of decisions to be made increases, almost invariably does the number of potential solutions to the larger problem—whatever we are seeking to replicate may have been done in several distinctly different ways. An added difficulty comes from the frequent lack of archaeological and ethnographic evidence to serve as clues to the process, as is the case with both moai and megaliths (we have more secure knowledge of how they were made than how they were moved).

The experiments with stone and metal axes provided examples of how archaeologists may revisit earlier experiments and build upon them as they pursue new lines of research. They also illustrated the approach to quantification of key variables that is characteristic of many recent imitative experiments. Experiments such as the experimental earthworks at Overton Down and Wareham in Britain, while focusing primarily on long-term, noncultural transformation processes, were likewise designed to produce quantifiable results.

The case studies reviewed in the following chapter build upon these strategies and illustrate ways in which a series of interrelated experiments can be combined to replicate the construction of complex and sophisticated features such as Maya temples and measure the productivity of agricultural systems.

NOTES

[1] In a similar vein concerning their experiments using replicas of Maya chert axes to cut limestone blocks, Woods and Titmus comment:

> Initial uses of our axes were somewhat conservative as we attempted to determine the stress limits the handles and bifaces could endure. However, after becoming comfortable with the use of our replicas, we used our axes more aggressively and eventually recorded several timed cutting episodes. (1996:483)

[2] These experiments, like the one by Sonnenfeld discussed earlier, raise issues concerning the appropriateness of using genuine artifacts in experiments. There are two principal areas of concern. The first can be dealt with as part of the experimental design, and that concerns whether or not the performance of an artifact (as opposed to a new replica) will be compromised as a result of its age and past use. The second is more difficult because it centers on the ethics of using an archaeological specimen in a way that is always to some degree

destructive. Using a Neolithic axe head to chop wood will at the very least modify its surface and, at worst, destroy it. We are left to consider when, if ever, is an artifact expendable?

3 There are times when the archaeologist does not intend to carry out a typical imitative experiment but rather seeks to reproduce an artifact for display purposes. In these instances the greatest possible fidelity to each step believed to be associated with the original process is unnecessary. While Coles (1979:36–38) recognizes the educational value of these "simulations," he underestimates the complexity of the choices to be made, the problems to be solved, and the knowledge that can be gained from carrying them out, as is made clear by Whittaker (1996) in a discussion of his experiences in making a reproduction of a Bronze Age dagger from Britain.

4 Not all moai were placed on platforms. This honor appears to have been reserved only for the most prestigious statues (Flenley and Bahn 2003:145).

5 See Love's comments on a poorly executed experiment led by Van Tilburg in which the most difficult step was carried out using a crane (Love 2000:115).

6 Some of the issues that arose in the planning and execution of this experiment are outside the scope of those typically encountered in archaeological experiments and are discussed in chapter 6.

7 For a further discussion of the difficulties in using unhafted scapulae as shovels see Curwen (1926).

CHAPTER 5

CEREMONIAL CENTERS AND ANCIENT FARMS
ASSEMBLING THE BIG PICTURE, PIECE BY PIECE

The objective from the beginning of the Ancient Farm had been to . . . integrate all the different experiments so that not only can the individual experiments be studied per se but also foreseen relationships between the experiments can be evaluated and unforeseen relationships might be identified. (Reynolds 1999:6)

OVERVIEW

The case studies reviewed thus far have demonstrated that imitative experiments provide unique opportunities to test hypotheses about the manufacture and use of artifacts and features. They also have shown how experiments are especially useful in helping us to acquire quantitative measures of such variables as speed of operation, energetic efficiency, number of flakes produced, light output, maximum attainable temperature, and so on.

When activities that required a coordinated effort by sizeable groups of people or the services of specialists are replicated, the scope of the investigations may be expanded to include more nonmaterial aspects of the past. For instance, once we have a reasonable and persuasive model of how a large and heavy statue might have been transported or an example of how monumental architecture was constructed, we are in a position to place these efforts in their social context. Among the questions we may ask are ones concerning the social and political organizations that made them possible, and this naturally leads to an evaluation of their cost to society. And here we must be especially careful to avoid making unwarranted assumptions. Whenever the word "cost" is used, most people today quite naturally think first of money. Most of the large-scale projects undertaken in antiquity were the products of societies that did not have money as we know it and were organized in ways alien to capitalism. For instance, if Mendelssohn (1974) is correct in arguing that the construction of a pyramid in ancient Egypt was an endeavor whose most important function was to give jobs to those who built it and in the process strengthen their allegiance to and dependence on the Pharaoh, then minimizing costs by paying as little (in goods, not money in this case) and employing as few people as necessary to complete the monument might well have been counterproductive. The notion of time can also be problematic—when time is mentioned, the general assumption among Westerners is that time *is* money and speedy completion of a project was as desirable in the past as it typically is in the present. In nonindustrial societies, people are rarely in the sort of rush as they go about their business as is typically the order of the day for most members of technologically advanced societies.[1] Nonetheless, with the rise of social complexity and the associated concentration of power in the hands of an elite, swift completion of projects designed to glorify the achievements of the rulers and honor the deities they represented or served may often have been of high priority.

When it comes to projects of these kinds, archaeologists often seek an understanding of their social implications and the means by which they might have been organized and carried out. To achieve those goals, answers must be found to questions concerning the labor and material resources committed to such endeavors: How many person-days were required for the project? How large a workforce might have been involved? From how large an area might this workforce have been drawn? How many of the workers (if any) were specialists? How much stone or earth did they use? What kind of logistical problems had to be solved? How great a burden might the project have placed on those whose labor made it possible? Here we come close to the ancient mind in one important respect: undoubtedly some of these questions had to be answered by the architects and planners of the past before their monumental visions could become reality.

In the case of ancient subsistence systems, the approach is similar. Once again, the absolute speed with which tasks such as clearing land could have been completed is probably not worth pursuing, but labor and energy costs, the possible value of pooled labor resources, and most certainly productivity and sustainability are worth investigating. A key difference between an experiment that provides an estimate of the labor force and rate of movement associated with transporting a 15-ton block of stone one mile on a wooden sledge and one that assesses agricultural productivity is that the latter must be repeated over the course of many years in a climate comparable to that of ancient times before any confidence can be placed in the results. This requires an extraordinary commitment on the part of the archaeologist(s) carrying out the research as well as suitable tracts of land that can be secured and protected for more than a decade. Not surprisingly, experimental investigations of this kind are rare, and they are typically performed under the auspices of a research center, as we shall see below.

In this chapter we examine projects in which larger slices of ancient life are modeled by means of carefully assembled sets of experiments. The discussion begins with examples that focus on the technological and social dimensions involved in the construction of Maya ceremonial centers and then considers ones that investigate the labor costs and productivity of agricultural systems. The chapter concludes with the broad-based, long-term research of the Lejre Experimental Center in Denmark and the Butser Ancient Farm in Britain where virtually every aspect of Western European Iron Age life amenable to experimentation has been or is being investigated.

CASE STUDIES

CONSTRUCTING UXMAL

A classic study carried out by Charles Erasmus in 1965 provides an excellent example of how we may go about modeling the construction of very large structures. The approach featured a combination of ethnographic research and extrapolation from experiments that replicated key component activities. I describe this study in some detail in order to make clear the many interdependent steps that were required and, in the process, both the benefits and potential pitfalls of this kind of experiment.

The focus of Erasmus' ambitious exercise was the Maya city of Uxmal (Yucatan, Mexico), which belongs to the Terminal Classic period (approximately AD 800 to 925). The purpose of his experiments was twofold. His first goal

> was to obtain a measure of the man-days of labor invested in the construction of Maya ceremonial centers. I wanted to know how many man-days of labor went into a cubic meter of fill or masonry and into a square meter of sculptured stone veneer, so that I could then divide these figures into estimates of fill and masonry and of the area of sculptured walls of a ceremonial center. (1965:277)

He then planned to apply these results to estimate the amount of labor invested in constructing Uxmal, a center of a known time span, by first computing "the average annual man-day investment. This figure, compared with population density estimates, could help fix the number of man-days per year invested by each household" (1965:277). Erasmus was particularly interested in how the results of his experiments and comparisons with community projects in contemporary societies might shed light on the level of political development at Uxmal.

Step 1: Acquisition and Transport of Raw Materials. The primary building materials used in Maya construction were earth (for fill) and stone (for the facings of earth-filled walls and structural components of buildings). Erasmus began his experiment far from Uxmal, in northern Mexico (Sonora) by hiring several Mayo Indians to excavate and carry earth. Erasmus recorded the number of trips, total distance, total weight, and total volume carried by two men, one carrying to a point 50 meters away and the other 100 meters. Results were adjusted to reflect a typical five-hour workday (because of the afternoon heat, work began in the early morning and ended at midday). Two Maya from Tikul (Yucatan) were later employed to excavate surface rock. Both were skilled at this activity; one used an iron crowbar and the other a hardwood post. The man using the wooden tool was able to excavate one-third the amount of rock that was excavated by the other man. Trials were then conducted in which four men transported the excavated rock to obtain measures of the number of trips to points at various distances from the source that could be made in five hours and the total weight carried.

Erasmus then had to determine the average distance of transport appropriate for the center at Uxmal in order to arrive at the number of kilos of stone each worker could deliver to the site per day. To do this, he first had to estimate the total amount of fill (850,000 cubic meters) and from there calculate the number of tons of rock required ($1\frac{1}{2}$ tons per cubic meter, hence 1,275,000 tons in total). Knowing at this point that 5 tons of rock could easily be extracted from a 30-square-meter area, he calculated that a maximum of 7,650,000 square meters would have been required. From here he was able to estimate that the average distance the material would have been carried was 750 meters. Applying that figure to the results of his rock-carrying experiment, he concluded that 500 kilos of rock per person-day was a conservative estimate for Uxmal.

The next step was to combine data on the number of kilos of rock and earth required per cubic meter of masonry with the time required to obtain it. The results suggested that approximately three person-days would be needed for carrying the rock and one for the earth. The figures for excavating came to one for the rock and one-fourth for the earth. Adding these up produced an estimate of $5\frac{1}{4}$ person-days/cubic meter. That figure, when multiplied by an estimate of 850,000 cubic meters for the fill in the terraces and buildings at Uxmal, produced a total of 4,500,000 person-days.

Step 2: Construction of Masonry Walls. Once the raw materials were on site, construction could commence. Accordingly, Erasmus engaged a Maya stone mason to build a test wall with the 516 kilos of rock that had been carried by one man in the previous part of the experiment. He measured the volume of the resulting construction and the amount of mortar used. The mason's work was timed as well. The results showed that 1,400 kilos of rock, 100 kilos of lime, and 300 kilos of sascab (an abundant "powdery lime breccia" used in place of sand in this region) would be required per cubic meter of masonry. The testimony of local residents was relied on to estimate how much sascab could be excavated per person-day. Estimates were also made for transport of lime to the site.

Erasmus had, of course, to take into account the effort required to produce the lime. Key to that operation was an abundant supply of firewood. No stone tools were in use or available for chopping, so an estimate had to be made, which led to a figure of 225 person-days for wood-cutting, 30 person-days for stacking properly, and 10 days to break up the rock and arrange it on top of the pyre. On the basis of these estimates, he was eventually able to determine that 3½ person-days were probably required to produce the lime needed for 1 cubic meter of masonry.

A variety of estimates obtained from experienced Maya building contractors, together with the results of the construction of the test wall, led to a figure of four person-days of construction work per cubic meter of wall. Combining this figure with estimates in person-days of 4½ for the excavation and transport of rock and sascab, 3½ for making and ¼ for transporting lime, gave 12¼ person-days as the total labor investment required for 1 cubic meter of wall. Using an estimate of 40,000 cubic meters for the amount of masonry at Uxmal, Erasmus concluded that approximately half a million person-days of labor had been required.

Step 3: Cutting and Sculpturing Stone. Also to be taken into account were the cutting and sculpturing of limestone. Erasmus combined the time estimates he obtained from two grave-stone cutters with the results of an experiment in which an admittedly rather crude design was created by the mason who built the test wall. These figures supported an estimate provided by one of the expert stonecutters that it would take three days to sculpt 1,000 square meters using stone tools. Because this work was not nearly as physically exhausting as digging and carrying, an eight-hour workday was assumed. Estimates for stonecutting pointed to 30 person-days per square meter of building exterior featuring cut stone veneer, and an additional 30 person-days per square meter for areas that were also sculptured.

Erasmus was now able to calculate an expenditure of about 2½ million person-days to produce approximately 75,000 square meters of cut stone, 10,000 square meters of which were also sculptured. The estimate for the total labor for the ceremonial center at Uxmal came to 7½ million person-days. Allowing for 250 years of occupation, the average number of person-days per year came to 30,000. To get a sense of what this signified in social terms, he proceeded to estimate the population density, with the goal of calculating how much of this work might have fallen to each household.

Step 4: Exploring Social Implications. Erasmus began this part of his project by complementing his experimentation with some ethnographic fieldwork in which he questioned people in and around Tikul about family size and food consumption. On the basis of what he learned, he settled on a figure of five as an average family size and, from that, derived a corn consumption figure of 1,100 to 1,460 kilos per year per family. He noted that these numbers were higher than more carefully acquired figures dating back to possibly less prosperous times in the 1930s. He settled on a figure of 1,300 kilos per year. Production estimates pointed to the need of about five acres per family in an area in which production would likely be lower than in regions with higher forests and richer soils. He concluded that his estimates were quite liberal for the ancient Maya.

Erasmus' next assumption was that half of the cultivated lands used by each family was newly cleared each year and the other half was in its second year. His model also incorporated a reasonable fallow period of 12 years. The net result was that each family required 21 acres. So, how many people were supported by the land near Uxmal? On the basis of information provided by his informants that indicated a maximum walking distance between home and field of about 5 to 6 miles or 2–2½ hours, and the presence of the smaller center of Kabah 9 miles southeast of Uxmal, he decided to limit the area of Uxmal's jurisdiction to a radius of 5 miles around its center. If half of the 50,240 acres contained within that 5-mile radius could have been cultivated (a conservative estimate) and if that arable land was divided equally among the residents, some 1,200 families could have been supported. That figure yields a population density of 75 per square mile (a little more than twice the density of Yucatan at the time of his study).

Erasmus concluded his report by estimating that with a contribution of 40 person-days of labor per year, the 1,200 families together could have contributed an annual total of 48,000 person-days. This figure represents more than 1½ times the average annual amount he estimated would have been needed to build Uxmal in 250 years. He noted that work was probably not continuous, but instead occurred in bursts when specific projects were carried out. The largest complex that appears to have been constructed from a single plan, the Nunnery Quadrangle, (see Figure 5-1) would have required 650,000 person-days of labor. Using the estimate

Figure 5-1 The Nunnery Quadrangle at Uxmal.

of 40 person-days per year per family, it would have taken 13½ years. He adds, "with a little enthusiasm (80 days per year), it could have been finished in less than seven years" (1965:297).

MAYA OCCUPATIONAL SPECIALIZATION IN COPÁN

One area touched upon briefly by Erasmus in his study has provided the focus for a more recent set of three experiments by Elliot Abrams (1984). These were undertaken for the purpose of gaining some insight on occupational specialization among the ancient Maya—specifically, the number of sculptors that might have been supported in Late Classic society.

In Abrams' first experiment, steel tools were used to cut blocks from newly quarried green tuff. Professional masons from Copán were employed to cut blocks using chisels, hammers, and hatchets. Nineteen blocks were produced, with the average time of 1 hour and 13 minutes to cut a block measuring 30 × 21 × 36 cm. Fourteen blocks were produced in a second experiment in which stone tools—12 hatchets and 6 handaxes—were used. Abrams reports that with the exception of wire used to haft the stone heads on wooden handles, the tools were comparable to Maya originals. In this experiment the average time to produce a masonry block measuring 27 × 18 × 40 cm was 1 hour and 48 minutes. From these results, Abrams computed a steel to stone ratio of 1:1½ that included cutting time as well as reknapping and rehafting. In his discussion of this ratio, he noted how much more equal in performance steel and stone were than in experiments involving cutting wood.[2] He attributed the discrepancy to toughness of wood compared to tuff. He also noted that in Erasmus' experiment, an identical ratio of 1:1½ was obtained for sculpturing, with cutting and facing limestone resulting in a greater difference—1:3. Because Abrams' ratio of cutting and facing tuff was equal to Erasmus' result for sculpturing, he decided to use that ratio for both activities (1984:42). Abrams considered potential sources of error in the trials with stone tools and how they might have affected the comparison with steel tools. He concluded that they were minimal, noting that

> the workers were professional masons, and familiar with tool use in general, and cutting with stone tools was not markedly different than with steel tools. Each worker was given about one hour to practice cutting green tuff with the stone tools prior to the experiment. The lack of precision offered by the stone tool's edge which causes the worker to cut more off the block than is desired, and the need to reknap and rehaft the stone tool, were the major factors producing the differential. (1984:43–44)

In the third experiment the issue of quality had to be addressed. To accomplish this, an experienced sculptor from Copán was employed to replicate by means of steel tools simple and complex motifs comparable to those found on Maya sculptures. For the simple designs, the mean time was 70 minutes and the mean area was about 375 square cm; for the complex designs the mean time jumped to 370 minutes, with a mean area of 550 square cm.

Abrams then applied the results of his experiments first to the Hieroglyphic Stairway at Copán. The Hieroglyphic Stairway consists of approximately 63 steps with elaborately carved risers, a balustrade, a series of human figures that are centered on the steps, and a built-in altar (1984:44). Abrams calculated the total sculptured area on the risers to be 1,553,357 square m. He added another 37.89 square m of sculptured area on the balustrade, 4.96 square m for each human figure (with an estimate of six figures), and 14.8 square m of sculptured area on the altar built into the front of the stairway.

Working with the same assumption of an eight-hour workday used by Erasmus, and an estimate of 24 workdays per month, Abrams found that a minimum of two sculptors would have required eight years, two months, and ten days to complete the work. Noting that the stairway is dated to a 25-year period, he estimated that two men could have been responsible for all of the sculpturing. With ten sculptors, only one year, eight months, and six days would have been needed. He concluded:

> The point I wish to emphasize is . . . the absolute low amount of investment, most probably if not necessarily reflected in a low number of sculptors. This small number of sculptors, moreover, was the *maximum* number required. (1984:45)

Finally, Abrams considered the upright carved monuments known as *stelae* in order to gain a better sense of the number of sculptors that might typically have been at work in a place like Copán (see Figure 5-2). Stelae can be considered a more common source of work for sculptors than a special project such as the Hieroglyphic Stairway. His calculations produced an estimate of about six months for two sculptors to complete a stela, which led to the conclusion that "the overwhelming result is that monument carving was probably not very time-consuming and . . . very few sculptors were required to successfully meet the sculpturing demands at Copán" (1984:45). An assessment of sculptured structures in a district (*barrio*) outside of the center of Copán likewise pointed to a need for very few sculptors.

At the end of his report Abrams returned to the question of economic specialization and cautioned that sculpturing may not have been representative in its needs for specialists compared to other enterprises. In lieu of solid information on the numbers of "scribes, featherworkers, court musicians, accountants and assorted entertainers" he suggested that the number of elite-specialists in Copán may have been comparably low (1984:47). But he added that sculpture was produced for a small percentage of the population—the elite—and thus would not reflect the numbers of nonelite specialists.

Discussion

Experiments such as those performed by Erasmus and Abrams rely on first breaking an activity that cannot be fully replicated into its essential building blocks (sometimes quite literally!). These are then combined in a way that produces what we hope is a credible estimate of the total time and labor required to achieve a specific goal in antiquity (whether that be constructing a ceremonial center or clearing and farming a sufficiently large expanse of land to meet the needs of a village). Clearly, any errors in component experiments will be compounded as their various results are added and multiplied to produce projections for whatever is being modeled. Another problem is that of small sample sizes. For example, are results based on the work of a single sculptor over a very short period of time adequate for estimates of the total time required for projects such as constructing the Hieroglyphic Stairway or carving all the decorated panels on a large building? There is also the matter of scaling. Erasmus used data acquired from the construction of a small test wall as the basis for an estimate of the total number of person-days of labor required for the masonry at Uxmal. The architecture of Uxmal consists of more than low walls, so it would have been desirable to take into consideration the special difficulties and additional labor costs associated with moving building materials from the ground to the top of large and ever-rising structures.

(b)

(a)

Figure 5-2   Maya stelae from (a) Copán, Honduras and (b) Machaquilá, Guatemala.

Scaling up from an experiment that did not model all key component activities by multiplying its results by the estimated volume of masonry at Uxmal is problematic at best.

Additional errors in a reconstruction can be introduced if there are unwarranted assumptions in the guiding model. When it came to calculating the number of families that could be supported in the territory surrounding Uxmal, was it appropriate to assume that all agricultural production was devoted to the sustenance of the producers? If portions were siphoned off by the elite in the form of taxes, perhaps to be used for commercial purposes—trade for exotic stone, feathers, or whatever—the population estimate would have to be reduced. Ideally, we should expect hypothetical reconstructions to incorporate, when possible, some alternative scenarios (or at least suggest them as hypotheses to be tested), and, in the end, provide us with a range of values (minimum to maximum) for each component activity that presumably brackets the actual but ultimately unknowable figure.

AS YOU SOW, SO SHALL YOU REAP: EXPERIMENTS IN ANCIENT AGRICULTURE

Farming above all else is a single related whole, each activity connected to the next in a sequence of seasonal work. By treating each action in isolation, we cannot come to grips with overall rates of success or failure on the part of ancient farmers, and these matters are of the greatest importance in attempts to learn more about early settlers, communities, and societies. A logical way to attempt to overcome this problem is to create an entire Ancient Farm, in which all experimental work is directed towards the success of the farm rather than the single exercise alone. (Coles 1979:113–114)

Experiments that replicate ancient agricultural systems are necessarily complex, long-term efforts. They take what would otherwise be stand-alone experiments directed at how particular artifacts and features were made and used and combine them in coherent sets of subsistence-related activities. To obtain meaningful data concerning the productivity and environmental impact of a particular method of farming, the archaeologist must repeat the experiment annually for more than a decade. This requires exclusive access to suitable land and a commitment to a time-consuming project that few can afford to make. When executed properly, this type of experiment can lead to perspectives on the past unobtainable by any other approach, as the Butser Ancient Farm and the Lejre Experimental Center discussed at the end of this chapter make clear.

SEEING IS BELIEVING: AN EXPERIMENTAL CORNFIELD AT MESA VERDE

It was disbelief that provided the motivation behind the creation of an experimental cornfield by Franke and Watson (1936). But unlike the case of brain removal by ancient Egyptian embalmers in which it was the experimenter who had doubts (see chapter 3), in this instance it was outright refusal on the part of many visitors to Mesa Verde National Park (Colorado) to believe that the ancient people who lived there could have farmed successfully in such an arid climate without irrigation. To convince them otherwise, a cornfield covering about two acres was established in 1919. At the time Franke (assistant superintendent and park naturalist) and Watson (park ranger-historian) wrote their report, the field had been in use for 17 years.

The essentials of this experiment were as follows. The plot was cleared, plowed, and harrowed with modern equipment. Navajos who worked in the park then used their traditional methods to plant a variety of corn grown by a number of contemporary Native American communities in the Southwest. In the early years when older Navajos were in charge, digging sticks were used, while in later years younger Navajos chose to use shovels. But the method of planting remained the same. Hills were located five to eight feet apart and were distributed in no particular pattern; 10 to 12 kernels were placed in each one. Outside of being hoed once or twice during the summer, the field received no additional attention.

The results were impressive enough to dispel any doubts visitors may have had about the ability of the ancient residents at Mesa Verde to support themselves using dry farming. Franke and Watson reported that only twice in 17 years did the crop fail. In one of those years the spring rains failed to come and the young corn did not survive until the onset of the summer rains; in the other instance there was widespread drought, with very little snow the previous winter and hence little moisture in the ground at the start of the growing season. No attempts were ever made to measure yield, as the corn was not protected from birds and rodents; furthermore, Franke and Watson suspected that Navajos living in the park often helped themselves to some of it for their own use. Beans, squash, melons, and potatoes were also grown in the field (the bean shoots were always eaten by rabbits and squirrels, but the other plants produced decent yields).

In support of the applicability of the experimental results to past circumstances, Franke and Watson noted the apparent absence of any major change in climate since the time of the ancient pueblo dwellers (ending around AD 1300) and the success of contemporary Hopi dry farming in the Keams Canyon area where annual precipitation is typically 6½ inches less than at Mesa Verde. They concluded, "It would seem safe to assume that if the Hopis have farmed successfully for many centuries, then surely Indians using similar farming methods, could have lived an agricultural life in the Mesa Verde" (1936:39).

Discussion

Although Franke and Watson replicated an ancient cornfield, their project was clearly much more a demonstration than a proper experiment. Its intended purpose was simply to provide the public with tangible proof that dry farming was a viable approach to producing corn at Mesa Verde. On that count it clearly succeeded. Although archaeologists at that time had no doubts about the use of this farming method by prehistoric peoples in the Southwest (and as noted, it was still being used in areas not suitable for irrigation by the Hopi and other Native

Americans in the region), the information on long-term productivity was useful. However, with some modifications, an effort of this sort could be of considerably greater value to archaeological research.

An experiment that carefully replicated all activities associated with dry farming would add more to our understanding of the characteristics of this method of cultivation, such as its costs, productivity, and sustainability. Let's consider productivity first, as this is a matter touched upon by Franke and Watson. It would come as a surprise to no one that yield varied from year to year, and this is why any experiment that seeks to evaluate agricultural production must be a long-term one. The results of one or two years cannot be used to generalize about dry farming in the Mesa Verde area or any other farming method in any other place, as experience with the experimental cornfield made clear. Careful measurement of each year's production would be essential. The field would have to be tended throughout the growing season in order to limit the destruction caused by pests, and all corn, beans, and squash would need to be carefully harvested (melons and potatoes were not grown in prehistoric times). This would allow yield to be computed (bushels/acre, which in turn could be converted into calories, grams of protein, and so on). These figures would then be used to calculate the number of acres required to feed a typical family (a figure that, as noted above, helped Erasmus to estimate the population of Uxmal). Of course, only aboriginal agricultural methods would be used—no shovels, even though their use had no noticeable effect on the crop at Mesa Verde—and the manure that Franke and Watson allowed to be spread on their cornfield on four occasions over the 17-year period (only because it "would otherwise have gone to waste" [1936:36]) would be excluded. The types of corn planted at Mesa Verde were related to those grown in ancient times and were well suited to dry farming in an arid environment. However, before attempting an experiment from which quantitative data on yield are desired, consultation with a botanist with expertise in ancient varieties of all crops to be grown would be in order, with the goal of obtaining seed as genetically similar to that used in the past as possible.

When a plot or set of plots is planted each year, it becomes possible to assess the impact of a particular type of agriculture on the soil and hence its sustainability as a food production strategy. In this instance, Franke and Watson were well aware of the fragility of soils in the arid Southwest:

> One question that often arises concerns the problem of soil depletion. The soil of the Mesa Verde is not a soil that could quickly revivify itself as do some tropical soils. The question may well be raised as to whether the Indians were able to farm a plot many years before the soil fertility was exhausted. (1936:40)[3]

The method of planting they used, which was copied from the contemporary Hopi, helped insure that the soil was not overtaxed—hills were widely spaced and in no definite order and the stubble left in place from the previous year's crop showed where not to plant in the following year. The soils in the experimental cornfield, while not tested in a laboratory as they would be in a proper experiment, showed no signs of degradation; Franke and Watson noted that the "finest crop ever produced" was in the fifteenth year of the experiment. They also consulted with Alvin Kezer, chief agronomist at Colorado State College of Agriculture, on this important matter. His response is significant:

> We have been growing crops at our Akron Dryland Station since 1907 and have not yet depleted the soil. Our yields go up and down with the rainfall and we have more fertility than the ordinary rainfall will utilize. Within twenty-five miles of Akron, however, we have sandy dry lands that grow about two crops of corn and no more unless the land is given a rest or is fertilized. These two cases show that no one statement can be made about how long it takes corn to deplete the soil under dry farming methods. In the one case thirty years of continuous corn growing have not depleted the soil, and only a few miles away two or three years cropping will deplete the available nitrogen fertility. (Franke and Watson 1936:40–41)

As to the matter of nitrogen, Franke and Watson point out that the Native American practice of planting beans (nitrogen fixing plants) with corn helps to maintain levels of that key element. Beans and corn were alternated in the Akron region for precisely that purpose.

ONE STEP FURTHER: MODELING ENERGY FLOW IN SUBSISTENCE SYSTEMS

When authentic methods are used to clear and prepare a plot of land and then plant, tend, and harvest the crops, estimates of the number of person-days and the amount of acreage required to produce enough food to support a population of a given size can be calculated. If production (output) of a subsistence system is measured, why not input—the effort that had to be expended to produce the measured output? A useful approach to investigating subsistence systems in terms of inputs and outputs is provided by energy flow analysis (see Kemp 1971, Rappaport 1971, and Thomas 1973 for examples of energy flow studies of living populations). In an imitative experiment designed to investigate energy flow, limited trials may be used to evaluate component activities such as clearance, plowing, planting, hoeing, and harvesting in terms of energy expenditure per hour (or whatever unit is most useful), with those results providing the basis for extrapolation for plots of any desired size. Output will simply be the food energy of the harvested products (and, as always, reliable data will come only from long-term experiments).

An archaeological approach to modeling prehistoric subsistence systems in terms of energy flow was incorporated into the second experiment Izumi Shimada and I performed with stone and steel axes (Saraydar and Shimada 1973). For our demonstration (unfortunately an incomplete one), we created two, 30 ft. × 30 ft. test plots. One was termed "primitive" and was cleared with the help of a stone axe and planted with a digging stick. The other served as our "modern" plot, and on it we used steel tools: an axe, a shovel, a warren hoe, and a mechanical sowing device. A variety of circumstances conspired against the experiment, with unusually dry weather, too much shading by the trees that surrounded the plots, and an inability to protect the plants from wildlife, resulting in little harvestable corn and hence no energy output worth measuring (see Figure 5-3). If this approach were incorporated into full-scale, long-term experiments on ancient agriculture like those at the Butser Ancient Farm and the Lejre Experimental Center (discussed below), it would provide energy flow data useful for comparisons of different systems—ancient and contemporary. An energy flow analysis is also amenable to computer-based simulations in which the effects of hypothetical variations in key variables on system performance are investigated (Saraydar and Shimada 1973:349–350).

PRIMITIVE PLOT:			**MODERN PLOT:**		
Tree cutting: stone axe			**Tree cutting: steel axe**		
(2.0 in blade, 30 in handle)			**(5.5 in blade, 30 in handle)**		
Energy expended per minute	8.40	kcal	Energy expended per minute	9.18	kcal
Total time	75.5	min	Total time	32	min
Total energy expended	634	kcal	Total energy expended	294	kcal
			Clearing		
			Energy expended per minute	5.73	kcal
			Total time	30	min
			Total energy expended	172	kcal
			Digging: shovel		
			Energy expended per minute	6.07	kcal
			Total time	720	min
			Total energy expended	4370	kcal
			Furrowing: warren hoe		
			Energy expended per minute	4.83	kcal
			Total time	66	min
			Total energy expended	319	kcal
Planting: pointed stick			**Planting: corn planter**		
Energy expended per minute	3.65	kcal	Energy expended per minute	3.49	kcal
Total time	121	min	Total time	55	min
Total energy expended	442	kcal	Total energy expended	192	kcal
Weeding			**Weeding**		
Energy expended per minute	6.60	kcal	Energy expended per minute	6.60	kcal
Total time	370	min	Total time	15	min
Total energy expended	2442	kcal	Total energy expended	99	kcal

All activities were performed by a single test subject.

Figure 5-3 "Primitive" and "modern" comparison. Energy expenditures are expressed in kilocalories.

IT TAKES A VILLAGE: LEJRE AND BUTSER

I conclude my survey with a look at the most elaborate and longest running experimental projects: the Lejre Experimental Center in Denmark and the Butser Ancient Farm in the United Kingdom. Experiments conducted at these facilities rarely stand in isolation; that is, they normally figure in the reconstruction of a coherent whole—village life in the Iron Age (ca. 400 BC to AD 400). Since both have been in operation and highly productive for over 30 years, I must limit my discussion to a brief account of several of their more significant achievements. Lejre and Butser maintain Web sites (http://www.english.lejrecenter.dk and http://www.butserancientfarm.co.uk) that provide up-to-date information on their research and educational efforts along with many color photographs. Each also regularly issues publications documenting its work, and these are highly recommended for anyone wishing to dig deeper (unfortunately most of those produced by the Lejre Center are available only in Danish).

LEJRE EXPERIMENTAL CENTER

The Lejre Experimental Center in Denmark, also known as the "Historical-Archaeological Research Centre at Lejre," offers a unique combination of educational programs and research opportunities. According to its statutes:

> The Experimental Centre's purpose is to run a research centre for the carrying out of ethnological, historical, and archaeological experiments, execution of associated research tasks and dissemination of the results through scientific channels and through active communication and instruction. (http://www.english.lejrecenter.dk/ABOUTLEJRE.449.0.html)

Lejre owes its origin to the work of Hans-Ole Hansen, whose interest in the lifeways of prehistoric people began in his adolescence. His first major achievement in experimental archaeology was the reconstruction of three Neolithic houses featuring wattle and daub walls (a construction in which mud or clay mixed with straw is plastered on a framework consisting of vertical wooden poles interwoven with horizontal twigs or small branches) and thatched roofs (see Figure 5-4). This was a pioneering effort that produced valuable information on the quantities of materials (clay, straw, reeds and rushes, poles, etc.), and (roughly) the length of time and size of the workforce likely to have been required in antiquity. It also provided insight into the possible appearance and character of the houses and (perhaps more importantly) the archaeological evidence resulting from gradual decay as well as from destruction by fire.

This initial project led to more precise reconstructions (this time of Iron Age houses), followed by a greatly improved approach to the study of the effects of burning on the remains that would present themselves to an archaeologist (Hansen 1977). Prior to setting a house on fire, Hansen ingeniously fitted the structural members of the building with numbered metal tags to facilitate their identification when the remains were excavated. That excavation was carefully undertaken to recover all details, including the characteristics of the ash produced by the different types of wood from which they were constructed. The results were then compared to evidence in reports of excavations of ancient houses, which led to revised interpretations of their structural characteristics.

From those early efforts, a center occupying 50 acres has emerged, in which experiments have been and continue to be performed in a variety of areas central to life in the Iron Age and in more recent (historical) periods, such as agriculture, metalworking, production of textiles, ceramics, and animal husbandry. One area of the Center's grounds is reserved for an Iron Age village, featuring a stockade surrounding a group of seven reconstructed houses based on plans from several archaeological sites in Denmark and representing the time period spanning approximately 200 BC to AD 200. Another corner of the facility is occupied by a reconstructed family farm of a type dating to about AD 1850. Lejre is also home to extensive and dynamic educational efforts that feature a wide variety of programs for the general public and teachers (for descriptions, see the Center's Web site at http://www.english.lejrecenter.dk). I will have more to say about the educational component of Lejre in chapter 6.

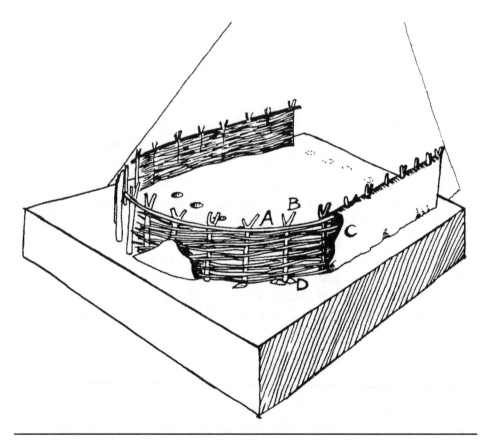

Figure 5-4 Wattle and daub construction. **A** is wattle wall, **B** is forked post support, **C** daubed wall, **D** tops of stones used to hold posts in place.

Experiments with replicated houses at Lejre have touched on more than their construction and destruction. They have also included investigations of thermal performance and other operating characteristics:

> One of the best experiments performed in Lejre dealt with this problem. Partly in 1967 (January–February) and partly in 1972 (February–March) experiments based on intensive temperature reading were carried out. In this way objective measurings replaced personal feelings. The basis of our judgements must come from data documenting the actual temperatures reached under certain outer conditions (wind, snow) and certain interior factors such as animals housed within, the use of fire places, etc.
>
> These factors and their effects can be observed by measuring the following: heavy or low burning in the hearth, substantial layers of cow dung accumulated in the stable; partially penetrable walls and roofs, . . . wind's direction and velocity; insulation and apertures; e.g., ventilation holes and the door in the wall of the house. (Hansen 1977:18)

The data acquired were obtained from thermometers located throughout the structure (and at various heights above floor level), and this information was correlated with data obtained from "meteorological observations." During periods when these measurements were made, a variety of tasks that simulated ancient life were performed, such as tending to the animals stabled in the house. The results of this exceptional effort provided a wealth of information about the internal environment of the house, one of the most interesting of which was that simply hanging a blanket between the fireplace and the stable end of the structure produced a significant increase in temperature in the living quarters—a difference of up to 20°C was observed when measuring on opposite sides of the blanket (Hansen 1977:19).

Other aspects of life in the Iron Age that have been investigated by means of experiment at Lejre include weaving and the production of garments, with in-depth investigation of the production and use of plant dyes as colorants; the replication of kilns, which were then used to fire replicas of prehistoric pottery; tilling ground for cultivation using a replicated ard (a simple plow featuring a pointed share that creates a narrow furrow) and trained oxen to learn more about the process, including methods of plowing field borders and corners and turning teams; comparisons of wear patterns on ancient ards and replicas used in plowing experiments as well as the traces left in the soil by these implements; and smelting iron in replicated furnaces. In addition, Lejre has played an important role in helping to save from extinction the few remaining examples of ancient breeds of cattle and sheep. In recent years the experiments at Lejre have been quite wide ranging, as the list of investigations from 2002 to the present on its Web site amply demonstrates (http://www.english.lejrecenter.dk/SCIENTIFICALRESEARCH.192.0.html).

BUTSER ANCIENT FARM

The Butser Ancient Farm Research Project was established in 1972 by Peter Reynolds largely in response to a dearth of documentary evidence on Celtic Britain and what he saw as a need for scientific experiments in prehistoric archaeology (Figure 5-5). In his words,

Its object is to reconstruct a farm dating to about 300 BC, in the mainstream of the Iron Age period. In reality it is an open-air scientific research laboratory. . . . The purpose is to explore all the aspects of such a farm, the structures and processes, the plant cultivation and animal husbandry, and to consider not only how each particular aspect itself may operate but also how all the aspects integrate together. . . . It sets out to define the basic evidence, to evaluate and test ideas and theories, and to focus attention upon the essential details. (Reynolds 1979:17)

The Ancient Farm continues to meet these objectives to this day.

Reynolds' initial goal was to construct three or four round-houses with associated barns, byres, and other structures to serve as the nucleus of the farm. He also envisioned an encircling ditch and bank complete with a palisade fence. The fields that would lie outside this central area were to be planted with crops as genetically close as possible to those raised prehistorically, and the paddocks were to be stocked with appropriate livestock. Above all else: "Everything had to be accomplished within the strictest scientific limits possible and correlated directly to archaeological evidence" (Reynolds 1979:22). Once established, this was to be a working farm to be studied in all its many interrelated aspects. The other primary goal of the research program was an improved understanding of the archaeological record of the Iron Age, through experiments in data retrieval and recording (Reynolds 1979:23).

In the first few years of the project two sites were established, one on the northerly spur of Butser Hill and the second on its southern slopes. The latter extended the research capa-

Figure 5-5 Replicated Iron Age houses at Butser Ancient Farm.

bilities of the facility but had public education as its primary focus and served both as an open-air museum and a resource for schoolchildren. During this early time period, two round-houses were constructed and five fields were established and planted with cereals. The livestock at the farm included five breeds of sheep, Old English goats, long-legged Dexter cattle, an Exmoor pony, Old English game fowl, and (occasionally) Tamworth/European wild boar cross-pigs (Reynolds 1979:27–28, 1991:1).

Round-Houses. To maximize the value of the reconstructed round-houses (see Figure 5-6) as tools for the interpretation of the archaeological record, a color photograph of each newly dug posthole was taken prior to setting its post in place. This was done to allow the changes that occurred over the lifetime of the structure to be documented for the purpose of increasing understanding of the postholes, which are the primary evidence left behind by Iron Age buildings. The construction itself provided a variety of challenges. Reynolds relied on evidence recovered from excavations at Maiden Castle and Balksbury for the plans on which to base his reconstructions as well as the material to be used for their walls (daub). Further clues were found in historical references that pointed to thatched roofs and the use of lumber in its natural (i.e., not squared-off) form. Unfortunately, both the historical record and the post patterns of prehistoric structures are mute on the matters of the height of the walls and the pitch of the roof.[4] So how did Reynolds proceed?

Figure 5-6 The Great Round House at Butser Ancient Farm.

The only solid evidence available was provided by surviving stone structures of the same time period from Scotland and coastal Spain and Portugal. From these a doorway height of 1½ m was adopted. As to the pitch of the roof, Reynolds was well aware that a minimum angle of 45° was required in order for a thatched roof to shed water effectively enough to remain sound and resist rotting. Although the range for contemporary thatched roofs was between 45° and 55°, the geometry of a round-house made the former figure more attractive in terms of minimizing both the surface area to be thatched and the lateral (outward) thrust the roof would produce (Reynolds 1979:33, 1993:2–3; see also the discussion of "Structures" at http://www.butser.org.uk/iafres_hcc.html).

The relatively simple framework of the 6-m diameter Maiden Castle house featured basketwork walls made from upright posts interwoven with hazel rods, a simple wall plate consisting of triple hazel rods tied to the posts, and a roof made of rafters lashed to the wall posts, with their upper ends set in the notch of a 4½ -m tall, forked center post. Construction was not an entirely straightforward process, and bringing it to an acceptable conclusion required Reynolds to solve several problems that ultimately provided insight into the likely configuration of key components of the original structures, such as the use of a support ring near the apex to accommodate the many rafters that converge on that point and that would otherwise distort the line of the roof (unacceptable when thatch is used). Another construction detail concerned the center post that was included as a roof support in response to a center posthole in the remains of the prehistoric structure that provided the model. Once the house was completed,

> it was possible to prove that the central posthole was unlikely to have been used by a central roof support. A house of this size simply does not require such a support. For example, it could have been a potstand . . . or it could have supported a mezzanine floor in the roof area for storage purposes; or it could have supported a cauldron over a hearth; or it could have been a pivot for room dividers. What is lacking is more precise archaeological data from the floor area of the house. (Reynolds 1979:35–36; for an interesting discussion on an issue that closely parallels this one and points to the absence of closed roofs on wood henges, see Wainwright 1989:117–118)

It should also be noted that although modern examples were used, all of the tools used in the reconstruction were available in Iron Age Britain.

The posthole pattern of the ancient structure that provided the plan for the 9.1-m-diameter Balksbury house argued strongly for timber frame, rather than the basketwork wall construction used in the Maiden Castle house (Reynolds 1979:36). More sophisticated but entirely appropriate joinery was also used, with each timber making up the wall plate joined to its neighbor with a pegged scarf-joint (a type of joint in which the pieces being joined overlap one another) and the continuous wall plate itself attached to the uprights with mortise and tenon joints; the primary roof rafters were notched and pegged to the wall plate. The lack of any evidence of a central support for the apex of the roof led to a design that incorporated a free span exceeding 9 meters. Wall panels were made of split hazel rods and covered with daub. Three tons of thatch were required for this structure, compared with somewhat more than one ton for the Maiden Castle house. In both cases, the roofs proved waterproof and able to withstand hurricane-force winds.

What Goes Up. . . . Construction of a larger round-house, measuring 12.8 m in diameter and based on careful interpretation of data obtained from the excavation of the Pimperne House in Dorset, was begun in 1976 (Reynolds 1979:94–103). After serving as both an object of research in its construction and the central display of a demonstration area for the public, the house was carefully dismantled in 1990, at which time its components were found to be in generally sound condition (for a detailed discussion of the Pimperne House project see Reynolds 1993, 1995a). It should be noted that Reynolds had originally planned to allow the reconstructed house to decay *in situ* to increase understanding of the archaeological evidence that would be produced when an ancient house was abandoned. The dismantling was the sad result of a dispute with the Hampshire County Council that forced the Farm to vacate its sites on Butser Hill. Reynolds explained that, "Rather than the dramatic disposal of the Pimperne House by fire, it was decided to take the structure apart in order to examine its real physical state after fifteen years of life and use" (1993:15).

One interesting observation from the dismantling concerned the early stages of decay of the structural supports. It was discovered that the pith wood had rotted from exposure to moisture, but left an "air gap" between the still intact bark and the hard wood making up the core of the timber. This gap helped to keep the center wood dry, which would have added to its longevity. Since the function of the post is to provide vertical support, the loss of the pith wood had no effect on the strength of the structure. Of significance for archaeological interpretation of postholes is the likelihood that as decay progressed, the gap would have increased, leading eventually to an infilling of just the sorts of artifacts and other materials typically found when postholes are excavated. These have tended to be viewed as postabandonment features rather than as associated with the early period of occupation, which has made their presence difficult to explain. Also relevant to interpretation of ancient houses is Reynolds' observation that the surface of the house's floor and the topmost surface of the packing material around the post are in the same plane: "The implication must be that, in the process of excavation, once the surface of the posthole packing is revealed the uppermost floor surface has been trowelled away. By the time the posthole itself has been clearly identified at the subsoil layer, all floor evidence has been totally destroyed" (Reynolds 1993:16–18; http://www.butser.org.uk/iaflphd_hcc.html).

Crops. The oldest and probably most significant aspect of the research program at Butser centers on prehistoric cereals. Currently, cropping trials are being carried out on a number of sites and soil types using emmer, spelt, einkorn, club wheat, and barley and employing a variety of practices, such as autumn and/or spring sowing, manuring/not manuring, weeding/not weeding, and crop rotation (cereal/legume, cereal/alternating crop, and fallow).

Records are kept on variables such as gross yields per hectare, stand height, size of ear, number and weight of grains per year, and the effects of burning ground cover prior to cultivating and manuring (Reynolds 1977; 1979:58, 61; 1981:5–10; 1992; http://www.butser.org.uk/iafpc_hcc.html). As the considerably less formal demonstration by Franke and Watson made clear, any attempts to evaluate the productivity of an agricultural system require an extended period of investigation. When he started, Reynolds anticipated a minimum of 20 consecutive years "to encompass all the natural variables of weather and land use" as well as to obtain maximum, minimum, and average yield figures (1979:21, 60). Confidence in the validity of the results obtained has been strengthened by evidence pointing to the similarity of contemporary weather conditions with those of the Iron Age.

Some of the early results at Butser are particularly interesting. Reynolds began with a small plot of 100 square meters with the idea of producing seed for a series of extensive comparative experiments. He reports that with the einkorn wheat late to emerge, the rapid regrowth of the grass seemed to point to failure. To his surprise the einkorn began to compete successfully with the grass and by early June he was able to hoe between rows of einkorn, guided by color differences in the plants (1979:59). Yield from the test plot translated to a "remarkable" figure of 1.4 tons/hectare. Reynolds adds: "In successive years, and most notably in 1976 when a period of sustained drought severely crippled all other cereals, the yield from the Einkorn experimental crops has never fallen below this first yield figure" (1979:59). Subsequent results were also "quite dramatic": "On a soil cover averaging ten centimeters thick over middle chalk, without any kind of fertilizer or any residual nutrient from previous land management, yield figures in excess of 2.5 tonnes to the hectare have been achieved while an average of 2 tonnes is not uncommon" (1979:61; see Reynolds 1981 and 1992 for crop yield data and further discussion of variables).

As would be expected, the methods used to prepare the soil, plant the seed, hoe, and harvest the crop were each the subject of experiments. These involved the use of reconstructed ards and "sowing sticks" to produce furrows, dibble sticks to make small holes for the seed, and flint tools used as sickles (Reynolds 1981:2–5; 1979:57–69). Interestingly, when reconstructed sickles were used, they were quickly abandoned in favor of hand-stripping the grain from einkorn and spelt. Unlike modern varieties, the seed heads of these wheat varieties appear at various levels, making it difficult if not impossible to hold several of them in one hand to be neatly cut with a sickle held in the other. Reynolds reports that hand-stripping was significantly faster and also quite easy as the heads broke easily at the rachis (the part of the plant that holds the seeds). As an alternative to use as sickles, he proposed that the tools may have served as spar-hooks, which would have been used to split hazel rods, willow withes, and brambles (1979:64–65; see also Reynolds 1992:10–14 for further discussion of harvesting and effects of impurities). Research at Butser has also (and necessarily) been devoted to weeds, many of which are edible and may have been deliberately collected. These studies face the limitation that some of these plants have become extinct and others are nearly so (Reynolds 1979:67–69; 1992:10).

Storage. Producing a bumper crop of grain was only a partial victory for the Iron Age farmer. After all, having a year's supply means little if it isn't stored in a way that prevents spoilage. Research on storage pits at Butser has had as its purpose the replication of variously shaped ancient pits with clay and basket linings, which were then monitored over an extended period of time. For these experiments,

> the grain is poured directly into a pit cut into surface chalk rock flush with the ground (sand and gravel or limestone pits work equally well); gas aspiration tubes for sampling purposes and bead thermistors [to measure temperature] are inserted at relevant points within the grain body; the pit is sealed with a plug of clay plastered directly onto the surface of the grain and extended for a further twenty centimetres beyond the edges of the pit . . . an earthcap is put onto the clay seal to keep it moist, so inhibiting the passage of rain water or oxygen into the pit. (Reynolds 1979:75)

A particularly significant finding was that as soon as the pit was sealed, the grain immediately below the clay plug responded to the moisture by increasing its respiration cycle, which resulted in the production of carbon dioxide that worked its way to the bottom of the pit and inhibited any further respiration of the grain as well as killing insect pests.

The experiments demonstrated that successful storage was normally assured when the following prerequisites were met: "low temperature during the storage period, an impermeable seal, a good production of carbon dioxide and finally, a subsoil which naturally inhibits lateral water flow" (Reynolds 1979:76). Grain stored under these conditions showed little decrease in germination ability, which demonstrated the suitability of pits for storage of seed grain. Physical loss in even an unlined pit was only about 2 percent. The experiments proved that the old idea that grain must be parched before storage was not true and, in the process, made the absence of any evidence of this practice in antiquity more significant. More speculative, but interesting and demonstrating excellent use of an integrated approach to Iron Age farming, was Reynolds' use of pit capacity in relation to production figures to estimate the number of "Celtic fields" (approximately .13 hectare in size) required to fill one. This led to the very reasonable conclusion that if only a relatively few of the large number of possible storage pits found on many sites were in simultaneous use for storage of grain, the amount of land under cultivation would have been enormous (a conclusion supported by evidence from aerial photography). What the experiments could not prove, of course, was that the pits uncovered in Iron Age sites *were* once used to store grain. Appropriately, Reynolds set out other possibilities, all potentially subject to investigation by experiment (1979:77–80).

Livestock. In choosing to discuss crops before livestock I have, I suppose, put the cart before the horse or, to be more appropriate, the ard before the cow. The most effective use of an ard to prepare a field for planting requires draft animals, and at Butser, a pair of long-legged Dexter cows were trained to the yoke for this purpose (for a report on an earlier experiment with an ard drawn by Dexters see Aberg and Bowen 1960). Maintaining animals requires that they be fed, of course, and this means that a functioning farm must make and store hay and perhaps silage. Provision for shelter for the animals, either within the dwellings as was the practice on the continent, or in byres (whose remains might be reflected in four- and five-posthole structures found on some sites) was also a necessity (Reynolds 1979:50-51).

The other animals were the closest equivalents of those that would have been kept on an Iron Age farm. An important aspect of this component of the Butser project was to learn more about the requirements for maintaining the animals and how those various maintenance activities might interact with one another (1979:55). One observation of archaeological interest concerns the fowl. Reynolds noted that

> chickens cheerfully scratch about and often will concentrate their activities around a specific post. In course of time they can enlarge a perfectly respectable tailored post-hole into a large post-pit. This simple activity alone distorts the evidence to such an extent that any arrangement of post-holes on the basis of similarity of type is suspect. (1979:55)

Another matter concerning the keeping of fowl is that of protecting them from predators. How was this done in the Iron Age? Reynolds was led to wonder if some of the four-post structures that have been found were, in fact, chicken houses.

Although the pig has not been a permanent inhabitant at the Farm, it hasn't been ignored. The importance of pigs as a source of food in Neolithic and later Britain is well documented. It has even been argued that pigs may have played a significant role in reclamation of farmland that had been lost to bracken infestation prior to the development of technological means to deal with this problem (Wainwright 1989:46). Pigs of the type raised in the Iron Age are extinct, and this led to a back-breeding experiment in which the European wild boar was crossed with the Tamworth pig. Reynolds reports that "the progeny were fairly small and rangy and almost impossible to contain . . . extremely fast of foot, they could easily outrun a dog" (1979:52–53). The primary interest in the pigs concerned discovery of evidence that might lead to the possibility of locating pig pannage archaeologically, although Reynolds also wished to explore the use of pigs to spare farmers the need to plough, by means of their ability to prepare land for planting by breaking up and manuring the soil as well as cleaning it up after the harvest (1979:53). Unfortunately, "financial constraints" forced postponement of these investigations and no further report is available.

Production of Metals. Finally, mention must be made of the many experiments carried out at the Farm on the discovery and use of metals. As Hamlin noted:

> It was realized early in the life of the project that the pyrochemical technologies of pottery and of metal production and exploitation were important inputs to Iron Age economy which should be included in the studies. Reasonable success was achieved in the re-creation of techniques for pottery production, but all attempts to produce useful data on metal production were unsuccessful. . . . Butser decided, therefore, to undertake a basic reexamination of the whole problem of metal discovery and exploitation. (1996:1)

That reexamination has led to a series of valuable experiments based on the key technological factors that had to come together to make metal production possible:

1. A supply of finely divided, relatively pure ore in oxide, hydroxide, or carbonate form

2. Heat that can be sustained at a high level for a long period

3. Means of producing and sustaining a reducing atmosphere around the ore at the high temperature

4. A mechanism for stabilizing the reduced metal (Hamlin 1996:3)

As with the experiment by Coghlan (see chapter 3), finely ground ore somehow had to have made its way into a reducing kiln capable of achieving a maximum temperature of at least 900°C. However, Hamlin offered the intriguing hypothesis that it was the processing of pigments, rather than pottery production, that led to the discovery of smelting and that the first metal thus produced was lead (1996:5–6, 12–13). He noted that people have always been attracted to color and that "the use of pigments, and hence their production, is known to predate the production of metals by millennia" (1996:4). Obtaining finely divided particles would have been labor intensive (pounding, crushing, grinding), but would be made easier by exposing the material to fire (which may well have been used in the process of extracting lumps from deposits). This "heat treatment" of ores would have had the fortuitous effect of converting them to the oxide form required for smelting; "without this unifying step, the smelting process would have had to have been worked out separately and empirically for every type of ore" (1996:6).

Although production of pottery may not have been the direct cause of the discovery of smelting as argued by Coghlan, it still plays a central role. As Hamlin explained:

> The only high temperature industry known to have existed at the time of the discovery of metals is pottery. A pigment industry would have been a small volume, high value industry easily operated in crucibles, for which it would have been dependent on pottery technology. To avoid excessive breakages, these crucibles would have had to have been heated in kilns in a way exactly similar to that required for the firing of pots. The high temperature technology available to the pigment manufacture would therefore have been essentially that of the potters. (1996:6)

He further noted, as did Coghlan, that at the time when the first metals were smelted, potters had at their disposal kilns capable of meeting the requirements of the process:

> A pigment industry would then have had available to it a firing technology capable of reaching and sustaining temperatures to 870°C. and above, and conditioned to long firing cycles. It would also have had the rudimentary technology of controlling the atmosphere of firing so as to give oxidising conditions . . . or reducing conditions. (Hamlin 1996:6).

Hamlin used kiln and furnace technology to investigate the production of a variety of metals, including copper, and was able to develop a list of possible indicators that might be found in archaeological sites where ores were prepared for pigment production or for early metallurgy (1996:68–69).

Although, like Coghlan, Hamlin did not attempt to replicate kilns based on examples recovered from excavations, he used modern materials such as firebrick and earthenware drainpipes to construct appropriately simple, yet effective kilns (see Figure 5-7) with excellent results (1996:54–56).

Discussion

The value of careful reconstruction of Iron Age houses followed by close attention to their "operating characteristics" and changes in their condition over time should be obvious. While we should never expect any replica to provide a representation of an original structure that is accurate on all counts, the approach taken by Reynolds and his colleagues (as with the earlier work by Hansen in Denmark), in which the archaeological and historical evidence was followed as closely as possible, adds to our confidence that in their most important aspects they mirror the originals. As with any interpretation, alternatives must be considered, as Reynolds made clear in his discussion of Balksbury "house": "It must be emphasised that this post-hole pattern does not necessarily belong to a house. Such a pattern could represent a number of other perfectly good alternatives" (1979:36). To make his point, he went on to construct a sheepfold based on the same set of postholes (1979:41–42).

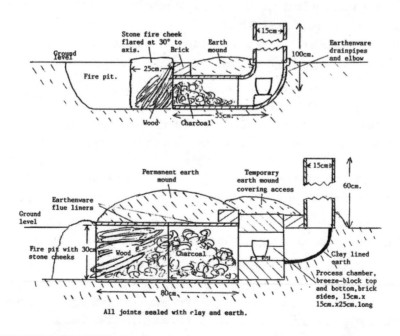

Figure 5-7   Schematic of kilns constructed by Hamlin at Butser Ancient Farm.

With a reconstructed house in place, changes relevant to the interpretation of the archeological record occur throughout the structure's life span. For example, Reynolds noted that rats, attracted to the grain and hay stored in the Maiden Castle house in winter, tunneled under the wall. This led to a transformation of postholes into "gulleys," a characteristic seen in the remains of some Iron Age houses (1979:36). Furthermore, the development of a shallow depression in the doorway, caused by foot traffic in wet weather, provided the basis for identification of the doorway in an excavated structure in the absence of any other evidence (1979:36).

Reynolds was justifiably cautious with respect to quantification of early results. As he noted:

> The time record is extremely interesting, but it begs entirely the question of skill. . . . If such reconstructions are accepted as valid structures, we are now in a position to build again, having acquired the basic skill and knowledge, and then the time taken would be a useful factor. Experiments which record time spent by unskilled operatives on skilled tasks, and use such information, are valueless in complex calculations. (1979:41)

Less problematic with respect to providing insight on the past were the quantities of materials used in thatching the roof and making the daub that was plastered on the basketwork wall of Maiden Castle house—a bit over 1 ton of straw for the roofing and 3½ tons each of clay and earth, 40 bales of straw, the hair from 40 pigs, "sundry" brambles, grass, hay, roots, and other vegetable matter for the daub (Reynolds 1979:34).[5] Also worthy of note was the excellent durability of the wall, which had required little in the way of attention after approximately five years of exposure. Data on thermal performance and interior air quality when being heated would be relatively easy to obtain for the houses reconstructed at Butser and would nicely complement the results of the Lejre experiments; unfortunately, nothing on this subject appears to have been published.

The Butser Ancient Farm, more than any other archaeological replication, demonstrates the value (and the necessity) of approaching ancient agricultural systems by means of long-term experiments that incorporate all the key interrelated activities that define them. If we wish to draw conclusions about any such system and its end products with a reasonable degree of confidence, the appropriate methods of preparing the soil as well as planting, tending, and harvesting the crops must be carefully followed in suitable environments over a much extended period of time. Doing this means, of course, that appropriate technology such as carefully replicated ards and suitable draft animals such as Dexter cows are required. And this in turn requires lengthy periods of training for the "farmers" and the animals. Keeping animals on site leads to additional areas of investigation, such as the provisioning of food and shelter and the effects of livestock on the landscape.

Only by replicating all of the interrelated components of an ancient system as thoroughly as possible can we hope to understand the operation of the whole. As the Butser project so admirably demonstrates, the potential of this sort of experimentation to increase our understanding of life in ancient communities is truly extraordinary, as extraordinary as is the commitment required to make it possible.[6]

CHAPTER SUMMARY

The experiments reviewed in this chapter demonstrate the value of "connecting the dots" to reveal a broader, more complete picture of the past. In the examples involving Maya monumental architecture, the modeling of the whole was based on the use of measurements and estimates of component processes; complete replicas of features at Uxmal and Copán were not constructed (for obvious reasons). As noted in the discussion of those experiments (the one by Erasmus in particular), some issues that would have a significant effect on the results may not reveal themselves directly when taking this approach. Even a complete reconstruction of a scale model of a wall or building may fail to present the experimenter with the full range of technical problems that had to be solved when original (full-size) structures were built. This should not be seen as a fatal flaw but as a limitation that must be kept in mind when the experimenter draws conclusions and the scientific community evaluates results.

A related problem presents itself with the reconstruction of subsistence systems if small test plots are cultivated and/or the trials are conducted over a short time period. In either case, the results will not be sufficiently reliable to allow for estimates of crop production, although we should be able to learn something of value about the process and the characteristics of the plants. The only solution to this problem is the one taken at Butser in which fields of authentic size are cultivated in a representative range of habitats. Data on yield, climate, and other variables are then compiled over a period of decades.

The results produced by the extraordinary range of experiments carried out at Lejre and Butser argue strongly for greater investment in ongoing research programs of the sort that provide an umbrella under which virtually all the types of experiments archaeologists normally perform may be carried out as part of an integrated effort. Living with our reconstructions of the past on a day-in day-out basis, year after year, provides the best opportunity we have to build detailed, coherent, and to the best of our abilities, accurate models of ancient life.

In the next and final chapter, we look at experiments as sources of valuable personal experience that I believe deserves inclusion in the reports written by those who perform them. Although the postprocessual challenge has helped to legitimize this sort of expression in contemporary archaeological reporting, it is not entirely new to experimental archeology, as we shall see. Finally, we look at the extraordinary potential of imitative experiments in the realm of education—both in terms of enlightening the general public about life in the past and in providing teachers with valuable new approaches to improving their students' critical thinking skills.

NOTES

[1] Sahlins (1972) has convincingly argued that leisure time is highly prized in hunting-gathering societies, where there is normally more of it than in those that rely on agriculture. And if we were to compare the typical work-

week and overall pace of life of the average Westerner today with those of a hunter-gatherer of the Kalahari (South Africa) or Arnhem Land (Australia) or, for that matter, a farmer in a community based on the kind of agriculture that typified the ancient Maya, we would probably have to wonder if modern technology has tended to enslave us rather than make us freer.

2 In a more recent set of experiments involving the use of carefully made and hafted chert axes to quarry limestone blocks at Tikal and Nakbe, Woods and Titmus (1996) obtained results very close to the 1:1.5 stone to steel ratio reported by Abrams.

3 The degree to which a subsistence economy based on agriculture is sustainable over extended periods of time has been the subject of increasing scrutiny by archaeologists in recent years (see, for example, Redman 1999 and Varien 1999).

4 For a discussion of roof pitch, wall height, and other closely related matters as they pertain to hypothetical reconstructions of wood henges, see Wainwright 1989:115–161.

5 The negative effects on the landscape brought about by farming can be significant. In an earlier period in Britain (prior to about 2500 BC), cutting turf for use as walling materials for houses may well have played a role in the destruction of once rich soils. As Wainwright notes, "It has been calculated . . . that the needs of one [not particularly large] turf-walled building . . . would have required one acre of turf. A village of twenty buildings would have devastated the surrounding pasture" (1989:163). Turf walls were quite likely features of some Iron Age buildings as well (Reynolds 1995:17–18).

6 I highly recommend Peter Reynolds' "Rural Life and Farming" (1995b) as an excellent example of how knowledge gained from long-term experimentation may be skillfully integrated with historical and more traditional archaeological evidence to provide a unique window on Iron Age life in Britain. Pryor's *Farmers in Prehistoric Britain* (1999) is also well worth reading.

CHAPTER 6

EXPERIMENTS, HUMANISTIC SCIENCE, AND EDUCATION

It is a wonderful experience to walk up and down a field behind a plow, your hand on its steering bar, and find yourself suddenly transported out of your own time into that of your forefathers.

My forefathers had plowed that field. In those days the fringe of the forest had been just beyond the rise and the plow must have kept twisting and sticking because of all the thousands of stones that raised their gray pates everywhere. They plowed the field this way and that, crisscross, and then sowed their wheat or barley in poorly weeded furrows. Since that day the sun has passed through the sky overhead more than a million times. So near and so inconceivably remote is the time when our Stone Age ancestors were alive.

My plow, I feel, has let me glimpse a little light in the darkness that prevails far down the ages, and I say to you:

Cherish the memory of the ancients and protect the few remaining traces of them. (Hansen 1964:77–79)

I have already suggested that imitative experiments may serve the needs of both processual and postprocessual archaeology. It is obvious that they can provide answers to questions that are of interest to all archaeologists, such as how an artifact might have been made and used. Those answers might then play into a straightforward reconstruction of the component parts of an agricultural system or into a more "poetic" account of life in an ancient farming village. There is no reason why these cannot coexist in the same report. Whatever the archaeologist's theoretical orientation, the act of performing the experiment provides firsthand experience and understanding unobtainable by other methods of inquiry into the past, and this, too, may figure into what is incorporated into the final report. There are dangers of possible excess here as well. While learning something about the function of an artifact may help explain its symbolic associations and hence facilitate an exploration of ideology, it is important to recognize that the experience gained by actually making and/or using it provides no direct access to the mind of an ancient person who did something similar. Likewise, living for a time in an replicated Iron Age village and performing tasks common to daily life in that period can greatly improve one's understanding but provides only limited insight on how Iron Age people experienced life in their villages, regardless of any feeling of "getting in touch" or "connecting" with them that we may get from the exercise. As Spiegelberg has put it, "the empathy theory, according to which a process of empathy, induced by a tendency to imitate another person's behavior, leads us to his mind is untenable" (1975:40–41). And he was certainly not thinking about an extreme case involving people separated in time from one another by thousands of years and living vastly different lives! Going "native" can thus be as intellectually dangerous for the archaeologist as it is for the historian or the cultural anthropologist. There is a cultural divide between there and then and here and now that we cannot cross. So, what can legitimately and productively be made of the personal experience gained by performing an experiment?

THE EXPERIMENT AND SENSUOUS–INTELLECTUAL COMPLEMENTARITY

In assessing the possible contributions of countercultural epistemology to the science of complex systems, physicist Thomas Blackburn considered the distinction between sensuous and intellectual knowing. He argued that

> by relying lopsidedly on abstract quantification as a method of knowing, scientists have been looking at the world with one eye closed. There is other knowledge besides reading the position of a pointer on a scale. The human mind and body process information with staggering sophistication and sensitivity by the direct sensuous experience with their surroundings. We have, in fact, in our very selves, "instruments" that are capable of confronting and understanding the blooming, buzzing, messy world outside the laboratory. If that were not so, Homo sapiens would never have survived the competitive pressure from predators who are also so equipped. (1971:1005)

In developing his notion of complementarity (based, not surprisingly, on the well-known work of physicist Niels Bohr), Blackburn defines "complementary realities" in terms that for the most part could be used to describe the relationship between processual and postprocessual archaeology. The key point is that there may be two (and probably more) valid ways to describe or model a phenomenon. Although these descriptions arise from different kinds of experience, each may be rational, with neither being subsumable into the other. Furthermore, since these descriptions refer to the same phenomenon, they cannot be entirely independent of each other. Accordingly, it can be argued that the fullest and most edifying account of the human past requires "enlarging the frame of reference to include both models as alternative truths, however irreconcilable their abstract contradictions may seem" (Blackburn 1971:1004).

I am confident that anyone who has done such things as make and use a stone tool or build a fire in the hearth of a replicated Iron Age house would readily agree that the experience was a source of both sensuous and intellectual knowledge. And I suspect that a desire for the former may be a more powerful motivating factor than is commonly recognized (or at least, admitted). I also think it is fair to say that the pleasure derived from the experience of replicating something from the past (or recovering it though an excavation) plays a significant role in convincing some students to opt for a career in archaeology. But there is a "disconnect" here: traditional approaches to science are geared toward the ultimately impossible task of excising the subjective, and as a result, the sensuous knowledge acquired from research projects has too seldom been communicated. Indeed, the archaeological literature is all the poorer for it. I lamented this state of affairs as a graduate student (Saraydar 1976:88–93), but it was not until the positivist philosophies that had dominated archaeological thought began to be challenged in the early 1980s that it became more widely acceptable for the archaeologist her/himself to make an appearance in reports of investigations as something other than a supposedly neutral observer/instrument.[1]

Communicating the most salient observations, feelings, and impressions that one has as an experiment (or a survey or excavation) is carried out and perhaps adding supplementary material from relevant but nontraditional sources can greatly enrich the final report and make it easier to comprehend and evaluate, as well as more enjoyable to read. This approach brings with it the added benefit (or danger, depending on one's point of view) of providing insight on the observer—his or her motivations and biases, for instance. In the classroom, I have found student response to reports that convey in one way or another the investigators' personal reactions to the material they write about (e.g., Ascher and Fairbanks 1971 and Spector 1996) to be far more enthusiastic than to those that follow conventional approaches to scientific reporting.[2] Creative approaches such as these carry the added benefit of preparing students to appreciate more fully and communicate more effectively their own archaeological experiences. And, as Hansen's (1964) delightful account of building "a stone-age house" demonstrates so well, exercises based on imitative experiments provide an especially good source of experiences to be articulated and shared.

EXPERIMENTS IN EDUCATION

Experiments have long served as teaching tools in the sciences. They are routinely used to demonstrate and provide an introduction to hypothesis testing, methods of observation, the proper use of instruments and other laboratory equipment, analysis and interpretation of data, and the art of presenting results in a clear and concise fashion. Ideally, they also enliven, clarify and reinforce material presented in lectures and textbooks through the firsthand experience they provide. Learning through experience is vital to the development of formal knowledge and to the growth of the kind of "intuitive" understanding that so often guides the organization and interpretation of research (Figures 6-1 and 6-2). Purely verbal (spoken or written) instruction cannot convey sufficient information to transform students into competent professionals or even allow them to gain a full appreciation of a field that they might pursue as a career; this is as true of art and auto mechanics as it is of archaeology and chemistry. Much of the "knowing" in these and virtually all other fields is dependent on their practice, that is, upon their "doing."

Figure 6-1 The State University of New York at Oswego has an area set aside exclusively for teaching and research initiatives in experimental archaeology.

The imitative experiments performed by archaeologists can play an educational role that goes beyond training the next generation of researchers; many of these experiments are perfect for demonstrations of interest to the general public, as the success in attracting visitors achieved by the Butser Ancient Farm and Lejre Experimental Center amply demonstrates. Used as an outreach tool, imitative experiments are a means of counteracting misleading popular images of the discipline and its practitioners while at the same time enlightening the public about the past.

EXPERIMENTS IN THE CLASSROOM

Many of the experiments discussed in chapter 3, as well as the smaller-scale examples in chapter 4, would make for interesting class projects to which a variety of lessons about ancient life could be attached. For example, every archaeology student learns the terminology of lithic technology: striking platforms, hard and soft hammer percussion, indirect percussion, core reduction, bulbs of percussion, edge angle, retouch, pressure flaking, and so

Figure 6-2 Students at SUNY Oswego processing a deer leg with obsidian tools. Remains of this activity were buried and left for excavation by the following semester's class.

on. And then there are the various artifact types produced by these processes, such as hand-axes, end scrapers, points, burins, and celts. An introduction to this subject matter typically comes through a combination of verbal descriptions, photographs, diagrams, and occasionally films, and most students leave the classroom relating to lithic technology at about the same level as they would to neurosurgical techniques after being introduced to that subject by a similar array of educational materials. As Gilborn (1968:25) has explained, "Performance is itself a form of knowledge quite apart from a verbal relation, symbolic representation or an observation of whatever is being performed." Fortunately, and unlike the case of neurosurgery, the archaeology curriculum can easily incorporate exercises that enable all students to acquire the kind of sensuous knowledge gained from firsthand experience with lithics that makes esoteric terminology and concepts "real," while at the same time having some fun in the process. Once a student has succeeded in detaching a suitably large flake from a core, dulled one edge by retouch and used the resulting tool as a cutting implement, mastery of concepts relating to lithic technology almost invariably improves, as does the level of enthusiasm for the subject matter.

There is a larger educational issue at stake here. We live in a time when what Gilborn (1968) has termed "the denial of experience," that is, the substitution of the use of language and the services of machines and specialists for firsthand experience has become increasingly the norm. The result of this trend, in Gilborn's view, is that "our knowledge of our world becomes less actively perceptual and increasingly conceptual, mechanical, or unthinking as machines and specialists continue their work to make life more secure" (1968:27). In response to the easily reached conclusion that education relies too heavily on the printed word and a concomitant belief that exploration is critical to learning, an increasing number of educators are working to create teaching materials that "present the students (and teachers) with the same sort of problems that challenge and motivate the scientist and scholar in their pursuit of knowledge" (28–29). Gilborn cited examples of what is termed "inductive" or "discovery" learning that include "assignments in libraries, labs, museums, or on historical or archaeological sites" (29).

Exercises based on archaeological experiments provide an excellent means of learning by discovery (as can, of course, experiments in many other disciplines such as chemistry and biology) but carry the added benefit of being able to address directly the relationship between people and the technology we have come increasingly to rely on (and from which many often feel alienated). Archaeology is uniquely situated to include hands-on exercises in its lessons on the evolution of technology, and there is no reason why the lessons and the experiments must necessarily stop with the technology of 50 or 100 years ago or some other arbitrary date in the past. If we choose to see archaeology as a science of material culture, then the objects we make and use today are as much fair game for study as are Upper Palaeolithic harpoons.

There is another important area in which hands-on exercises based on archaeological replication can be of considerable educational value and that is in the improvement of "critical thinking" skills. Although critical thinking has long been emphasized in K–12 education, it has become an especially prominent concept in the United States with its inclusion in the National Curriculum Content Area Standards (Davis 2000:60–61). An ability to think critically, that is to reason logically both in constructing one's own arguments and evaluating those of others, is a skill that everyone needs to develop. Science education in particular should arm students with an understanding of and appreciation for the reasoning processes that guide research and interpretation of data; in short, it should develop their capabilities for the "doing" of science by encouraging them to think like scientists. But there is more at stake here than the preparation of future scientists. The greater value of being able to approach and solve problems as scientists do goes well beyond the confines of any science curriculum (see Matthews 1994:83ff). An understanding of the logic on which sound interpretation is based is valuable in any subject and in everyday life. The "systematized common sense" to which Conan Doyle's Sherlock Holmes once referred in describing his craft is an apt description of scientific method, so it shouldn't come as a surprise that the types of reasoning used by the scientist or detective to solve a puzzle serve us equally well in our efforts to make intelligent decisions concerning the many claims and options that present themselves as we make our way through a typical day. Or, at least they would, if more people were capable of discriminating between sound and unsound reasoning.

On this last point, Matthews (1994:88–93) confirmed the distressing conclusions reached independently by many teachers at the high school and college levels concerning the poor ability of the average student to evaluate the validity of even simple arguments. He cites one study that documents the inability of the vast majority of science students in their first year of college to recognize fallacious reasoning (most notably they typically believe that "if X then Y" also means "if Y then X," which brings us squarely back to the abductions discussed in chapter 2). Another study, which examined the reasoning abilities of 600 students from grades 9 to 12 and 400 trainee teachers (all science graduates) in three countries, produced similarly distressing performance when it came to awareness of logical fallacies of the following kinds:

1. Assuming that events which follow from others are caused by them

2. Drawing conclusions on the basis of an insufficient number of instances

3. Drawing conclusions on the basis of nonrepresentative instances

4. Assuming that something that is true in specific circumstances is true in general

5. Imputing causal significance to correlations

6. Tautological reasoning

Matthews found the results especially troubling, "given the importance of reasoning not just to science, but to social and personal functioning more generally—voting in an election, buying a car, deciding on school-board policy, determining what went wrong with the baked cake and so on" (Matthews 1994:91). His response to this sorry situation is to call for the integration of formal and informal reasoning in science courses. Specifically, he recommends that students should be trained to recognize and avoid several common forms of fallacious reasoning, including, among others, the fallacy of *denying the antecedent*—If X then Y. Not X, therefore not Y—and the now-familiar fallacy of *affirming the consequent*—If X then Y. Y, therefore X (Matthews 1994:92).

Of course, there are many ways to improve reasoning skills. An approach that combines some instruction in formal logic with illustrative examples taken from case studies in scientific interpretation and everyday life works well. Archaeology can be a source of interesting and memorable lessons in reasoning that carry with them the added benefit of teaching about the past, how we reconstruct it, and why we need to conserve archaeological resources. For example, the relationship in ancient Mesopotamia between the growth of centralized administration and increasingly large and complex irrigation systems works well in demonstrating that a positive correlation does not in itself imply a causal relationship. The perils of working from too small a sample can be demonstrated by an exercise in which generalizations are made about a particular time and region on the basis of the contents of a small number of sites from a specified region that a larger (more representative) sample later reveals to be atypical.[3] The claim investigated by Hartenberg and Schmidt (1969) that the Egyptian drill represented the earliest example of the crank and the subsequent more thorough experiments by Stocks (1993, 2003) illustrate the dangers of making inferences on the basis of problematic assumptions and then failing to acquire the data necessary to evaluate their validity. And here again we see the special value of the imitative exercise: I am confident that everyone who has the opportunity to experiment with a replica of the drill will find the experience as interesting and memorable as I did. For a slightly different sort of experimental exercise suitable for any group of individuals to try, see the Appendix.

EXPERIMENTS IN WHICH THE PUBLIC CAN PARTICIPATE

The educational value of imitative experiments is not limited to the classroom—they can be used as the basis for lessons that can be taught anywhere. The past brought to life is a powerful draw and provides the archaeologist with an especially effective tool that can be used to educate schoolchildren and the general public about a broad range of archaeological issues. Facilities such as the Lejre Experimental Center and the Butser Ancient Farm have always attracted large numbers of visitors who come both to observe and to take part in hands-on activities (Figure 6-3). Comparable lessons can also be taught effectively (if not quite so dramatically) in the absence of reconstructed villages and farms through programs in which demonstrations and exercises are constructed around simulated digs and smaller-scale replications of past technology and behavior.

Regardless of venue, the most effective lessons are almost always multidimensional:

> For older children the implications of "hands-on" experience leads to understanding of the integration of system, lines of supply and demand, sequences of work and ultimately human impact on environment. It is, perhaps, the infinite cross-curricular nature of the Ancient Farm which initiates and substantiates an appreciation of the complexity [of] the real world. It is possible to range from the simplest activities like spinning and weaving to the complexities of the climatic impact on plant growth, from the base techniques of applying daub to a wickerwork wall to the mathematical determination of the forces exerted by a cone upon a cylinder. This diversity of academic disciplines . . . provides on the one hand a rich and flexible educational tool, on the other a continuously increasing data resource. (Reynolds 1999:8)

Likewise at Lejre, workshops and the reconstructed village provide the basis for "camp schools" lasting five days and more intensive courses for teachers and students that emphasize interrelationships as seen through the lens of a cultural ecological model. In all cases of instruction designed for visiting elementary and secondary school classes, working closely with teachers in advance of the students' visit is essential. With the imposition of increasingly more national and, in the case of the U.S., state curriculum standards, the lessons the

Figure 6-3 Experiencing the ambiance of a replicated Iron Age longhouse at Lejre, Denmark.

archaeologist provides should most often be designed to help teachers meet specific curricular requirements. If not, the teachers find what the archaeologist has to offer interesting but insufficiently relevant to the lengthy list of topics they must include in their lesson plans.

When it comes to the general public, such restrictions do not apply. For many casual visitors to places such as Lejre and the Butser Ancient Farm, viewing exhibits and reenactments will suffice to satisfy their curiosity. But for those who want more, both centers provide the opportunity to register for "do-it-yourself" activities such as preparing meals from Stone Age and Iron Age menus; building replicas of ancient ovens to make pottery, extract iron, and cook food; making textiles, knapping flint, and, for the especially fit and energetic at Lejre, working with a group of 150 to 200 people to move a very heavy stone. Similar demonstrations and exercises geared for general audiences are also easily within the realm of what might be offered on weekends by faculty and students at colleges and universities, with the added benefit of improving "town-gown" relations.

One final and unusual educational experiment deserves mention here. At Lejre, several families each year experience "living in the past," an ambitious program that affords them the opportunity to live in the Iron Age village or the "country cottages" for a period ranging from one weekend to an entire week. During this time they are expected to participate in the

Center's public activities while they carry out the full range of activities associated with life in the time period they've chosen. Some of the consequences of this exercise have been unexpected. When the program was first started in 1970, several adventurous families were invited to spend up to two weeks living in the long houses. The idea behind this, according to Hansen, was to "challenge their ingenuity and powers of observation," while adding to the vividness of the reconstructed Iron Age environment presented to the public (1977:22).

From the very start, Hansen was quite impressed by the families' "persistence," especially given the thousands of visitors, many of whom asked the same questions—"Where is your toilet?", "Why aren't you ill from eating such primitive food?", "Why doesn't the house burn down with the open fire in the hearth?", "Are you paid to do this?", "Do you sleep together in the straw beds?" were especially common (Hansen 1977:22). He also noted that very few visitors actually asked questions about the past! He was even more surprised by entries in the diaries kept by the "prehistoric" families in which they expressed the feeling that visitors often looked down on them as a "peculiar minority" (Hansen 1977:23). They also noted, apparently with displeasure, that some visitors would help themselves to their food and sit on their beds without asking for an invitation. According to Hansen, "Through the disguise of Iron Age attire, and strange surroundings, 'nice' Danes became foreigners" (1977:23). The responses of participants and visitors were found sufficiently interesting that a follow-up experiment in social behavior was undertaken. In this instance, what was intended as a lesson on the past provided a perhaps more significant lesson on the discrimination in the present. Today, the programs at Lejre continue to be built around three principles that reflect such early experiences.

1. Understanding—of the links between culture, view of nature, and resource exploitation
2. Responsibility—for sustainable administration of the cultural and natural heritage
3. Tolerance—between people regardless of culture and understanding of the surrounding world. (Holten 2003:1)

This leads to a final, related matter, and that concerns the issue of cross-cultural sensitivity in the design and execution of experiments.

WHO OWNS THE PAST?

In chapter 2 I made the point that experimental archaeology can provide some relief for the frustration archaeologists may occasionally feel with the fragmentary and chance nature of their primary data and the impossibility of "redoing" an excavation. It brings other benefits as well. Archaeologists often face the hurdle of obtaining permits before an excavation may begin, while a permit of any sort would only very rarely be required for an experiment. Furthermore, the logistics associated with the typical experiment are normally far less complicated than are those associated with more typical fieldwork. On another front, when archaeologists perform an imitative experiment they avoid a particularly difficult issue confronting their discipline today: the rights descendant populations may exercise over the material remains of their ancestors. In the United States, legislation such as the Archaeological Resources Protection Act and the Native American Graves Protection and Repatriation Act place constraints on excavation as well as on the study and retention of the materials excavation brings to light (for excellent discussions of this important matter see Watkins 2000 and 2003). While there are no similar restrictions on imitative experiments, and most experiments run negligible risk of being found culturally offensive by anyone, it is still possible for conflict to develop with the descendants of the people whose past is replicated.

The most notable incident of this sort involved the 60-foot replica of a Polynesian sailing vessel—the Hokule'a—discussed in chapter 4. In this case, it was not the replication of the vessel that led to trouble, but the publicity surrounding its cultural significance. In Finney's words:

> Launch a magnificent double-canoe amidst much publicity and fanfare proclaiming it to be a faithful reconstruction of an ancient voyaging canoe; campaign it around the islands advertising it to Hawaiians as their ancestral spaceship; then encourage them to step aboard and make of it whatever they wish. That became our self-made recipe for trouble.
>
> [We] had unwittingly opened the Hawaiian equivalent of Pandora's box. We had sailed into the uncharted waters of an awakening Hawaiian consciousness and were being buffeted by strange winds and currents. (1979:32)

Finney noted that trouble first came from kahunas (Hawaiian "priests") who were apparently insulted that they had not been the ones chosen to lead the ritual performed at the launching ceremony. Pronouncements of ill fortune for the vessel and its voyage came next, followed by reports of strange illnesses attributed to spiritual factors by some of the Hawaiians participating in the project. Some even ceased to work on it. "It might have been possible to have extricated the project from the spiritualistic depths into which it was sliding had the situation not been complicated by a vigorous 'Hokule'a for Hawaiians only' movement" (1979:35).

Although the crew of the Hokule'a was multiracial, an emerging "ethnic sensitivity" that Finney likened to "that of the blacks, Chicanos, Indians and other American minority groups" (1979:37) made the presence of haoles (non-Polynesians, Caucasians in particular) unacceptable. Tying cultural revival to scientific research, although a well-intended goal of a project member who was himself part-Hawaiian, proved "naïve" in contemporary Hawaii, where, in Finney's view:

> Scientific research is part of that haole world and must be rejected, especially if it aims to tell [Hawaiians] more about their own past. Their way to find out about the past is to ask the elders, not look in books, dig in the ground or perform experiments. (1979:38)

The potential for situations of this kind to occur increases with the scale and scope of the experiment. As larger "slices" of past lifeways are replicated and the experimental project becomes more visible to the general public, its appropriateness and relevance may be questioned by descendant communities. As in the case of the Hokule'a, issues may also arise concerning the ethnicity of the participants. Clearly this sort of situation will not occur with the research at Butser and Lejre, where the experimenters explore their own heritage and present it to the public. But what if archaeologists were to create an experimental seventeenth-century Iroquois (Haudenosaunee) village open to the public and featuring actors in period costume?

The primary point to be made here is that scientific research never takes place in a vacuum. As members of a larger community of human beings, archaeologists must do their best to respect the feelings of descendant communities and to make their efforts to understand the past as multivocal and inclusive as possible. Communication with descendant communities as well as with the general public on the aims of planned archaeological research and the dissemination of the knowledge gained from completed projects, whatever their subject matter, is essential not only for reasons of ethics but also for the continued prosperity of the discipline.[4] Does this mean that without at least the tacit approval of descendent communities, projects like the construction and sailing of the Hokule'a should be scuttled? Absolutely not. I am opposed to any group having veto power over the study of humanity's past.

Fortunately, replicative experiments can, more often than not, be quite useful to efforts to work with descendant groups, even those that are uneasy with the ways in which archaeology typically recovers the past. By their very nature replicative experiments have several important advantages that normally keep them out of troubled waters: most notably, they do not involve excavation of ancient sites and the artifacts and features employed are only replicas. Furthermore, these replicas are used in activities that ancient communities would almost certainly not have hidden from outsiders (e.g., cooking, clearing a field, making stone tools and pottery), so the subject matter of the experiment is unlikely to be found offensive. In addition, the results of experiments often demonstrate the great ingenuity of past people in solving difficult problems such as smelting ore, casting with the lost-wax method, drilling of stone, transporting a multiton statue on a sledge drawn only by humans, and growing corn and beans in a desert without fertilizer or irrigation, to name a few. This works to increase the public's respect for other cultures by clearly demonstrating what they were able to accomplish without the benefit of the modern technology, on which most people today so thoroughly depend, and with no need for extraterrestrial assistance.

When there is to be a public component to an experiment or a demonstration is to be performed to highlight achievements of an ancient people, collaboration with any available descendants willing to add their own personal and cultural perspectives can add measurably to the richness and ultimate success of the effort.[5] It has been my experience that even those whose beliefs and traditions lead them to oppose removing relics of the past from the ground generally find efforts to increase understanding of and respect for their ancestors and their traditions among the general public worth pursuing. For instance, while archaeology may not be the path to the past followed by most contemporary Easter Islanders and Maya, pride in demonstrating the accomplishments of their ancestors to the outside world has motivated members of both societies to participate in some of the experiments described in this book. This suggests to me that as valuable as imitative experiments are as tools for unlocking ancient mysteries, they may be equally important as bridges connecting people to one another and helping us, at least in some small way, to create a more enlightened and tolerant future.

NOTES

[1] Long before it became fashionable to deviate from a "just the facts" approach to site reports, some archaeologists did attempt to be more creative. In a retrospective essay, my late mentor and friend, Paul S. Martin commented:

> From 1930 to about 1939 my reports often ended with a section labeled "Conjectures" or "Synthesis." In these sections I summed up our results but also added sections that might be dubbed imaginative, fanciful, or visionary. (Martin 1974:18)

By 1940, he had backed away from "expressing any radical ideas" (1974:18). His tentative explanation for this change is telling:

> I am perplexed about why I slackened and permitted my views to take on a pseudo-objectivity, to become sterile and unoriginal. . . . One [possible] reason is that my previous reports had drawn a considerable amount of criticism and ridicule. I was told that my reports lacked objectivity; and to be "scientific" and unbiased, one should present only facts and not make "interpretations." I had thought that by presenting all the cold data as carefully as possible and by then separating my "conjectures" very carefully from the actual details, I was not overstepping the bounds of propriety. Anyone could then take our "facts" and make his own interpretations. But, perhaps, I had violated some unwritten code. . . . I [also] felt that my reports were out of line with others. (1974:18–19)

Martin concludes his essay by observing that

> we are becoming aware that the scientific method with its creation of an hypothesis, test implications and so on may not be the only approach to good archaeology. We have emphasized the processual view or the study of the reasons for changes in culture through time. But there is the humanistic approach; the focus on social organization as a method of getting at human interactions; and many other ways of getting at the explanation of human behavior which is one important aspect of the millennia of human history at our command. We do not feel we have *the* answer. My guess is that there are many roads to truth. (1974:27)

[2] These two are perennial class favorites. Ascher and Fairbanks take a novel approach to their report on an excavation of a slave cabin in Georgia:

> Our presentation includes a sound track and pictures. The sound track is composed from eye-witness accounts, slave narratives, and other sources. You are encouraged to sound out the words; the sound track selections are based on their auditory value and on their connection with the archaeological findings. The organization follows a modular plan; each module begins with a sound track and ends at the start of the next sound track. You are invited to reassemble the components to best suit yourself. Artifacts are three dimensional: they are visual and tactile and sometimes they smell and make noise. Word pictures and flat representations in photographs and drawings offer only limited help. (1971:4)

Spector (1996) pairs a fictional narrative that conveys the meaning she found in a Wahpeton (Eastern Dakota) awl with a traditional, depersonalized set of descriptions of such objects.

[3] The site selection options in *Adventures in Fugawiland: A Computer Simulation in Archaeology* (Price and Gebauer 2002) allow for an especially effective lesson on the effects of working from a nonrepresentative sample.

4 For a discussion of these and other issues related to ethics, I recommend Vitelli (1996).

5 Perhaps the best example of how this sort of collaboration may bring benefits to all concerned is provided by the Ozette site, in the state of Washington. This case did not involve archaeological experiments but rather the excavation and preservation of an early seventeenth-century Makah village that had been covered by a mud-slide and was remarkably well preserved. Archaeologists and Makah worked together on the excavation and interpretation of the finds, which are now preserved and displayed in a museum built and run by the Makah (see Kehoe 1992:452; http://www.makah.com/mcrchome.htm; http://www.makah.com/ozette.htm; http://www.northolympic.com/makah/).

APPENDIX

LESSONS FROM EXPERIMENTAL SITES[1]

A special kind of imitative exercise deserves mention here. While not an experiment in the typical sense, the creation of a site to be excavated as part of a class project clearly involves replication of a sort. Indeed, typical experimental exercises such as making and using simple stone tools can provide an excellent set of formation activities for a site to be excavated by another group of students at a later time. Experimental sites of this kind can provide the basis for particularly engaging lessons that help improve critical thinking skills while simultaneously providing an introduction to archaeological field methods and interpretation.

I have incorporated exercises designed around such sites in my introductory course in theory and methods to increase the number of hands-on activities. My primary goal has been to give students a chance to practice what they learn about methods in the classroom and from reading assignments and then proceed, albeit to a much more limited extent than if a genuine site were excavated, to analysis and interpretation (again, adding personal experience to their knowledge of these two phases of research). They get both a taste of archaeological fieldwork (and teamwork) and an opportunity to reconstruct some events of the recent past (that is, work from results back to possible causes) by explicit application of scientific methods and reasoning.

While the term "artificial" might be applied to sites created for teaching purposes, the activities that lead to their formation are always "real" in the sense that objects are not just placed in a pit for others to dig up; rather, meaningful sets of activities are performed so that there is something legitimate to reconstruct. For example: a small site is created by digging out a roughly square area 1 or 2 m on a side to a depth of 3 or 4 cm., and a fire pit ringed with stones is constructed and a wood fire is started. Some food is cooked on site while other items are prepared elsewhere (Kentucky Fried Chicken is a favorite). People then sit along the perimeter of the site and eat, toss bones or whatever into the area near the fire pit; beverage containers with return-deposits may be carted away, while ones with no cash value might be discarded at the site; the square plastic "closers" on packages of hot dog buns may be left behind, while the bags that contained the buns are not, and so on. (This exercise also serves, I suppose, as an illustration of how ecologically insensitive behavior works to the advantage of archaeologists!) Four to five such squares can accommodate a class of 15 to 20 students. Individual squares may contain unrelated activities or simulate portions of a single, larger site. A site with a decidedly contemporary character makes it easier for many students to gain a sound understanding of site-formation processes and helps prepare them for more difficult reconstructions of ancient behavior.

In my comparison between the tasks facing detectives and archaeologists in chapter 2, I offered a tongue-in-cheek lament on the lack of anything in archaeology comparable to the videotape that sometimes documents the commission of crimes and the outright confessions that may bring closure to a criminal investigation. In the case of experimental sites, there are no such limitations: all formation behaviors are videotaped, the site is photographed before being covered and several of the "perpetrators" may even be interrogated at the end of the exercise. After the students present their site reports in class (the exercise requires both oral and written communication), they then examine the set of photographs and view the video of the site's creation. This is followed by discussion in which reconstructions are compared with reality, and data recovery, analysis, and interpretation are critiqued. In addition, each semester's students are responsible for replacing the sites they excavate with new ones they help to design, thus further facilitating understanding of how the archaeological record is formed.

This particular type of exercise is easily adapted to all grade levels and a variety of pedagogical purposes. It is especially useful for teaching students to think critically (see Chiarulli, Bedell, and Sturdevant 2000:218). A specially created site such as the one described above provides students with interpretive problems that highlight the processes by which conclusions are reached while avoiding esoteric scenarios and terminology. For students with a background in prehistoric archaeology, similar analytic and interpretive challenges can be provided by having them excavate a stone tool workshop in which cores were reduced, blanks trimmed, and tools made and then used in an adjacent area to work a variety of materials. The possibilities are virtually unlimited.[2] So here we have a simple way to encourage students to think critically about how they reason while also teaching them something they will remember about the means by which we come to know the past through archaeology. By encouraging them to formulate multiple working hypotheses, derive appropriate test implications, and search for corroborative evidence, they learn to be more cautious in reaching conclusions about the human behavior responsible for the material traces archaeologists study. When we create a setting in which reasoning "backwards" is called for, we also establish a laboratory ideal for the exploration of sound and unsound reasoning methods. This type of exercise can also be used to highlight the difference between science and pseudoscience by contrasting the procedures and results of real archaeology with flights of fancy passed off as legitimate explanation of the past (see, for example, the discussion of Erich von Däniken's "extraterrestrial intervention" approach to human history and the related critical thinking exercise in Feder 2008:225–251. See also Feder 1984 on the subject of "Irrationality and Popular Archaeology.").

Another benefit of excavating and interpreting an artificial site comes from firsthand exposure to the permanent loss of information that goes along with site destruction—through proper excavation, looting, or other human or natural activities. I always encourage my students to think about how much less they would have been able to learn about the behavior that produced the site without the knowledge of provenience and association obtained through systematic excavation and careful recovery of evidence. I have them do this as they excavate and then again when they present their interpretations. After attempting careful excavations of their own, they always seem to have increased appreciation for the technical precision and intellectual rigor that characterize the case studies they read about and discuss in class.

Looked at broadly, the dig exercise and its ancillary activities can be used as an effective means of introducing some key curricular reforms in education that an increasing number of archaeologists and other educators are demanding. Out of a list of seven reforms for education in archaeology discussed by Bender (2000:32–39), stewardship, ethics and values, written and oral communication, fundamental archaeological skills, and real-world problem solving stand out as especially amenable to exercises centering around excavation and analysis of a simulated site. With respect to the last item in this list, Bender observes:

> One of the most difficult things for undergraduates to do is to connect the classroom and the real world. In the realm of coursework, helping students make this connection often involves emphasizing main points and demonstrating applicability to their lives and professions. (2000:37)

Hansen expressed the same concern over 20 years earlier:

> When the pupils get stuck in the theoretical material, they show less and less motivation to try and comprehend the subject. . . . Education must turn to the real world, returning to the classroom after the student has obtained stimulus and experience from his own world. History is a most vulnerable victim of disinterest stemming from the seeming unrelatedness of the subject to the real world of today. Because the past has gone and can not always be easily read from the physical environment and museum exhibitions, it seems completely unreal. . . . Large sums of money are often wasted on theoretical teaching, for burdened under numerous uses of the media, children do not retain what they are taught because they can not relate it to reality. They see everything on a television screen and there it remains. (1977:43)

The connection between the classroom and the world outside can be made in a number of ways. One, of course, is by providing students with the opportunity to gain firsthand experience by experimenting with replicas of the material culture of the past. Another is by demonstrating the value of improved problem-solving and decision-making skills to all facets of life—on the job, in the home, and so on. And there is at least one more bonus that comes with using archaeological subject matter to improve the ability to think critically: in the process of contemplating the nature and significance of the archaeological record, students can also be taught valuable lessons in archaeological ethics and the need for cultural sensitivity in the pursuit of knowledge.

NOTES

[1] Portions of this section appeared in abbreviated form in Saraydar 2004.

[2] Bedell and Sturdevant have had success with an excavation of a simulated, multicomponent Anasazi site in a program for ninth-grade students. Their admirable and ambitious program is designed to teach students about the Anasazi as well as about archaeological methods and reasoning (Chiarulli, Bedell, and Sturdevant 2000).

BIBLIOGRAPHY

Aberg, F. A. and H. C. Bowen. 1960. Ploughing Experiments with a Reconstructed Donneruplund Ard. *Antiquity* 34:144–147.

Abrams, E. 1984. Replicative Experimentation at Copan, Honduras: Implications for Ancient Economic Specialization. *Journal of New World Archaeology* 6:39–48.

Ascher, R. 1960. Archaeology and the Public Image. *American Antiquity* 25:402–403.

_____. 1961. Experimental Archaeology. *American Anthropologist* 63:793–816.

_____. 1970. CUES I: Design and Construction of an Experimental Archaeological Structure. *American Antiquity* 35:215–216.

Ascher R. and C. Fairbanks. 1971. Excavation of a Slave Cabin: Georgia, U.S.A. *Historical Archaeology* 5:3–17.

Ashbee, P. and I. Cornwall. 1961. An Experiment in Field Archaeology. *Antiquity* 35:129–134.

Ashbee, P. and P. Jewell. 1998. The Experimental Earthwork Revisited. *Antiquity* 72:485–504.

Atkinson, R. J. C. 1956. *Stonehenge*. London: Hamilton.

Balkansky, A. K., G. M. Feinman and L. M. Nicholas. 1997. Pottery Kilns of Ancient Ejutla, Oaxaca, Mexico. *Journal of Field Archaeology* 24(2):139–160.

Bauman, Z. 1978. *Hermeneutics and Social Science*. New York: Columbia University Press.

Beaune, S. A. de. 1987. Palaeolithic Lamps and Their Specialization: A Hypothesis. *Current Anthropology* 28:569–577.

Bell, M., M. J. Fowler and S. W. Hillson. 1996. *The Experimental Earthwork Project, 1960–1992*. Research Report 100. York, UK: Council for British Archaeology.

Bender, S. J., ed. 2000. A Proposal to Guide Curricular Reform for the Twenty-first Century. In *Teaching Archaeology in the Twenty-first Century*, ed. S. J. Bender and G. S. Smith, pp. 31–48. Washington, DC: Society for American Archaeology.

Berlin, A. M. 1999. What's For Dinner? The Answer Is in the Pot. *Biblical Archaeology Review* 25(6):46–55, 62.

Bimson, M. 1956. The Technique of Greek Black and Terra Sigillata Red. *Antiquaries Journal* 36:200–204.

Binford, L. 1968. Archeological Perspectives. In *New Perspectives in Archeology*, ed. L. Binford and S. Binford, pp. 5–32. Chicago: Aldine.

_____. 1977 *For Theory Building in Archaeology*. New York: Academic Press.

_____. 1978. *Nunamiut Ethnoarchaeology*. New York: Academic Press.

_____. 2002. *In Pursuit of the Past: Decoding the Archaeological Record*. Berkeley: University of California Press.

Binford, L. and S. Binford, eds. 1968. *New Perspectives in Archeology*. Chicago: Aldine.

Binneman, J. and J. Deacon. 1985. Experimental Determination of Use Wear on Stone Adzes from Boomplaas Cave, South Africa. *Journal of Archaeological Science* 13:219–228.

Blackburn, T. 1971. Sensuous-Intellectual Complementarity in Science. *Science* 172:1003–1007.

Bordes, F. 1968. *The Old Stone Age*. New York: McGraw-Hill.

Bordes, F. and D. Crabtree. 1969. The Corbiac Blade Technique and Other Experiments. *Tebiwa* 12(2):1–21.

Brain, C. K. 1967. Bone Weathering and the Problem of Bone Pseudo-Tools. *South African Journal of Science* 63(3):97–99.

Brier, B. 2001. A Thoroughly Modern Mummy. *Archaeology* 54(1):44–50.

Brier, B. and R. S. Wade. 2001. Surgical Procedures During Ancient Egyptian Mummification. *Chungará (Arica)* 33(1) [online] http://www.scielo.cl/scielo.php?script=sci_arttext&pid=S0717-73562001000100021&lng=en&nrm=iso.

Brightwell, A., G. Demetriou, M. Massey and N. Neagy. 1972. The Horniman Museum Kiln Experiment at Highgate Wood. Parts 1 and 2. *The London Archaeologist* 2:12–17 (part 1), 2:53–59 (part 2).

Bronitsky, G. and R. Hamer. 1986. Experiments in Ceramic Technology: The Effects of Various Tempering Materials on Impact and Thermal-Shock Resistance. *American Antiquity* 51:89–101.

Browne, J. 1940. Projectile Points. *American Antiquity* 5:209–213.

Calvin, W. H. 1990. *The Ascent of Mind: Ice Age Climates and the Evolution of Intelligence*. New York: Bantam Books.

Chamberlin, T. C. 1904. The Methods of the Earth-Sciences. *Popular Science Monthly* 66:66–75.

Cheshier, J. and R. L. Kelly. 2006. Projectile Point Shape and Durability: The Effect of Thickness:Length. *American Antiquity* 71(2):353–363.

Chiarulli, B. A., E. D. Bedell and C. L. Sturdevant. 2000. Simulated Excavations and Critical Thinking Skills. In *The Archaeology Education Handbook: Sharing the Past with Kids*, ed. K. Smardz and S. J. Smith, pp. 217–233. Walnut Creek, CA: Altamira Press

Clarke, J. G. D. and M. W. Thompson. 1953. The Groove and Splinter Technique of Working Antler in Upper Palaeolithic and Mesolithic Europe, with Special Reference of the Material from Star Carr. *Proceedings of The Prehistoric Society* 19:148–160.

Coe, Michael D. 1993. *The Maya*. New York: Thames and Hudson.

Coghlan, H. H. 1940. Prehistoric Copper and Some Experiments in Smelting. *Transactions of the Newcomen Society* 20:49–65.

Coles, J. 1962. European Bronze Age Shields. *Proceedings of the Prehistoric Society* 28:156–190.

_____. 1973. *Archaeology by Experiment*. New York: Charles Scribner's Sons.

_____. 1979. *Experimental Archaeology*. New York: Academic Press.

Conkey, M. 1980. The Identification of Prehistoric Hunter-Gatherer Aggregation Sites: The Case of Altamira. *Current Anthropology* 21:609–639.

Cosner, A. J. 1951. Arrowshaft Straightening with a Grooved Stone. *American Antiquity* 17:147–148.

Crabtree, D. E. 1972. An Introduction to Flintworking. Part 1. An Introduction to the Technology of Stone Tools. *Occasional Papers of the Idaho State University* 28.

Crabtree, D. E. and B. R. Butler. 1964. Notes on Experiment in Flint Knapping: 1. Heat Treatment of Silica Materials. *Tebiwa* 7(3):1–6.

Crabtree D. E. and E. L. Davis. 1968. Experimental Manufacture of Wooden Implements with Tools of Flaked Stone. *Science* 159:426–428.

Curwen, E. C. 1926. On the Use of Scapulae as Shovels. *Sussex Archaeological Collections* 67:139–145.

_____. 1930. Prehistoric Flint Sickles. *Antiquity* 4:179–186.

_____. 1935. Agriculture and the Flint Sickle in Palestine. *Antiquity* 9:62–66

Dahling, B. H. and W. J. Litzinger. 1986. Old Bottle, New Wine: The Function of Chultuns in the Maya Lowlands. *American Antiquity* 51:721–736.

Daniel, G. 1964. *The Idea of Prehistory.* Hammondsworth, UK: Pelican Books.

Davis, M. E. 2000. Governmental Education Standards and K–12 Archaeology Programs. In *The Archaeology Education Handbook: Sharing the Past with Kids*, ed. K. Smardz and S. J. Smith, pp. 54–71. Walnut Creek, CA: Altamira Press.

D'Errico, F. G. Giacobini and P-F. Puech. 1984. Varnish Replicas: A New Method for the Study of Worked Bone Surfaces. *Ossa. International Journal of Skeletal Research* 9/10:29–51.

Dibble, H. L. and J. C. Whittaker. 1981. New Experimental Evidence on the Relationship between Percussion Flaking and Flake Variation. *Journal of Archaeological Science* 8:283–296.

Eighmy, J. L. and R. S. Sternberg. 1990. *Archaeomagnetic Dating.* Tucson: University of Arizona Press.

Erasmus, C. 1965. Monument Building: Some Field Experiments. *Southwestern Journal of Anthropology* 21:277–301.

Evans, J. G. and S. Limbrey. 1974. The Experimental Earthwork on Morden Bog, Wareham, Dorset, England: 1963–1972. *Proceedings of the Prehistoric Society* 40:170–202.

Evans, O. F. 1957. Probable Uses of Stone Projectile Points. *American Antiquity* 23:83–84.

Feder, K. L. 1984. Irrationality and Popular Archaeology. *American Antiquity* 49:525–541.

_____. 2008. *Frauds, Myths, and Mysteries: Science and Pseudoscience in Archaeology*, 6th ed. New York: McGraw-Hill.

Fedje, D. 1979. Scanning Electron Microscopy Analysis of Use-Striae. In *Lithic Use-Wear Analysis*, ed. B. Hayden, pp. 179–187. New York: Academic Press.

Finney, B. R. 1979. *Hokule'a: The Way to Tahiti.* New York: Dodd, Mead.

Fischer, S. R. 2005. *Island at the End of the World: The Turbulent History of Easter Island.* London: Reaktion Books.

Flenley, J. and P. Bahn. 2003. *The Enigmas of Easter Island.* New York: Oxford University Press.

Flennikin, J. J. 1978. Reevaluation of the Lindenmeier Folsom: A Replication Experiment in Lithic Technology. *American Antiquity* 43:473–480.

Franke, P. R. and D. Watson. 1936. An Experimental Cornfield in Mesa Verde National Park. In *Symposium on Prehistoric Agriculture* 1, ed. Donald M. Brand, pp. 35–41. Albuquerque: University of New Mexico Bulletin, Anthropological Series.

Frison, G. C. 1989. Clovis Tools and Weaponry Efficiency in an African Elephant Context. *American Antiquity* 54:766–778.

Gifford-Gonzalez, D., D. B. Bamrosch, D. R. Damrosch, J. Pryor, and R. Thunen. 1985. The Third Dimension in Site Structure: An Experiment in Trampling and Vertical Dispersal. *American Antiquity* 50:803–818.

Gilborn, C. 1968. Words and Machines: The Denial of Experience. *Museum News* 47:25–29.

Gonzalez-Urquijo, J. E. and J. J. Ibáñez-Estévez. 2003. The Quantification of Use-Wear Polish Using Image Analysis. First Results. *Journal of Archaeological Science* 30:481–489.

Gould, R. A., ed. 1978. *Explorations in Ethnoarchaeology.* Albuquerque: University of New Mexico Press.

———. 1980. *Living Archaeology.* Cambridge, UK: Cambridge University Press.

Griffin J. B. and C. W. Angell. 1935. An Experimental Study of the Techniques of Pottery Decoration. *Papers of the Michigan Academy of Science, Arts and Letters* 20:1–6.

Hamlin, A. G. 1996. *The Discovery and Exploitation of Metals.* Monograph Series No. 1. Waterlooville, Hampshire, UK: Butser Ancient Farm.

Hansen, H-O. 1964. *I Built a Stone Age House.* New York: The John Day Company.

———. 1977 *The Prehistoric Village at Lejre.* Lejre, Denmark: Historical-Archaeological Research Centre.

Hanson, N. R. 1969. *Patterns of Discovery.* Cambridge, UK: Cambridge University Press.

Hardy B. L. and G. T. Garufi. 1997. Identification of Woodworking on Stone Tools through Residue and Use-Wear Analyses: Experimental Results. *Journal of Archaeological Science* 25:177–184.

Harlan, J. R. 1967. A Wild Wheat Harvest in Turkey. *Archaeology* 20:197–201.

Hartenberg R. S. and J. Schmidt, Jr. 1969. The Egyptian Drill and the Origin of the Crank. *Technology and Culture* 10:155–165.

Hayden, B. 1976. *Australian Western Desert Lithic Technology: An Ethnoarchaeological Study of Variability in Material Culture.* Ph.D. dissertation, University of Toronto.

———. 1977. Stone Tool Functions in the Western Desert. In *Stone Tools and Cultural Markers,* ed. R. V. S. Wright, pp. 178–188. Canberra: Australian Institute of Aboriginal Studies.

Hegmon, M. 2003. Setting Theoretical Egos Aside: Issues and Theory in North American Archaeology. *American Antiquity* 68:213–243.

Heizer, R. F., ed. 1959. *The Archaeologist at Work.* New York: Harper and Row.

Herschel, J. F. W. 1830. *A Preliminary Discourse on the Study of Natural Philosophy.* London: Longman, Rees, Orme, Brown & Green.

Hester, T. R. and R. F. Heizer. 1973. *Bibliography of Archaeology I: Experiments, Lithic Technology and Petrography.* Reading, MA: Addison-Wesley.

Heyerdahl, T. 1950. *The Kon-Tiki Expedition. By Raft Across the South Seas.* London: Allen and Unwin.

———. 1971. *The Ra Expeditions.* London: Allen and Unwin.

Hodder, I. 1982. *Symbols in Action.* New York: Cambridge University Press.

———. 1986. *Reading the Past: Current Approaches to Interpretation in Archaeology.* New York: Cambridge University Press.

———. 1991. Interpretive Archaeology and its Role. *American Antiquity* 56:7–18

———. 1999 *The Archaeological Process: An Introduction.* Oxford, UK: Oxford University Press.

Hodges, H. W. M. 1964. *Artifacts: An Introduction to Primitive Technology.* New York: F. A. Praeger.

Holly, G. A. and T. A. Del Bene. 1981. An Evaluation of Keeley's Microwear Approach. *Journal of Archaeological Science* 8:337–348.

Holten, L. 2003. Lejre—Background, Goals and Possibilities. Paper presented at EXARC (European Exchange on Archaeological Research and Communication) meeting, March 14–16, 2003.

Horvath, S. M. and B. R. Finney. 1969. Paddling Experiments and the Question of Polynesian Voyaging. *American Anthropologist* 71:271–276.

Hutchings, W. K. and L. W. Brüchert. 1997. Spearthrower Performance: Ethnographic and Experimental Research. *Antiquity* 71:890–897.

Ingersoll, D., J. E Yellen and W. MacDonald, eds. 1977. *Experimental Archaeology*. New York: Columbia University Press.

Iversen, J. 1956. Forest Clearance in the Stone Age. *Scientific American* 194:36–41.

Jahren, A. H., N. Toth, K. Schick, J. D. Clark and R. G. Amundson. 1997. Determining Stone Tool Use: Chemical and Morphological Analyses of Residues on Experimentally Manufactured Stone Tools. *Journal of Archaeological Science* 24:245–250.

Jennings, B. 1983. Interpretive Social Science and Policy Analysis. In *Ethics, the Social Sciences, and Policy Analysis*, ed. Daniel Callahan and Bruce Jennings, pp. 3–35. New York: Plenum Press.

Jewell, P. A. 1963. *The Experimental Earthwork at Overton Down, Wiltshire*. London: British Association for the Advancement of Science.

Jewell. P. A. and G. W. Dimbleby. 1966. The Experimental Earthwork on Overton Down, Wiltshire, England: The First Four Years. *Proceedings of the Prehistoric Society* 32:313–342.

Johnson, L. L. 1978. A History of Flint-Knapping Experimentation, 1838–1976. *Current Anthropology* 19:337–372.

Johnson, M. 1999. *Archaeological Theory: An Introduction*. Oxford, UK: Blackwell.

Johnson, T. 1957. An Experiment with Cave-Painting Media. *South African Archaeological Bulletin* 47:98–101.

Jones, P. R. 1980. Experimental Butchery with Modern Stone Tools and its Relevance for Palaeolithic Archaeology. *World Archaeology* 12:153–165.

Keeley, L. H. 1980. *Experimental Determination of Stone Tool Uses: A Microwear Analysis*. Chicago: University of Chicago Press.

———. 1981. Reply to Holly and Del Bene. *Journal of Archaeological Science* 8:348–352.

Kehoe, A. B. 1992. *North American Indians: A Comprehensive Account*. Upper Saddle River, NJ: Prentice-Hall.

Kemp, W. B. 1971. The Flow of Energy in a Hunting Society. *Scientific American* 225(3):104–115.

Kingery W. D. and J. D. Frierman. 1974. The Firing Temperature of a Karanova Sherd and Inferences about South-East European Chalcolithic Refractory Technology. *Proceedings of the Prehistoric Society* 40:204–205.

Kosso, P. 1991. Method in Archaeology: Middle-Range Theory as Hermeneutics. *American Antiquity* 56:621–627.

Kramer, C., ed. 1979. *Ethnoarchaeology: Implications of Ethnography for Archaeology*. New York: Columbia University Press.

Kuhn, T. S. 1970. *The Structure of Scientific Revolutions*. Chicago: University of Chicago Press.

Lambert J. D. H. and T. Arnason. 1978. Distribution of Vegetation on Maya Ruins and Its Relationship to Ancient Land-use at Lamanai, Belize. *Turrialba* 28:33–41.

Lechtman, H., A. Erlij and E. J. Barry, Jr. 1982. New Perspectives on Moche Metallurgy: Techniques of Gilding Copper at Loma Negra, Northern Peru. *American Antiquity* 47:3–30.

Leek, F. F. 1969. The Problem of Brain Removal During Embalming by the Ancient Egyptians. *Journal of Egyptian Archaeology* 55:112–116.

Leone, M. P., ed. 1972. *Contemporary Archaeology: A Guide to Theory and Contributions.* Carbondale: Southern Illinois University Press.

Lewis-Williams, J. D. and T. A. Dowson. 1988. The Signs of All Times. *Current Anthropology* 29:201–217.

Liddell, D. M. 1929. New Light on an Old Problem. *Antiquity* 3:283–291.

Long, S. 1964. Cire Perdue Copper Casting in Pre-Columbian Mexico: An Experimental Approach. *American Antiquity* 30:189–192.

Longacre, W. A. and J. M. Skibo, eds. 1994. *Kalinga Ethnoarchaeology: Expanding Archaeological Method and Theory.* Washington DC: Smithsonian Institution Press.

López Varela, S. L., A. van Gijn and L. Jacobs. 2002. De-mystifying Pottery Production in the Maya Lowlands: Detection of Traces of Use-Wear on Pottery Sherds through Microscopic Analysis and Experimental Replication. *Journal of Archaeological Science* 29:1133–1147.

Lorblanchet, M. 1991. Spitting Images: Replicating the Spotted Horses of Pech Merle. *Archaeology* 44(6):24–31.

Love, C. M. 1990. How to Make and Move an Easter Island Statue. In *State and Perspectives of Scientific Research in Easter Island Culture*, ed. H-M Esen-Bauer, pp. 139–140. Frankfurt: Courier Forsch.-Inst. Senckenberg.

————. 2000. More on Moving Easter Island Statues, with Comments on the *NOVA* Program. *Rapa Nui Journal* 14:115–118.

Lucas, A. 1962. *Ancient Egyptian Materials and Industries.* London: Edward Arnold.

MacIntyre, F. 1999. Walking Moai? *Rapa Nui Journal* 13:70–78.

MacIver, R. 1921. On the Manufacture of Etruscan and Other Ancient Black Wares. *Man* 21:86–88.

Macphail, R. I., J. Crowther, T. G. Alcott, M. G. Bell and J. M. Cruise. 2003. The Experimental Earthwork at Wareham, Dorset After 33 Years: Changes to the Buried LFH and Ah Horizons. *Journal of Archaeological Science* 30:77–93.

Martin, Paul S. 1971. The Revolution in Archaeology. *American Antiquity* 36:1–8.

————. 1974 Early Development in Mogollon Research. In *Archaeological Researches in Retrospect*, ed. Gordon R. Willey, pp. 3–29. Cambridge, MA: Winthrop.

Mathieu, J. and D. Meyer. 1997. Comparing Axe Heads of Stone, Bronze, and Steel: Studies in Experimental Archaeology. *Journal of Field Archaeology* 24:333–351.

Matthews, M. R. 1994. *Science Teaching: The Role of History an Philosophy of Science.* New York: Routledge.

Mayes, P. 1961. The Firing of a Pottery Kiln of a Romano-British Type at Boston, Lincs. *Archaeometry* 4:4–30.

————. 1962. The Firing of a Second Pottery Kiln of Romano-British Type at Boston, Lincolnshire. *Archaeometry* 5:80–107.

McGrail, S. 1974. *The Building and Trials of the Replica of an Ancient Boat: The Gokstad Faering. 1. Building the Replica.* Maritime Monographs and Reports 11, Greenwich, UK.

McKee, E. 1974. *The Building and Trials of the Replica of an Ancient Boat: The Gokstad Faering. 2. The Seas Trials.* Maritime Monographs and Reports 11, Greenwich, UK.

Medawar, P. B. 1963. Is the Scientific Paper a Fraud? *The Listener* September 12:377–378.

Mendelssohn, K. 1974. *The Riddle of the Pyramids.* New York: Praeger.

Michels, J. W. 1973. *Dating Methods in Archaeology.* New York: Seminar Press.

Miksicek, C. H., K. J. Elsesser, I. A. Wuebber, K. O. Bruhns and N. Hammond. 1981. Rethinking Ramon: A Comment on Reina and Hill's Lowland Maya Subsistence. *American Antiquity* 46:916–919.

Miller, R., E. McEwen and C. Bergman. 1986. Experimental Approaches to Ancient Near Eastern Archery. *World Archaeology* 18:178–195.

Mithen, S. J. 1996. Ecological Interpretations of Palaeolithic Art. In *Contemporary Archaeology in Theory: A Reader*, ed. R. W. Preucel and I. Hodder, pp. 79–96. Oxford, UK: Blackwell.

Newcomer, M. 1971. Some Quantitative Experiments in Handaxe Manufacture. *World Archaeology* 3:85–93.

Newcomer, M. H. and L. H. Keeley. 1979. Testing a Method of Microwear Analysis with Experimental Flint Tools. In *Lithic Use-Wear Analysis*, ed. Brian Hayden, pp. 195–205. New York: Academic Press.

Nielsen, A. E. 1991. Trampling the Archaeological Record: An Experimental Study. *American Antiquity* 56:483–503.

O'Brien, E. M. 1981. The Projectile Capabilities of an Acheulian Handaxe from Olorgesailie. *Current Anthropology* 22:76–79.

_____. 1984. What Was the Acheulian Hand Ax? *Natural History* 93(7):20–24.

Odell, G. H. 2000. Stone Tool Research at the End of the Millennium: Procurement and Technology. *Journal of Archaeological Research* 8(4):269–331.

_____. 2001. Stone Tool Research at the End of the Millennium: Classification, Function and Behavior. *Journal of Archaeological Research* 9(1):45–100.

_____. 2003. *Lithic Analysis*. New York: Springer.

Olgyay, V. 1963. *Design with Climate*. Princeton University Press, Princeton.

Orliac, C. and M. Orliac. 1988. *Easter Island: Mystery of the Stone Giants*. New York: Harry N. Abrams.

Osenton, C. J. 2001. Megalithic Engineering Techniques: Experiments using Axe-based Technology. *Antiquity* 75:293–298.

Pareto, V. 1935. *The Mind and Society*. Vol. 1. New York: Harcourt, Brace.

Pavel, P. 1990. Reconstruction of the Transport of Moai. In *State and Perspectives of Scientific Research in Easter Island Culture*, ed. H-M Esen-Bauer, pp. 141–144. Frankfurt: Courier Forsch.-Inst. Senckenberg.

_____. 1992. Raising the Stonehenge Lintels in Czechoslovakia. *Antiquity* 66:389–391.

_____. 1995. Reconstruction of the Transport of the Moai Statues and Pukao Hats. *Rapa Nui Journal* 9:69–72.

Peets, O. H. 1960. Experiments in the Use of Atlatl Weights. *American Antiquity* 26:108–110.

Peirce, C. S. 1931. *Collected Papers*. Volume 5. Cambridge: Harvard University Press.

Peregrine P. N., C. R. Ember and M. Ember, eds. 2002. *Archaeology: Original Readings in Method and Practice*. Upper Saddle River, NJ: Prentice-Hall.

Pitts, M. and M. Roberts. 1998. *Fairweather Eden. Life in Britain Half a Million Years Ago as Revealed by the Excavations at Boxgrove*. New York: Fromm International.

Platt, J. R. 1964. Strong Inference. *Science* 146:347–353.

Pokines, J. T. 1998. Experimental Replication and Use of Cantabrian Lower Magdalenian Antler Projectile Points. *Journal of Archaeological Science* 25:875–886.

Pope, S. T. 1923. A Study of Bows and Arrows. *University of California Publications in American Archaeology and Ethnology* 13(9):329–414.

Popper, K. 1962. *Conjectures and Refutations*. New York: Basic Books.

Price, T. D. and G. M. Feinman. 2008. *Images of the Past*, 5th ed. New York: McGraw-Hill.

Price, T. D. and A. B. Gebauer. 2002. *Adventures in Fugawiland: A Computer Simulation in Archaeology*. New York: McGraw-Hill.

Preucel, R. W. and I. Hodder, eds. 1996. *Contemporary Archaeology in Theory: A Reader.* Blackwell Publishers, Oxford, UK.

Pryor, F. 1999. *Farmers in Prehistoric Britain.* Gloucestershire, UK: Tempus.

Puleston, D. E. 1971. An Experimental Approach to the Function of Classic Maya Chultuns. *American Antiquity* 36(3):322–335.

Purdy, B. A. and H. K. Brooks. 1971. Thermal Alteration of Silica Minerals: An Archaeological Approach. *Science* 173:322–325.

Quimby, G. I., Jr. 1949. A Hopewell Tool for Decorating Pottery. *American Antiquity* 14:344.

Raab, L. M. and A. C. Goodyear. 1984. Middle-Range Theory in Archaeology: A Critical Review of Origins and Applications. *American Antiquity* 49:255–268.

Rappaport, R. A. 1971. The Flow of Energy in an Agricultural Society. *Scientific American* 225(3):116–132.

Rathje, W. L. 1974. The Garbage Project: A New Way of Looking at the Problems of Archaeology. *Archaeology* 27(4):236–241.

Redman, C. L. 1999. *Human Impact on Ancient Environments.* Tucson: University of Arizona Press.

Reina, R. E. and R. M. Hill, II. 1980. Lowland Maya Subsistence: Notes from Ethnohistory and Ethnography. *American Antiquity* 45:74–79.

Renfrew, C. and P. Bahn. 2004. *Archaeology: Theories, Methods, and Practice.* New York: Thames and Hudson.

Reynolds, P. J. 1977. Slash and Burn Experiment. In *Butser Farm Occasional Papers* 3, pp. 27–36. Waterlooville, Hampshire, UK: Butser Ancient Farm.

_____. 1979. *Iron-Age Farm: The Butser Experiment.* London: Colonnade Books.

_____. 1981. Deadstock and Livestock. In *Butser Farm Occasional Papers* 2, pp. 1–16. Waterlooville, Hampshire, UK: Butser Ancient Farm.

_____. 1992. Crop Yields of the Prehistoric Cereal Types Emmer and Spelt: The Worst Option. In *Butser Farm Occasional Papers* 2, pp. 17–28. Waterlooville, Hampshire, UK: Butser Ancient Farm.

_____. 1993. Experimental Reconstruction. In *Butser Farm Occasional Papers* 4, pp. 1–22. Waterlooville, Hampshire, UK: Butser Ancient Farm.

_____. 1995a. The Life and Death of a Post-Hole. In *Butser Farm Occasional Papers* 1, pp. 27–32. Waterlooville, Hampshire, UK: Butser Ancient Farm.

_____. 1995b. Rural Life and Farming. In *Butser Farm Occasional Papers* 3, pp. 1–26. Waterlooville, Hampshire, UK: Butser Ancient Farm.

_____. 1999. Butser Ancient Farm: A Unique Research and Educational Establishment. In *Butser Farm Occasional Papers* 1, pp. 1–10. Waterlooville, Hampshire, UK: Butser Ancient Farm

Rice, P. and A. Patterson. 1985. Cave Art and Bones: Exploring the Interrelationships. *American Anthropologist* 87:94–100.

Richards, J. and M. Whitby. 1997. The Engineering of Stonehenge. In *Science and Stonehenge*, 231–256. Oxford, UK: The British Academy.

Rorty, R. 1979. *Philosophy and the Mirror of Nature.* Princeton, NJ: Princeton University Press.

Rosch, E. 1977. Human Categorization. In *Studies in Cross-cultural Psychology* 1, ed. Neil Warren, pp. 1–49. New York: Academic Press.

Ryder, M. L. 1966. Can One Cook in a Skin? *Antiquity* 40:225–227.

_____. 1969. Paunch Cooking. *Antiquity* 43:218–220.

Rye, O. S. 1981. *Pottery Technology: Principles and Reconstruction.* Washington, DC: Taraxacum.

Sahlins, M. 1972. *Stone Age Economics.* Chicago: Aldine-Atherton.

Salisbury, R. F. 1962. *From Stone to Steel: Economic Consequences of a Technological Change in New Guinea.* Melbourne: Melbourne University Press.

Saraydar, S. C. 1976. *Quantitative Experiments in Archaeology: New Approaches to the Study of Prehistoric Human Adaptations.* Ph.D. dissertation. Cornell University, Ithaca, New York.

_____. 1981. Thermal Behavior of Primitive Houses: Scale Model Analysis. *Archaeometry* 23:115–121.

_____. 2004. Archaeology and Critical Thinking: Exercises for Educators. *SAA Archaeological Record* 4(1):12–14.

Saraydar, S. C. and I. Shimada. 1971. A Quantitative Comparison of Efficiency between a Stone Axe and a Steel Axe. *American Antiquity* 36:216–217.

_____. 1973 Experimental Archaeology: A New Outlook. *American Antiquity* 38:344–350.

Schiffer, M. B., J. M. Skibo, T. C. Boelke, M. A. Neupert and M. Aronson. 1994. New Perspectives on Experimental Archaeology: Surface Treatments and Thermal Response of the Clay Cooking Pot. *American Antiquity* 59:197–217.

Schmidt P. and D. H. Avery. 1978. Complex Iron Smelting and Prehistoric Culture in Tanzania. *Science* 201:1085–1089.

Schmidt, D., S. E. Churchill and W. L. Hylander. 2003. Experimental Evidence Concerning Spear Use in Neandertals and Early Modern Humans. *Journal of Archaeological Science* 30:103–114.

Semenov, S. A. 1964. *Prehistoric Technology.* London; Cory, Adams, and Mackay.

Severin, T. 1978. *The Brendan Voyage.* London; Hutchinson.

Shanks, M. and C. Tilley. 1987. *Re-Constructing Archaeology.* Cambridge, MA: Cambridge University Press.

Sharer, R. and W. Ashmore. 2003. *Archaeology: Discovering Our Past.* New York: McGraw-Hill.

Sharp, L. 1952. Steel Axes for Stone-Age Australians. *Human Organization* 11:17–22.

Shea, J. J. and J. D. Klenck. 1993. An Experimental Investigation of the Effects of Trampling on the Results of Lithic Microwear Analysis. *Journal of Archaeological Science* 20:175–194.

Shimada, I. and J. F. Merkel. 1991. Copper-Alloy Metallurgy in Ancient Peru. *Scientific American* 265(1):80–86.

Skibo, J. M. 1992. Ethnoarchaeology, experimental archaeology and inference building in ceramic research. *Archaeologia Polona* 30-27-38.

Skibo, J. M., M. B. Schiffer and K. C. Reid. 1989. Organic-tempered Pottery: An Experimental Study. *American Antiquity* 54:122–146.

Sonnenfeld, J. 1962. Interpreting the Function of Primitive Implements. *American Antiquity* 28:56–64.

Spaulding, A. C. 1968. Explanation in Archeology. In *New Perspectives in Archeology*, ed. L. Binford and S. Binford, pp. 33–39. Chicago; Aldine Publishing.

Spector, J. 1996. What This Awl Means to Me: Towards a Feminist Archaeology. In *Contemporary Archaeology in Theory: A Reader*, ed. R. W. Preucel and I. Hodder, pp. 485–500. Oxford, UK: Blackwell.

Speth, J. D. 1977. Experimental Investigations of Hard-Hammer Percussion Flaking. In *Experimental Archaeology*, ed. D. Ingersoll, J. E. Yellen and W. Macdonald, pp. 3–37. New York: Columbia University Press.

Spiegelberg, H. 1975. *Doing Phenomenology: Essays on and in Phenomenology.* The Hague: Martinus Nijoff.

Stafford, M. 1993. The Parallel-flaked Flint Daggers of Late Neolithic Denmark: An Experimental Perspective. *Journal of Archaeological Science* 30:1537–1550.

Steensberg, A. 1943. *Ancient Harvesting Implements*. National Museum, Copenhagen.

Stocks, D. A. 1993. Making Stone Vessels in Ancient Mesopotamia and Egypt. *Antiquity* 67:596–603.

_____. 1999. Stone Sarcophagus Manufacture in Ancient Egypt. *Antiquity* 73:918–922.

_____. 2001. Testing Ancient Egyptian Granite-Working Methods in Aswan, Upper Egypt. *Antiquity* 75:89–94.

_____. 2003. *Experiments in Egyptian Archaeology: Stoneworking Technology in Ancient Egypt*. Oxford, UK: Routledge.

Stout, D. 2002. Skill and Cognition in Stone Tool Manufacture: An Ethnographic Case Study from Irian Jaya. *Current Anthropology* 43:693–722.

Taylor, W. W. 1948. *A Study of Archaeology*. American Anthropological Association Memoir 69, Menasha, Wisconsin.

Thomas, R. B. 1973. *Human Adaptation to a High Andean Energy Flow System*. University Park: Occasional Papers of the Pennsylvania State University.

Thompson, M. W. 1954. Azilian Harpoons. *Proceedings of the Prehistoric Society* 20:193–211.

Toth, N., D. Clark and G. Ligabue. 1992. The Last Stone Ax Makers. *Scientific American* 267(1):66–71.

Toulmin, S. 2003. *The Uses of Argument*. Cambridge, UK: Cambridge University Press.

Toulmin, S., R. Rieke and A. Janik. 1984. *An Introduction to Reasoning*. New York: Macmillan.

Trigger, B. G. 1989. *A History of Archaeological Thought*. Cambridge, UK: Cambridge University Press.

Tweney, R. D., M. E. Doherty and C. R. Mynatt, eds. 1981. *On Scientific Thinking*. New York: Columbia University Press.

Tylecote, R. F. 1973. Casting Copper and Bronze into Stone Moulds. *Bulletin of History of Metallurgy Group* 7:1–5.

_____. 1986. *The Prehistory of Metallurgy in the British Isles*. London: Institute of Metals.

Varien, M. D. 1999. *Sedentism and Mobility in a Social Landscape: Mesa Verde and Beyond*. Tucson: University of Arizona Press.

Vitelli, K. D., ed. 1996. *Archaeological Ethics*. Walnut Creek, CA: Altamira.

Wainwright, G. 1989. *The Henge Monuments: Ceremony and Society in Prehistoric Britain*. London: Thames and Hudson.

Watkins, J. E. 2000. *Indigenous Archaeology: American Indian Values and Scientific Practice*. Walnut Creek, CA: Altamira.

_____. 2003. Beyond the Margin: American Indians, First Nations, and Archaeology in North America. *American Antiquity* 68:273–285.

Watson, P. J., S. A. LeBlanc and C. L. Redman. 1971. *Explanation in Archaeology: An Explicitly Scientific Approach*. New York: Columbia University Press.

White, L. 1949. *The Science of Culture*. New York: Grove Press.

White, T. D. 1992. *Prehistoric Cannibalism at Mancos 5MTUMR-2346*. Princeton, NJ: Princeton University Press.

Whittaker, J. C. 1994. *Flintknapping: Making and Understanding Stone Tools*. Austin: University of Texas Press.

———. 1996. Reproducing a Bronze Age Dagger from the Thames: Statements and Questions. *London Archaeologist* 8(2):51–54.

Whittaker, J. C. and G. McCall. 2001. Handaxe-Hurling Hominids: An Unlikely Story. *Current Anthropology* 42:566–572.

Willey, G. R. 1953. *Prehistoric Settlement Patterns in the Virú Valley, Peru.* Bulletin 155. Washington, DC: Bureau of American Ethnology.

Willey, G. R. and J. A. Sabloff. 1993. *A History of American Archaeology.* New York: W. H. Freeman.

Woods, J. C. and G. L. Titmus. 1996. Stone on Stone: Perspectives on Maya Civilization from Lithic Studies. In *Eighth Palenque Roundtable, 1993*, ed. M. J. Macri and J. McHargue, pp. 479–489. San Francisco: Pre-Columbian Art Research Institute.

Zuckerman, D. 2000. Experimental Archaeology at Sha'ar Hagolan: A Reconstruction of Neolithic Pottery in the Jordan Valley. *Near Eastern Archaeology* 63:45–50.

INDEX

167

CREDITS

Figure 1-1. From *Introduction to Southwestern Archaeology*, by A. V. Kidder and I. Rouse. Copyright © 1962. By permission of Yale University Press.

Figure 2-1. Adapted from *The Uses of Argument* by Stephen E. Toulmin. Cambridge University Press, 2003.

Figure 3-1a. Adapted from "Egyptian Civilization: Daily Life, Trades and Crafts" (http://www.civilization.ca/civil/Egypt/egc105e.html).

Figures 3-1b, 3-2 and 3-3. Adapted from "The Egyptian Drill and the Origin of the Crank" by R. S. Hartenberg and J. Schmidt, Jr. *Technology and Culture*, vol. 10, 1969.

Figure 3-4. Adapted from a drawing attributed to H. Hodges (http://www.geocities.com/ unforbidden_geology/ancient_egyptian_copper_coring_drills.html.

Figures 3-5 and 3-6. Photos by the author.

Figure 3-7. From *Flintknapping: Making and Understanding Stone Tools*, by John C. Whittaker. Copyright © 1994. By permission of the University of Texas Press.

Figure 3-8. Reprinted by permission from "Scanning Electron Microscopy Analysis of Use Striae" by D. Fedje. In *Lithic Use-Wear Analysis*, edited by B. Hayden. Copyright © Elsevier 1979.

Figure 3-9. Photo by the author.

Figure 3-10. From "An Experimental Approach to the Function of Classic Maya Chultuns" by D. Puleston, *American Antiquity* 36(3), 1971. By permission of the Society for American Archaeology.

Figure 4-1. From "Comparing Axe Heads of Stone, Bronze, and Steel: Studies in Experimental Archaeology" by J. Mathieu and D. Meyer. *Journal of Field Archaeology* 24, 1997. By permission of the Trustees of Boston University. All rights reserved.

Figures 4-2 and 4-3. From "Cire Perdue Copper Casting in Pre-Columbian Mexico: An Experimental Approach" by S. Long, *American Antiquity* 30(2), 1964. By permission of the Society for American Archaeology.

Figure 4-4. From "The Firing of a Pottery Kiln of a Romano-British Type at Boston, Lincs" by P. Mayes, *Archaeometry* 4, 1961. By permission of Blackwell Publishing and the Research Laboratory for Archaeology and the History of Art.

Figure 4-6. From "Walking Moai?" by F. MacIntyre. *Rapa Nui Journal* 13, 1999. By permission of the Easter Island Foundation.

Figure 4-7. From "Raising Stonehenge Lintels in Czechoslovakia" by P. Pavel. *Antiquity* 66, 1992. By permission of Antiquity Publications Ltd.

Figure 4-8. From "Reconstruction of the Transport of the Moai Statues and Pukao Hats" by P. Pavel, *Rapa Nui Journal* 9, 1995. By permission of the Easter Island Foundation.

Figure 4-9. From "Thermal Behavior of Primitive Houses: Scale Model Analysis" by S. Saraydar, *Archaeometry* 23, 1981. By permission of Blackwell Publishing and the Research Laboratory for Archaeology and the History of Art.

Figure 4-10. Photo by Werner Karrasch. Copyright © 2007. By permission of The Viking Ship Museum, Denmark.

Figure 4-11. From "The Experimental Earthwork Revisited" by P. Ashbee and P. Jewell, *Antiquity* 72, 1998. By permission of Antiquity Publications Ltd.

Figure 4-12. From "The Experimental Earthwork at Overton Down, Wiltshire, England: The First Four Years" by P. Jewell and G. Dimbleby. *Proceedings of the Prehistoric Society* 32, 1966. By permission of The Prehistoric Society.

Figure 5-2 a. Drawing by Ian Graham. Reproduced with his permission.

Figure 5-3. From "Experimental Archaeology: A New Outlook" by S. Saraydar and I. Shimada, *American Antiquity* 38, 1973. By permission of the Society for American Archaeology.

Figure 5-4. From H. O. Hansen, *I Built a Stone Age House.* John Day, 1964.

Figures 5-5 and 5-6. By permission of Butser Ancient Farm Ltd.

Figure 5-7. From A. G. Hamlin, *The Discovery and Exploitation of Metals*, 1996. Reproduced by permission of Friends of Butser.

Figures 6-1 and 6-2. Photos by the author.

Figure 6-3. By permission of the Historical-Archaeological Experimental Centre, Lejre.